POVERTY

OPPOSING VIEWPOINTS®

Other Books of Related Interest in the
Opposing Viewpoints Series:

POVERTY

OPPOSING VIEWPOINTS®

David L. Bender & Bruno Leone, *Series Editors*

Katie de Koster, *Book Editor*

Bruno Leone, *Assistant Editor*

OPPOSING
VIEWPOINTS
SERIES®

Greenhaven Press, Inc.   PO Box 289009   San Diego, CA 92198-9009

Cover photo: Worldwide Photo

Library of Congress Cataloging-in-Publication Data

Poverty : opposing viewpoints / Katie de Koster, book editor; Bruno Leone, assistant editor.
        p.   cm. — (Opposing viewpoints series)
    Includes bibliographical references and index.
    Summary: A collection of articles debating issues related to poverty in America, including its causes, how it affects minorities, government policies, and how poverty can be reduced.
    ISBN 1-56510-066-2 (lib. : acid-free paper) — ISBN 1-56510-065-4 (pbk. : acid-free paper)
    1. Poor—United States. 2. Economic assistance, Domestic—United States. 3. Public welfare—United States. [1. Poor. 2. Poverty. 3. Public welfare.] I. de Koster, Katie, 1948- . II. Leone, Bruno, 1939- . III. Series: Opposing viewpoints series (Unnumbered)
HC110.P6P63 1994
362.5'0973—dc20   93-22397
                                                          CIP0
                                                           AC

"Congress shall make no law . . .
abridging the freedom of speech,
or of the press."

First Amendment to the U.S. Constitution

The basic foundation of our democracy is the first amendment guarantee of freedom of expression. The Opposing Viewpoints Series is dedicated to the concept of this basic freedom and the idea that it is more important to practice it than to enshrine it.

Contents

Why Consider Opposing Viewpoints?

"The only way in which a human being can make some approach to knowing the whole of a subject is by hearing what can be said about it by persons of every variety of opinion and studying all modes in which it can be looked at by every character of mind. No wise man ever acquired his wisdom in any mode but this."

John Stuart Mill

In our media-intensive culture it is not difficult to find differing opinions. Thousands of newspapers and magazines and dozens of radio and television talk shows resound with differing points of view. The difficulty lies in deciding which opinion to agree with and which "experts" seem the most credible. The more inundated we become with differing opinions and claims, the more essential it is to hone critical reading and thinking skills to evaluate these ideas. Opposing Viewpoints books address this problem directly by presenting stimulating debates that can be used to enhance and teach these skills. The varied opinions contained in each book examine many different aspects of a single issue. While examining these conveniently edited opposing views, readers can develop critical thinking skills such as the ability to compare and contrast authors' credibility, facts, argumentation styles, use of persuasive techniques, and other stylistic tools. In short, the Opposing Viewpoints Series is an ideal way to attain the higher-level thinking and reading skills so essential in a culture of diverse and contradictory opinions.

In addition to providing a tool for critical thinking, Opposing Viewpoints books challenge readers to question their own strongly held opinions and assumptions. Most people form their opinions on the basis of upbringing, peer pressure, and personal, cultural, or professional bias. By reading carefully balanced opposing views, readers must directly confront new ideas as well as the opinions of those with whom they disagree. This is not to simplistically argue that everyone who reads opposing views will—or should—change his or her opinion. Instead, the series enhances readers' depth of understanding of their own views by encouraging confrontation with opposing ideas. Careful examination of others' views can lead to the readers' understanding of the logical inconsistencies in their own opinions, perspective on why they hold an opinion, and the consideration of the possibility that their opinion requires further evaluation.

Evaluating Other Opinions

To ensure that this type of examination occurs, Opposing Viewpoints books present all types of opinions. Prominent spokespeople on different sides of each issue as well as well-known professionals from many disciplines challenge the reader. An additional goal of the series is to provide a forum for other, less known, or even unpopular viewpoints. The opinion of an ordinary person who has had to make the decision to cut off life support from a terminally ill relative, for example, may be just as valuable and provide just as much insight as a medical ethicist's professional opinion. The editors have two additional purposes in including these less known views. One, the editors encourage readers to respect others' opinions—even when not enhanced by professional credibility. It is only by reading or listening to and objectively evaluating others' ideas that one can determine whether they are worthy of consideration. Two, the inclusion of such viewpoints encourages the important critical thinking skill of objectively evaluating an author's credentials and bias. This evaluation will illuminate an author's reasons for taking a particular stance on an issue and will aid in readers' evaluation of the author's ideas.

As series editors of the Opposing Viewpoints Series, it is our hope that these books will give readers a deeper understanding of the issues debated and an appreciation of the complexity of even seemingly simple issues when good and honest people disagree. This awareness is particularly important in a democratic society such as ours in which people enter into public debate to determine the common good. Those with whom one disagrees should not be regarded as enemies but rather as people whose views deserve careful examination and may shed light on one's own.

Thomas Jefferson once said that "difference of opinion leads to inquiry, and inquiry to truth." Jefferson, a broadly educated man, argued that "if a nation expects to be ignorant and free . . . it expects what never was and never will be." As individuals and as a nation, it is imperative that we consider the opinions of others and examine them with skill and discernment. The Opposing Viewpoints Series is intended to help readers achieve this goal.

David L. Bender & Bruno Leone,
Series Editors

Introduction

"If the misery of our poor be caused not by laws of nature, but by our institutions, great is our sin. "

Charles Darwin, *Voyage of the Beagle*

The United States has spent trillions of dollars since 1964 in an effort to eradicate poverty. When President Lyndon Johnson's War on Poverty began, the official poverty rate was just under 15 percent of the population. Thirty years later, the official poverty rate is essentially unchanged.

If poverty is a lack of money, and so much money has been spent to eradicate poverty, why has the poverty rate remained the same? Some quarrel with the definition of poverty itself, maintaining that the poverty rate is much lower than the numbers would indicate. These people take issue with the fact that certain sources of income and in-kind benefits (such as food and housing assistance) are not counted when assessing poverty levels. Others, however, believe the situation is worse than official figures show. They claim the poverty line is set so low that many people living in poverty are not included in the statistics. A related debate blames the lack of success in eradicating poverty on a "welfare industry" that enriches members of the bureaucracy instead of being funneled to the poor themselves. The evolution of this industry and whether it helps or harms the poor is the greatest debate.

Although most European countries had some form of social security by the early years of the twentieth century, many Americans did not believe that government should have to help the aged, disabled, or needy. The Great Depression of the 1930s altered that attitude, when the unemployment rate reached 25 percent and so many banks and businesses were failing that people felt only the federal government could reverse the situation. The Social Security Act of 1935 was the first national law to provide for unemployment insurance for U.S. workers; the idea of making such benefits a right signaled a new attitude toward helping the poor. At the same time, an associated welfare program, another part of President Franklin Roosevelt's New Deal, began providing Aid to Dependent Children, which has

12

grown into today's basic welfare program, Aid to Families with Dependent Children (AFDC). Although the New Deal programs "did not end the depression, these measures and others relieved hardship for many and established a commitment on the part of the federal government to deal with American economic problems," according to researchers Ted Yanak and Pam Cornelison.

That commitment remained, even though it took mobilization of all the country's resources during World War II and a concerted effort to meet wartime production needs to eventually put the United States on a sound financial footing again. During the period of prosperity that followed the end of the war, the poverty level dropped steadily from 32 percent in 1950 to 14.7 percent in 1966.

Then the War on Poverty began. And the poverty level stopped dropping.

Conservatives see a direct link between subsequent soaring welfare spending and "behavioral poverty," defined by the Heritage Foundation's Robert Rector as

> a breakdown in the values and conduct that lead to the formation of healthy families, stable personalities, and self-sufficiency. Behavioral poverty is a cluster of social pathologies including: dependency and eroded work ethic, lack of educational aspiration and achievement, inability or unwillingness to control one's children, increased single parenthood and illegitimacy, criminal activity, and drug and alcohol use.

In this view, welfare creates a disincentive to marry because marriage can cut welfare benefits and to work because taking a job may end eligibility for housing and food assistance, medical care, and other benefits. When children in the inner cities are raised on welfare, they learn to accept it as the neighborhood lifestyle. Thus, the argument goes, behavioral poverty becomes generational poverty. For those who believe welfare causes the problem rather than ends it, cutting off benefits seems to be the proper cure.

Liberals point out that welfare stipends provide the barest subsistence living, which sufficiently discourages a life on welfare. The problem with the current system, they believe, is that it does not offer enough help to boost people out of poverty. Roger Wilkins is one of those who believe that more help, not less, is needed. He contends that many of the poor "have tried like hell to climb out of the hole they're in, but there have been no jobs and few services to help them. I'm all for personal responsibility and empowerment," he adds, "but people have to have something to stand on before they can begin to climb."

When Charles Darwin wrote of the "institutions" that might cause misery for the poor, the idea of a massive welfare apparatus as one of those institutions never crossed his mind. But when society's structures and problems affect an individual's ability to earn a living, society must judge whether, when, and how much to help. Finding a balance between helping those who cannot help themselves and taking over responsibility for those who could help themselves is a delicate task. Erring on either side may have disastrous consequences. Finding that balance is among the subjects covered in *Poverty: Opposing Viewpoints*, which examines the causes of and proposed cures for poverty in America today. Its authors debate the following questions: Is Poverty a Serious Problem in the United States? What Are the Causes of Poverty? Why Does Poverty Disproportionately Affect Certain Groups? Why Does an American Underclass Exist? Can Government Efforts Alleviate Poverty? In *We're Number One*, Andrew Shapiro reports that America has the largest percentage of children living in poverty of the major industrial nations—and the largest number of billionaires in the world. It remains to be seen whether the American dream is still able to bridge that gap.

Is Poverty a Serious Problem in the United States?

POVERTY

Chapter Preface

Poverty in America is not thousands of homeless urchins on city streets. It is not millions dying of starvation and disease, entire generations wiped out in the kinds of crises evoked by the names *Ethiopia* and *Somalia*. Homeless and hungry people exist in the United States, but their poverty is perhaps most tellingly a failure of the American dream. And it is in relation to that American dream that the extent of poverty is defined.

This view of poverty as more than simple economic necessity is spelled out by Paul L. Wachtel in *The Poverty of Affluence:*

> The misery of those at the bottom of our society is not due simply to a lack of goods. It has elements of real material deprivation, to be sure, but it is also social and psychological. It is the invidious quality in their lives that particularly constitutes their poverty; it is having less than everyone else that continually redefines and upgrades what are regarded as necessities for a decent life.

Liberals maintain that the dream of being able to afford the "necessities for a decent life" and get ahead through hard work is out of reach of an increasing number of Americans. They see a poverty of opportunity, a social and economic inequality that seems antithetical to the American spirit. Among other factors, they point to what Irving Howe calls "a steady decline in wage levels, so that we now have in America a group that is called the working poor—people who do have jobs, who work hard, who try desperately to stay afloat . . . but who earn such wretchedly low wages that they sink below the poverty line."

Many conservatives, on the other hand, believe that the American dream is still available to those who are willing to work hard and endure a little sacrifice. They agree with Myron Magnet, who finds that "poverty is less an economic matter than a cultural one. In many cases, . . . 'have-nots' lack the inner resources to seize their chance, and they pass on to their children a self-defeating set of values and attitudes." Contending that the economic resources to escape poverty are within reach for most of the poor—as the Heritage Foundation's Robert Rector asserts, "The material living standards of poor Americans are far higher than is generally understood"—they maintain that where there is poverty in America, it is often a poverty of faith and of values.

In their attempts to define the extent of poverty in the United States, the authors of the following viewpoints debate whether the American dream is still available to anyone who wants to achieve it.

16

"The overwhelming majority of persons officially identified as 'poor' are in fact well fed and well housed."

Poverty Is Overestimated

Robert Rector

The Census Bureau provides the official estimates of the extent of poverty in the United States. Robert Rector, author of the following viewpoint, points out that these figures consistently ignore evidence from other government agencies showing that most "poor" people have adequate food and shelter. In fact, he states, living conditions for America's poor are improving, and are already better than those of average families in other industrialized countries and average families in America's recent past. Rector is a policy analyst for welfare and family issues at the Heritage Foundation, a conservative think tank in Washington, D.C.

As you read, consider the following questions:

1. Why does Rector believe that many people who are out of work or who have suffered heavy business losses should not be classified as "poor"?
2. How much money does the author say is spent in assistance programs for the poor that is not counted by the Census Bureau when it measures poverty levels? Does the author say that poor households actually receive this money?
3. What evidence does Rector offer to back up his assertion that low income does not necessarily indicate poor living conditions?

From Robert Rector, "How the Poor Really Live: Lessons for Welfare Reform," The Heritage Foundation *Backgrounder*, January 31, 1992. Reprinted with permission.

Each year for the past decade the United States Census Bureau has reported that at least 30 million Americans live in poverty. For ordinary Americans, the word "poverty" suggests destitution, and the idea of widespread and unremitting poverty in a land of prosperity is of course deeply distressing. The vision is one of over 10 percent of the entire population being hungry and malnourished, living in overcrowded, poorly heated, filthy apartments.

Yet, this simply is not the case.

Sophisticated surveys of the actual living conditions of America's poor by the Census Bureau, the U.S. Department of Agriculture, and other government agencies, paint a very different picture. These surveys show that the overwhelming majority of persons officially identified as "poor" are in fact well fed and well housed.

That has major implications for the design of American welfare policy. A distorted picture of the conditions of low-income families has led to misdirected policies that, in too many instances, give the wrong help to the wrong people while ignoring the real needs of many lower income Americans.

Crucial Data Ignored

The reason that an inaccurate picture of poverty continues to drive federal policy is that policy makers, curiously, are not looking at the federal government's own data. For instance, because lawmakers and federal officials ignore crucial data on nutrition from the U.S. Department of Agriculture and the U.S. Centers for Disease Control, many believe there is widespread hunger in America. In fact, there is almost no poverty-induced malnutrition in America, and the poor have virtually the same level of nutrient consumption as the middle class.

A distorted picture of the housing conditions of Americans classified as poor by the Census Bureau is also prevalent among policy makers. Again, readily available data refute many of the impressions driving policy. For example, among the little-known facts about poor housing from the 1989 "American Housing Survey," a joint project of the U.S. Bureau of the Census and the Department of Housing and Urban Development, are:

• Nearly 40 percent of all "poor" households actually own their own homes. The median value of the homes of these households is 58 percent of the median value of all homes owned in America. Over one million poor households owned homes worth over $80,000.

• The average home owned by persons classified as poor in the U.S. is a three-bedroom house with a garage and porch or patio. Contrary to popular impression, the majority of these households who own their own homes are not elderly.

• According to the Census Bureau, only 8 percent of poor households are overcrowded. Nearly two-thirds have more than two rooms per person.

• The average American defined as poor has twice as much living space as the average Japanese and four times as much living space as the average Russian. Note: These comparisons are to the average citizens in these countries, not to those classified as poor.

• The homes and apartments of the poor typically are in good condition. The Census Bureau reports that only 5 percent of all housing of the poor have even "moderate upkeep" problems.

• Some 53 percent of poor households, owners as well as renters, have air conditioning. By contrast, just twenty years ago only 36 percent of the entire U.S. population enjoyed air conditioning.

• Contrary to popular impression, housing costs for many poor households are quite low; half of all poor households either live in taxpayer-subsidized public housing or own their own homes with mortgages fully paid.

Overall, the actual housing and living standards of the "poor" are far higher than the public would imagine. . . .

Unscrambling the Poverty Puzzle

Government surveys measuring actual food consumption, nutritional status, housing, and property ownership show that few of the households defined as "poor" by the Census are poor in the sense understood by most Americans. Furthermore, in contrast to the official Census poverty count, measures of the actual living standards of the poor show improvement over time. How can the contradiction between the official poverty numbers and these other data be explained? There are five reasons for this disagreement:

Reason #1: A large number of the poor, as defined by the Census Bureau, are only "temporarily poor." This category would include many individuals thrown out of work. Included also are the families of businessmen who suffer losses in a given year. Such families may have reasonable amounts of savings which they spend during the period of lost or reduced income. Despite temporarily low income, their life-style may not change dramatically. Few Americans would consider these households as "poor." They are radically different from families trapped in welfare dependence and permanent poverty. . . .

Reason #2: Significant numbers of poor and low-income families have cash earnings which they do not report to the Census Bureau or the Internal Revenue Service. There are large numbers of individuals working primarily for cash payments rather than salaries. These include waitresses, housekeepers, handymen, repairmen, and many other self-employed persons. Census Bureau officials admit that those who have not fully reported cash earnings to the IRS are unlikely to report those same earnings to Census takers. A recent study of welfare mothers in an unidentified major midwestern city, for example, found that over 90 percent had jobs and income they had concealed from government authorities. . . . Government surveys of expenditures show that low-income households typically spend $1.94 for every $1.00 of income reported to the Census Bureau. . . .

Americans Have It Good

Few residents of our worst ghettos would swap their assets for a one-way ticket back to Africa, Mexico, Eastern Europe or Vietnam. One would concede that the quality of the life led by the average American, measured in space, leisure, and cost of daily living, compares favorably with that of the average crowded, hard-worked Japanese, and is not markedly inferior to that of the dwellers in such socialized high-tech utopias as Switzerland, Sweden, and the united Germany—all of which, recently, evince their own discontents. Americans still have it good.

John Updike, *Forbes*, September 14, 1992.

Reason #3: The Census Bureau does not count much welfare assistance in its calculation of poverty. A family is defined as poor by comparing family income to an official income level, or "poverty threshold." The poverty threshold for a family of four was $13,359 in 1990. But in excluding nearly all welfare assistance from its calculation of family income, the Census Bureau gives the public an erroneous picture of poverty in America.

Total annual federal, state, and local welfare spending amounted to $184 billion in 1988. This figure excludes programs for the middle class such as Social Security and Medicare. But of this total welfare spending, the Census Bureau counts only $27 billion as income. Thus, $158 billion of welfare assistance is devoted to helping the disadvantaged but is not counted by the Census Bureau. This is equal to an average of $11,200 for each poor household. . . .

Reason #4: The Census Bureau ignores all assets and savings in determining whether or not a family is "in poverty." But a family which has fully paid for and furnished a house, and paid for a car, will not necessarily have a poverty life-style even if its annual cash income is regularly below the official poverty level. This point is particularly important among the elderly.

Reason #5: Low family income does not automatically indicate des-

titute living conditions. . . . The median annual housing costs for the average poor household of two persons, including utilities and taxes, came to $2916 in 1989. According to the U.S. Department of Agriculture, a thrifty but nutritious diet for that same household would cost about $1980 per year. So, the combined food and housing costs would amount to $4896, or 61 percent of the official poverty threshold in that year for a household of that size. Similarly, food and median housing costs for a poor married couple with two children living in non-subsidized rental housing is $8267 per year.

This figure is 65 percent of the poverty threshold for a family of that size. Over half of all poor households, of course, actually have housing costs below the median figures given above. Given the typical cost of basic food and housing in the U.S., it is simply incorrect to assume that most families with incomes below the poverty level must be inadequately housed and fed. . . .

Of course, America's poor do not live lavishly. But few households are "poor" in the sense of being destitute. The average poor family is well fed and well housed in a two-bedroom house or apartment that is structurally sound, in good repair, and well heated. Very few poor persons live in crowded conditions. Forty percent of all poor households own their own homes. And the average home owned by a poor household is a three-bedroom house in good repair with a value equal to 58 percent of the average value of all homes owned in America.

Moreover, the housing conditions of the poor have improved dramatically over the last thirty years. In 1960 some 25 to 30 percent of poor households actually lacked an indoor toilet. Today such situations are virtually non-existent. Today 53 percent of poor households have air-conditioning, compared to 36 percent among all U.S. households, both poor and non-poor, just twenty years ago.

For state legislators and Members of Congress to devise sound welfare policies, they need accurate information. They do not have it today. The federal government should revise its surveys to provide more accurate information about the financial resources and actual living conditions of "poor" Americans. Such good information is the necessary first step in reforming America's failed welfare system.

"The government's misleading poverty statistics
disguise the problem of the working poor."

Poverty Is Underestimated

John E. Schwarz and Thomas J. Volgy

In the following viewpoint, John E. Schwarz and Thomas J.
Volgy, authors of *The Forgotten Americans: Thirty Million Working
Poor in the Land of Opportunity*, argue that the official formula
for deciding who is poor in America is flawed. Schwarz and
Volgy contend that the poverty line—the smallest amount of
money needed to live adequately—should be much higher than
the figures used by the Census Bureau. The bureau's misleading
statistics, they charge, hide the fact that many full-time workers
are actually living in poverty. Schwarz is a professor of political
science at the University of Arizona at Tucson. Volgy, an associate professor of political science at the university, is a former
mayor of Tucson.

As you read, consider the following questions:

1. According to the authors, how did the government define
   poverty during the 1960s?
2. What has changed since the 1960s, according to Schwarz and
   Volgy, to make the Census Bureau's poverty formula out of
   date? Why do they believe this change has skewed poverty
   statistics?
3. What differences between the full-time working poor and the
   stereotype of the poor do Schwarz and Volgy see?

John E. Schwarz and Thomas J. Volgy, "Out of Line," *The New Republic*, November 23, 1992.
Reprinted by permission of *The New Republic*, © 1992, The New Republic, Inc.

Paul and Jane Lambert are married with three children. He heads a department in a retail store on the outskirts of Cleveland, and she manages an office. Both are employed full-time. They budget their combined $22,300 income with consummate skill, but it is too little to make ends meet. The family never eats out or goes to a movie. They haven't bought new clothing in years, and they don't go for Sunday drives with the children because they can't afford the gas. They are able to put food on the table and have regular meals only because Jane's parents give them money, and they have none to cover co-payments for needed medical care. Yet the federal government does not consider the Lamberts poor. To the Census Bureau, their income is nearly 50 percent above the official poverty line for a family of five.

The Lamberts escape official poverty figures because the government's poverty line, first formulated in the 1960s, is ludicrously inaccurate. In September 1992, the Census Bureau reported that in 1991 nearly 36 million Americans were living in poverty. Most people think the government's poverty line refers to a specific idea or concept of a minimal standard of living. It once did, but no longer. Divorced from any real definition of poverty, the official measure has fallen far below economic reality, masking particularly the number of working poor. The number of year-round, full-time American workers who live in poverty is actually three times what official census figures would have us believe.

The Origin of the Poverty Line

When the government adopted the poverty line measure in the mid-'60s, it defined poverty as the smallest amount of income required to afford basic necessities at the lowest level of living for an average family, purchased at the lowest realistic cost. To fall beneath this standard of living was to live in poverty. Mollie Orshansky, an official in the Social Security Administration, was most responsible for the creation of the poverty line. She started by calculating the lowest amount of money necessary to feed a family of a given size with minimum nutrition. (Food was used as the starting point of the measure for good reason. Of all consumption items, food alone had an accepted minimum standard of need.) Since the average American family at the time spent one-third of its income on food, Orshansky set the poverty line for a household at around three times the amount of the lowest realistic food budget, calculating that the family could meet the rest of its basic needs with the two-thirds not spent on food. In 1959, for example, the Orshansky formula found that a family of four needed an after-tax minimum of around $3,000 to avoid poverty.

From then on, the poverty line was adjusted each year. Initially this was done simply by reapplying Orshansky's formula. But in the late '60s the government changed the formula, choosing instead to peg the poverty line to the consumer price index. That may seem like a mere technical distinction. It isn't. The CPI measures price changes in all consumer goods, while Orshansky's formula focused on basic necessities. Over the years the cost to obtain basic necessities at the lowest standard increased more than the general inflation rate. As a result, the modified formula—the one still used today—produced a skewed result. If applied to 1990, for instance (the last year for which full data are available), the formula Orshansky devised would exceed the government's official poverty line by more than 50 percent. Had the government measured poverty consistently over time by retaining the original Orshansky formula, the poverty line for 1990 would have been more than $20,000 for a family of four, not the government's figure of around $13,000.

Hard Work Is No Guarantee Against Poverty

Americans are brought up to believe that hard-working and responsible people can make a decent living. Yet for millions of workers and their families, harsh economic realities dictate that they resort to selling their blood, going without medical care, depending on charity or subsisting on a diet of potatoes for days at a time to make ends meet. Working hard and working full-time are not enough to lift millions of people to self-sufficiency.

John E. Schwarz and Thomas J. Volgy, *Governing*, November 1992.

This higher number matches the public's perception. Seven times during the 1980s, Gallup asked Americans what they thought was the least amount of money required to live adequately. Repeatedly the dollar amounts they gave were in excess of 150 percent of the government's poverty line. To illustrate this point, assume a family of four spends about $76 a week, or $3,952 a year, on food—a very modest budget based on the lowest realistic amount needed to meet minimum nutritional requirements, according to the Department of Agriculture. Then add other necessities at the lowest and most frugal living standard of an average family. The cost to rent a two-bedroom apartment defined by the government as a low-cost unit for its public assistance programs averaged $6,192 a year ($516 a month) across the nation in 1990, including all utilities and a small allowance for telephone.

Add to that $1,500 for medical expenses for a family of four; another $1,000 for clothing and shoes for two adults and two children; and $3,200 for transportation (15 percent beneath the average 1990 cost of running a single automobile 10,000 miles yearly over a life of ten years, including fuel, tires, maintenance, repair, insurance, taxes, and financing). Throw in a modest $1,700 for everything else: soap, cleansers, personal hygiene products, furniture and appliance repairs, sheets, blankets, and towels. And, of course, $2,975 for taxes. The total: approximately $20,600 for a family of four.

A No-Frills Budget

Remember, this budget is extremely frugal. It allots no spending money for children, none to hire baby sitters or for child care, to buy books, toys, or records for the children, or for school field trips, a family pet, or even a haircut. Nor does it allow any money to pay for a meal out or to go to a movie, a ball game, or any other form of paid entertainment. And the budget has no space for savings of any kind, whether to send the children to college, to prepare for an emergency, to provide for retirement, or to help an ill or elderly parent.

In order to afford any of these so-called frills, the family would have to give up other necessities. And even without them, families living on this budget don't have enough for all the necessities. Eighty percent can't afford the cost of their shelter. Families around the country we interviewed ended up having to forgo medical or dental care (Paul and Jane Lambert's children, for example, had never been to a dentist), or spend less on food, or turn off their heat in winter. And even then they had to accept regular handouts from relatives or take charity. In several of the families, members resorted to selling their blood.

The government's misleading poverty statistics disguise the problem of the working poor. The officially reported poverty figures tell us that fewer than 2 million year-round, full-time workers were living beneath the poverty line in 1989, the end of the last recovery. But the more accurate poverty line tells a starker truth. In 1989 nearly 6 million people who worked full-time year-round were living in poverty (18 million when their spouses and children are included). This is three times the number of full-time workers that the official poverty figures said were poor, and nearly double the 3.4 million adults on the welfare rolls.

The official poverty figures say that barely 26 percent of those heading poor households who were able-bodied, non-elderly adults—people we would most expect to be working—were employed year-round full-time in 1989. By our calculation, virtually half of the household heads who lived in poverty (49 percent) were employed year-round full-time. In fact, nearly 40 percent of all year-round, full-time workers made too little to lift a family of four above the real poverty line.

The full-time working poor do not fit the stereotype of the poor in other ways, either. More than half are over age 30 and nearly three-quarters have a high school degree or have gone to college. About one-seventh of them have college degrees. In making it appear as if poverty is confined predominantly to those who do not work, or do not work steadily, the official figures have reinforced a dominant but erroneous American notion, namely that poverty is primarily the product of idleness. The more accurate poverty line proves the opposite: that the narrow economic opportunities that exist for poor and average full-time workers have left millions of working families poor or on the verge of poverty. The official poverty line has, in effect, allowed us to define our problems away.

"Those of us born in the 1920s . . . simply know how much better things are today."

The Condition of America's Poor Is Improving

James W. Michaels

Seventy-five years ago, the average middle-class family worked harder and had fewer comforts than the average poor do today, charges James W. Michaels in the following viewpoint. Michaels, editor of *Forbes* magazine, examines the nation's economic improvement since the early years of this century. The economic system is in fine shape, he concludes, as evidenced by the waiting lists of people around the world seeking to immigrate to America.

As you read, consider the following questions:

1. How does the picture of America in the 1920s drawn by Michaels compare with the picture of America today?
2. According to the author, what might keep today's American poor from having more comforts than the average American did 75 years ago?
3. It isn't the American economic system that needs to be repaired, according to Michaels. What system does need attention, in his view?

From James W. Michaels, "Oh, Our Aching Angst," *Forbes*, September 14, 1992. Reprinted by permission of *Forbes* magazine, © Forbes Inc., 1992.

When you're my age you don't have to ask: Are Americans really materially better off than they were in the recent past? Those of us born in the 1920s and with vivid memories of the Depression simply *know* how much better things are today. The improvement is implicit in almost our every memory, every experience.

Even for comfortable middle-class people life was much more difficult and insecure in the 1920s than it is today. If he was fortunate enough to have central heating (less than one-third of the population in 1920 did), middle-class Dad had to pull himself from bed at 4 a.m. on cold winter mornings to unbank the furnace and shovel coal; if he overslept, the pipes froze. But he usually didn't have to rake leaves or shovel snow. Not in the 1930s. That was done by shabby, humble men who knocked at the back door mornings, asking for a warm meal in return for doing chores.

In 1921 the typical American workweek was 60 hours, and many people worked longer. The most common American household appliance was a woman, who worked a lot more than 60 hours in her home. Leisure-time industries scarcely existed because few people had leisure. For more than half the population, the family toilet was a hole in the backyard with a shack built over it. In those shacks, Scott Paper products competed with difficulty against old Sears and Montgomery Ward catalogs; real toilet paper was a luxury.

Senior citizens? We called them old folks, and they were old in their 50s; if they were lucky, one of their kids had a spare room for them, maybe in the attic. Life expectancy was about 54 years, which was just as well because there were few pensions beyond what the gold watch might bring at a pawnshop.

I'm not talking about the 19th century. I'm describing the first three or four decades in our own century. Unless they blow their money and energy on booze or drugs, the American poor have more physical comforts today than the *average* American did 75 years ago.

We've come a long way, and although the rate of improvement has slowed lately, our economy put on an amazing performance in this century. So amazing that almost every U.S. consulate has a waiting list for immigration visas.

Change America? To What?

Yet in 1992 on television I watched a sweating Bill Clinton harangue a midwestern audience. Work with me to change America, the candidate shouted, punching the air, Kennedy-like, with his fist. That cliché produced the expected cheers and waving of banners. Cut now to a local living room where a TV reporter interviews a well-dressed middle-aged woman. What did she think of the speech? "I liked it," she said. "God knows we need change in this country."

Change from what to what? The lady didn't say and the newscaster didn't even think to ask; everyone just assumes the country is in rotten shape. Where do they get their certainty? From the mass media that keep telling them that the economy is a mess, America is a mess.

Poverty Is Disappearing

Income is really only a proxy for something more important: material welfare. And in this regard, income proves to have been a highly misleading indicator.

With this realization, a growing number of social scientists are taking another look at the data and coming to surprising conclusions. . . .

"The corrected statistics show that the standard of living is rising, inequality is falling, and poverty is disappearing," asserts the distinguished Harvard economist Dale Jorgenson.

Jonathan Marshall, *Reason*, July 1993.

Peggy Noonan got it right: . . . "It is writers—journalists, screenwriters, novelists, newswriters—we turn to more than anyone to tell us exactly how our country is doing, and they are precisely the last people who would accurately point out that in the long tape of history this is a pretty good few inches. . . ."

But where do the media mandarins get their feeling that these are bad inches on history's tape? From writers and academicians, of course. Especially from writers and academicians who have a low opinion of capitalism and of American popular culture. The media machine turns this highbrow griping into sound bites and data bites and feeds them to the masses.

To mark *Forbes* magazine's 75th anniversary, the editors wanted to look behind the sour moroseness of the media and seek more profound explanations for the prevailing angst.

No Economists

At the start we decided: no economists. They have nothing to tell us about the real reasons for America's turn-of-the-millennium discontent. So eleven of America's best writers and scholars gave their noneconomic explanations for the blue funk oppressing Americans.

Each essay was an attempt by the author to answer our question: Why do Americans feel so bad when they've got it so good?

Varied as the answers are, there is a fairly common thread. It isn't the national debt or the unemployment rate or the current recession that bothers the nation's thinkers. It's not an economic mess that they see. It's a moral mess, a cultural mess. While the media natter about a need for economic change, these serious intellectuals worry about our psyches. Can the human race stand prosperity? Is the American experiment in freedom and equal opportunity morally bankrupt?

Reading the essays isn't a comfortable experience for one who believes deeply in this country and its values. Without exception these brainy Americans (and one Brit) see us in a moral crisis. . . . It isn't the economic system that needs fixing, most of [the] essayists say. It's our value system. As historian Gertrude Himmelfarb puts it: "I am not talking about . . . psychobabble. . . . I am talking of the justified discontent of the responsible citizen who discovers that economic and material goods are no compensation for social and moral ills."

Pessimism May Be Justified

Some conclude that pessimism is justified and that we are in grave risk of going to hell. Harvard historian Simon Schama writes: "More housing starts, a little leap in the 'consumer confidence' ratings, or a pickup in auto sales may signal some sort of return to short-term cheerfulness, but these indices say nothing about the deep systemic sicknesses that may in the end determine that the American Century will have lasted, in fact, for just 50 years.

"It's an old joke in our family that the Schamas have an uncanny knack for following collapsing empires. A century and a half ago we were subjects of the Ottoman Empire; then, as that disintegrated, took ourselves off to Habsburg Vienna; thence, in my parents' generation, to Edwardian Britain. And here I am."

It may be that the Schama family will have to flee once more. But it's well to remember that this is a country where the intellectuals have almost always felt cut off and unhappy. Just because people write well doesn't mean they can predict well or even accurately judge the present. Saul Bellow, the great novelist, dismisses a lot of the current doom-saying with these words:

"When I was young the great pundits were personalities like H.G. Wells or George Bernard Shaw or Havelock Ellis or Romain Rolland. We respectfully read what they had to say about communism, fascism, peace, eugenics, sex. I recall these celebrities unsentimentally. Wells, Shaw and Romain Rolland brought punditry into disrepute. The last of the world-class mental giants was Jean-Paul Sartre, one of whose contributions to world peace was to exhort the oppressed of the Third World to slaughter whites indiscriminately.

"Lincoln Steffens, playing the pundit in Russia after the Revolution, said, 'I have been over into the future, and it works.' Some secret wisdom! As a horseplayer he would have lost his shirt."

So, before you lose your shirt and your faith in the country, decide for yourself what is behind the American angst-amidst-abundance. I personally like what political scientist James Q. Wilson writes: "Cheer up, Americans. You are right to be grumpy, but there is no system for governing a large, free and complex society such as ours that is likely to do much better or make you less grumpy. If you don't believe it, travel."

And when you get back from Sweden and Japan, Germany and Cuba and hear our politicians and our ideamongers shouting about changing America, ask them: Change it to what? At what cost?

"People . . . who were children during the Great Depression . . . tend to romanticize poverty."

The Condition of America's Poor Is Deteriorating

Bettye Caldwell

Poor people in America's past suffered from a different kind of poverty—poverty with hope, according to Bettye Caldwell, author of the following viewpoint. Caldwell notes that an increasing number of poor children are born into a bleak future. The lack of hope that they can escape poverty compounds the problems of the disadvantaged, she asserts. Those born poor today, unlike the poor in America's past, are likely to remain so. Caldwell, professor of education at the University of Arkansas, Little Rock, and past president of the National Association for the Education of Young Children, began the first infant day-care program in America.

As you read, consider the following questions:

1. How does the description of the home environment of the child named Willie, quoted in the viewpoint, convey the impression of poverty without directly discussing money?
2. What statistics does the author cite as evidence that childhood poverty will continue to increase?
3. What threat is implicit in Caldwell's reference to the poor children of Hong Kong and Latin America?

From Bettye Caldwell, "Childhood Poverty." In *Buying America Back*, Jonathan Greenberg and William Kistler, editors. Tulsa: Council Oak Books, 1992. Reprinted by permission of the author.

Some years ago there was a wonderful Jules Feiffer cartoon showing a dyspeptic old man telling the readers that over the years he had been told at different times that he was poor, needy, deprived, underprivileged, or disadvantaged. The punch line of the cartoon, which I have long since lost and therefore cannot properly attribute, was something like, "I still don't have a dime, but I have a great vocabulary."

If disadvantaged children had the vocabulary, they could track backwards across those words to the crux of their problem: they are poor kids. Poor children in an age of affluence, children trapped in a cycle of failure in an era when everyone is supposed to succeed. That is the way childhood comes packaged for all too many children today. And, unfortunately, the package appears to be totally recyclable.

There are still a few people around who were children during the Great Depression, and many of them tend to romanticize poverty in childhood. In fact, for those who have "made it," a past childhood of poverty is almost a status symbol. A multimillionaire movie actor can speak with nostalgic braggadocio about having slept in a bureau drawer or in a double bed with three siblings. From the comfort of my paneled study with its two functioning computers I can reminisce about wearing dresses made from flour sacks (sometimes using prints from two sacks that neither matched nor blended) and taking a school lunch consisting only of a cold biscuit and maybe a little bacon. Many of us did know poverty—real poverty that went beyond the fashionable level. Furthermore, we often minimize its effects by claiming (inaccurately) that "everyone was poor." But it was perhaps poverty with a difference: it was poverty with hope. Prosperity was just around the corner, and happy days were going to be here again.

No Comparison

The kind of poverty and disadvantage experienced during the Great Depression probably did not compare to that described by Ned O'Gorman, a poet and educator who established a private school, The Storefront, located in the heart of Harlem. One cannot help but be moved by this description of the home environment of one of the Storefront children:

> When Willie first came to my nursery, he was mute. Till then he had never had a chance to talk to anyone, even with his limited use of words, about the world. He had gotten used to the silence.
>
> His mother, her husband, his two sisters and brother live in a flat that was a wreck when they came into it; it increased in horrors as the months went on; the plaster cracked and peeled; the plumbing gradually went to pot and a stink of

urine permeated everything. The kitchen was a lounge for roaches. They took command everywhere: in the butter dishes in the icebox, in the bread, in the rubber insulating lining of the icebox door, in the cutlery drawer, in the sink, around the faucets. They marched with their crisp brown bodies into the glasses on the drying rack and romped on the plates in the china closet. . . . One afternoon I found the father in a state of great anger and self-righteousness. The children had been acting up, and he had locked them in a closet, nailed a board across the door and let them stew in the dark for a few minutes. The children . . . hung like skinned rats in a little room, dumb with horror from their ordeal.

That, of course, is real poverty—soul-destroying, hope-demolishing, escape-barring poverty. And it is the children who experience this type of chronic, unrelenting poverty who are most completely at a disadvantage in today's world.

Ted Rall, reprinted by permission of Chronicle Features, San Francisco, California.

Contemporary demographic data all present the same bleak picture: we have many children living in poverty in this country, and the proportion of children living in such conditions is increasing rather than decreasing. A recent analysis by the Center for the Study of Social Policy of trends that reflect the well-being of children showed that child poverty increased during the 1980s by some 26%. By 1989 over 12 million children under 18, representing 20% of the total population of children, lived below the poverty line ($12,675 for a family of four). Black and Hispanic children were far more likely to live in poverty (43.8% and 38.2%, respectively, in comparison to 15.4% for whites). The increase over the decade, incidentally, was greatest for whites (36%); blacks showed the smallest increase (16%).

The National Center for Children in Poverty has published similar data for children younger than six—the group most vulnerable to the negative impact of poverty and the group least capable of doing anything about it. Ironically, this age group is more likely to be poor than any other. . . . The incidence of poverty is almost one out of four, or approximately 5 million children. Again, blacks and Hispanics are over-represented in the poverty population. Almost half (42%) of the poor children under six are white, but this represents only 13% of the total population of white children in that age group. In contrast, almost half of all black children and two-fifths of Hispanic children of comparable ages were poor.

Other demographics could be cited which would strengthen the case that we have too many disadvantaged children and that something must be done. Disadvantages, of course, tend to come in packages, not in isolation. For example, data from the 1990 census show that 29% of first births were born to single parents. As single parent households bring in less income, and as women generally earn less than men, this statistic signifies the increased likelihood of poverty in children. And poor children, when their mothers do work, are more likely to be in poor quality child care. When a family lives in poverty, there is little or no money to be used for sharing the joyful occasions that help to make up our memories of happy family life. In addition, the stresses associated with subsistence living increase the probability of child abuse. Thus poverty and disadvantage have a way of compounding themselves, of metastasizing into a tumor that invades the whole organism. That fact alone makes them difficult to eliminate. . . .

Poverty Threatens All of Society

"What shall I give my children, who are poor?" asked Gwendolyn Brooks in the opening line of a beautiful sonnet some years ago. In order to help America move ahead into the 21st Century, we have to make a firm commitment to answer that question with the resolute promise, "A great deal." Their needs threaten to pour forth like lava from an uncontrollable volcano. If society does not meet those needs, then adults, as well as the children themselves, will also be losers. Anyone who has seen the menacing threat in the eyes of boat children in Hong Kong

35

or experienced the hostility manifested by the army of homeless waifs roaming the cities of Latin America will know that, if the numbers multiply to a critical level, no one is safe—least of all the children, who deserve a safe haven.

I have cited current demographics to illustrate the magnitude of poverty in children in America at the end of the 20th century. Approximately one out of every five children lives in poverty, with almost as many living just above that cutting point. Just what the critical mass is that would signal a major social breakdown no one can specify exactly. However, a concerned society surely does not want it to be any greater than it is now.

"Over 30 million people . . . do not have the food
security they need to maintain an adequate diet."

Hunger in America
Is Increasing

Kevin Clarke

America's hungry have traditionally been the elderly, the long-term poor, and children. In the following viewpoint, Kevin Clarke enlarges this picture to include newly unemployed and underemployed people who never expected to go hungry. While some Americans are starving, he maintains, millions more—many of whom are not eligible for food stamps—are now chronically undernourished. Clarke is assistant editor for *Salt*, a magazine published by a Roman Catholic community, the Claretians, for Christians who seek social justice.

As you read, consider the following questions:

1. According to Clarke, what groups of people are experiencing hunger for the first time?
2. The author does not believe food banks should be the official answer to widespread hunger. Do you agree? Why or why not?
3. Why is it ironic that hunger can be most severe in rural communities, in Clarke's view?

From Kevin Clarke, "Who's Hungry Now?" *Salt*, March 1993. Reprinted by permission of Claretian Publications, 205 W. Monroe St., Chicago, IL 60606.

The tractor trailers somehow make the sharp turns from Chicago's narrow streets into the loading docks that are lined up in asphalt rows for blocks around Pulaski Avenue. The big trucks bring the food in; smaller ones come later to truck it out.

The Greater Chicago Food Depository looks no different from the warehouses that surround it in this otherwise residential neighborhood on Chicago's West Side. It has the same gray metal exterior as the others. And past the doors it's the same busy industrial interior—stacks of pallets, swirling warning lights, and shouting workers dodging hi-los, hand trucks, and conveyors.

What distinguishes this storage space, though, is the row of volunteers at work on a unique production line and the "product" itself that is stacked around them—food, tons of food. Huge shipping boxes of cereal, market overorders, misprints, discontinued products, dented cans of beans, crushed boxes—the depository is the last refuge of forgotten foods.

They're the factory rejects—production mistakes and marketing misdemeanors—that in the recent past would simply have been thrown away, buried by the ton in landfills. . . .

Now local supermarket chains like Jewel and Dominick's and big food manufacturers like Quaker Oats bring their excess or otherwise unsellable products to the depository. Once there the food is sorted, repackaged, and cleaned up as necessary, the beginning of a short journey to homes where the misfit food will be welcome, whatever its marketing flaws may have been.

The depository is a well-oiled testament to the increasing sophistication and efficiency of the food-relief distribution network in the United States. Last year, the Greater Chicago Food Depository distributed over 22 million pounds of food, representing 48,000 meals for every operating day—$45 million worth of food. Those numbers make it the largest food bank in the world.

It is also the primary food source for over 500 food pantries and other food programs at shelters and soup kitchens scattered throughout Chicago. The food depository is feeding a hungry city.

And other food banks like it are feeding a hungry country. Almost 30 years after the United States initiated its war on hunger with various federal food-assistance programs—food stamps, WIC (the Women, Infants, and Children supplemental food program), and school breakfast and lunch programs—the specter of chronic hunger is once again threatening the country's most vulnerable citizens.

A Distressing Milestone

In April 1992, the United States reached a distressing milestone. A record 25.8 million people—10.2 percent of the nation's population and 7 million more than in just 1989—were receiving food stamps. Advocates think as many as 20 million more

Americans may be economically eligible for food stamps but not receiving them. Most if not all of these people, advocates say, are hungry in the United States today.

In many ways the faces of the hungry are familiar: poor folks, people scraping by on public aid. America's older citizens remain hungry. Between one half million and 1 million of the country's senior citizens are malnourished; 30 percent of all senior citizens skip meals on a regular basis.

Native American populations, where people have trouble reaching government support services, remain often startling pockets of hunger. The hungry can be found among the nation's homeless and undocumented aliens.

Mostly, the United States' hungry are still its children. One in four children is growing up hungry, according to Bread for the World, a Washington-based international, interfaith hunger-policy agency.

But advocates say a new class of hungry are beginning to appear at food pantries across the nation.

"We've always had people who were unemployed or on S.S.I. (Social Security) or AFDC (Aid to Families with Dependent Children)," says Barbara McCormick, the director of the Interfaith Ministries' Hunger Coalition in Houston. "But today what we're seeing is more families, more long-term unemployed people, or people who are working but just don't have enough money to buy food."

The New Faces of Hunger

McCormick's experience is being repeated in urban and "post industrial" areas throughout the nation. The country's nouveau poor—recently laid-off workers, "permanent part-time" workers, industrial workers who can now only find jobs that offer a fraction of their previous salaries—are becoming the new faces of hunger.

Many of these new hungry—because they do have some kind of work or have acquired some property from a period when they did have jobs—are discovering that they cannot receive food stamps. For these working hungry, the aid from a local food pantry may be all they can expect to receive. The nation's mayors report a 26 percent increase last year alone in emergency food requests.

While the grim numbers indicate a serious hunger problem, advocates say people in the United States are not facing the same kind of food crisis being experienced by desperate people in other parts of the world. "Mostly it's chronic inadequacy," says Bread for the World's Barbara Howell.

John Colgan is the director of the Illinois Hunger Coalition. "People aren't hungry every day," he says. "It's usually in a monthly cycle. There's a week, a couple of days or maybe more, when the money runs out." His coalition's research indicates that the average family in Illinois has exhausted its monthly allotment of food stamps a little over two weeks into any given month.

"We don't have people starving to death in the streets, but we do have over 30 million people who do not have the food security they need to maintain an adequate diet."

While Colgan's assessment is generally accurate, advocates say specific cases of starvation and acute hunger do occur in the United States. "In urban areas, many of the homeless are going days without meals," says George Sanders, the director of the Alabama Coalition Against Hunger.

"We have people who are stuck way back in the woods. At the end of the month when the food stamps are running thin, they are not eating meals. And I know for a fact because I've seen it, that there are children in Alabama who are in the school lunch program who haven't eaten when they come back to school since the day before at school."

Food Security Is Threatened

Not since hunger became a focus of the war on poverty in the 1960s has "food security"—the ability of a typical family to maintain a level of nutrition necessary to good health and physical comfort—been as threatened as it is today.

That's true for several reasons. Up through the late 1970s, advocates say, federal food-assistance programs such as food stamps and school breakfast and lunch programs had been adequately addressing the problem of hunger. But the 1980s began a steady erosion of both the reach and effectiveness of those programs at the same time the advent of other, seemingly more imperative social ills like homelessness and the lack of affordable housing "bumped" hunger off the media's priority lists.

"But it has not gone away," Colgan says. "It has only gotten worse. Hunger is an invisible problem, though it certainly isn't to a trained eye. You walk by people every day who are hungry and lacking food security. They don't have name tags. . . ."

While homeless people represent a very visible problem on the nation's streets, Colgan says the hungry can be "someone who is dressed like you and me, and they may be going to work.". . .

Sister Evelyn Summers, who oversees service programs [for St. Basil's Food Pantry on Chicago's South Side], has been experiencing a slight increase in business of late.

"Mostly younger people have been coming, younger people who normally would be in the job market. They just closed a big Phar-Mor [grocery and pharmacy] nearby, and that put a lot of neighborhood people out of work. It sometimes puts a strain on us.

"There are a lot of first-timers. They're disjointed [by being laid off] and embarrassed that they have to come here. They feel like it's begging. They're confused by the system and angry. They've got that 'I don't believe this is happening to me' feeling," she says.

A lot of St. Basil's new pantry clients are being forced to make some hard choices about their monthly budgets for the first time.

"One of my new people was a woman who lost her job as a public school aide. She used the money she did have to pay her mortgage and her utilities because she thought they were more important, then she ran out of money for food. She told me, 'I didn't have to make those decisions before. I just took them for granted.'"

That response is pretty typical, according to John Colgan. His studies indicate that food is often the last item on a poor or struggling family's priority list. Paying for shelter—whether through a mortgage or as rent—and maintaining utility payments always come first. "They buy food with what's left over."

Colgan is quick to commend the work being done at the 50,000 private food banks and pantries like St. Basil's throughout the U.S., which he thinks represent a final, thin, and increasingly overburdened line of defense against a wholesale food disaster.

"They certainly have to be supported. They really are carrying the weight that is keeping people out of the starving mode."

Though government may have come to tacitly rely on private food pantries, Colgan likes to remind people that they hardly reflect a concrete answer to the problem of hunger.

"They've become an integral part of providing food security to people, but real security comes about when people have the income and the resources to buy what they need without going to charity."

And as the number of hungry increases in the U.S., the strain on the fragile pantry networks will become more obvious. Jo Ann Jensen of the Greater Chicago Food Depository thinks many of the pantries the depository serves have already begun stretching their monthly food budgets, much the same but on a larger scale than their individual family clients do. She explains that while the number of people who have been turned away from pantries (though referred elsewhere) because the pantries have run out of food has remained constant—about 2000 a month—the overall number of people the pantries are serving has increased.

Problems in Rural America

Rural America faces unique challenges in addressing its hunger problems. George Sanders, the director of the Alabama Coalition against Hunger, says the highest percentages of hungry are to be found in rural counties.

He is not unaware of the irony that hunger can be the severest in these rural communities—where the nation raises most of the food it uses to feed its citizens and a good number of the people of the world. That's because the infrastructure of rural communities, according to Sanders, is designed primarily to get food out, not to distribute the food within.

There are other roadblocks preventing the rural hungry from reaching food aid. Many, though eligible, do not receive food stamps or other government food support like WIC.

"Half of our counties [in Alabama] don't have municipalities of any size in them." These small communities simply don't have social-service agencies located in them. Visiting the right government office to maintain the food-assistance paperwork can mean a 60- to 100-mile round-trip odyssey.

"People in rural communities can't just walk down the street and jump on a bus and say, 'I'll be back with the documents,'" Sanders says. "There's no public transportation in most of these communities."

People in small, rural towns are also less willing to apply for food stamps because it's harder to protect their privacy. They may travel far out of their way to other communities to avoid buying food with stamps at the grocery where they've shopped all their lives.

And while urban food pantries can expect shipments of U.S. Department of Agriculture food surpluses pretty much on a monthly basis, rural pantries can expect such shipments only quarterly, making planning for such pantries difficult.

That is, it would make planning difficult, Sanders says, if rural communities *had* pantries. Most don't. Sanders says the fewer numbers of residents in sparsely populated counties can make maintaining a volunteer staff at a food pantry pretty challenging if not impossible.

In Alabama at least, Sanders says the rural hungry are less visible, harder to find. "We've got people up in the mountains, way up in the hollows," out of sight and out of reach of both government workers and advocates.

The System Doesn't Work Anymore

Advocates like Sanders say the contemporary problem of hunger cannot ultimately be resolved unless policymakers reappraise the nation's current food-assistance system. It's a system, they complain, that simply doesn't work anymore.

"When we see people on food stamps now we can almost assume they are in trouble," Colgan says, rather than the opposite, which would have been true as few as 12 years ago. "You'd be under attack if you used that as a standard," he allows, "but you wouldn't be wrong."

Worse news is that only 52 percent of the people who are income-eligible for food stamps are receiving them. Colgan blames that shortfall on the lack of a community outreach that had been a standardized component of the food-stamp program in the past. It was one of the aspects of the program cut during the 1980s. As a result, many working poor assume they are ineligible without getting the facts on the program.

"You're dealing with a proud group of folks. They may have assets, but they'll sell them down until they're flat broke before they'll apply for food stamps. Some people might say that's okay, but that's not within the aims of the food-stamp program."

Colgan argues that the designers of the country's food-assistance programs in the 1960s understood the importance of maintaining a well-fed population to national defense and a strong economy. Those designers might also be the first to argue that it is hardly logical for a country to allow its citizens to impoverish themselves in response to what may be a short-term economic crisis.

Sanders offers a concrete example. According to food-stamp regulations, families who possess an automobile valued at more than $4800 (a figure that has not been adjusted since the mid-

1970s) cannot join the program. "A guy working in a steel mill gets laid off—we've got a lot of folk like this now in Alabama—and he applies for food stamps and they tell him, 'You are income-eligible, but your pickup is worth more than $4800.' He has to sell that and use that money before he can get food stamps, but by selling that vehicle he entraps himself in a cycle of poverty; it makes it more difficult for him to find work again."

Food-stamp eligibility has also been reduced by how the federal government has redefined household and family. In response to the tightening economic times, many families have been doubling up in single households. But when two families live in one residence, they may be counted as "one household."

The total household income may then be used to determine eligibility for food stamps. That means if one family is drawing an adequate income, it may push the other family out of food-stamp eligibility—whether or not both families are sharing household food expenses.

Such efforts to restrict eligibility, advocates argue, are ultimately counterproductive.

It's a matter of dollars and sense, Barbara Howell says. She points out that chronic hunger directly contributes to the nation's increasingly expensive health-care dilemma, most obviously in the predicament of low-birth-weight babies. Health care for such fragile infants can reach astounding costs even on an individual basis.

That childhood "start-up" cost only grows with children who continue to be hungry and who experience a variety of "failure to thrive" health problems during their growing years.

Saving Money in the Long Run

Howell says programs like WIC and Head Start "save money in the long run." She explains that for every dollar spent to feed a hungry mother or child, government can save $4 it now spends in Medicare costs related to the health problems low-birth-weight infants and malnourished children typically have.

Hunger is also a silent contributor to education costs. A hungry child is irritable at school, has headaches, and has difficulty following classroom work. That means immediate higher short-term costs in education.

But Howell says the problem of hunger has even deeper implications if the long-term educational and social costs are factored in. She argues students graduating without the tools to find work and hold down a job are not going to be able to participate in a U.S. economy that must compete with a well-educated global work force.

The good news is that the country need not wait for such worst-case scenarios to evolve. Howell says the programs that can wipe out hunger are already established, they simply have to have their resources and vision restored.

"We don't have to start from ground zero. Things are in place now; it's a matter of making this a priority." Bills like the "Every Fifth Child Act" indicate a renewed interest in the nation's hunger problem. That act would fully fund programs like WIC and Head Start so that every eligible child could be included.

Hunger Could Be Eradicated

Colgan says that with the right commitment hunger as a specific social ill could be eradicated within five years. While hunger is inextricably bound to the other social dynamics that swirl around it—unemployment, poverty, education, industrial decline—he argues that it's not necessary to resolve these complex problems to do away with hunger.

"I don't think our long-term goal is to get people into federal entitlement programs and leave them there. But none of the [hunger] programs are being utilized in ways they should be utilized. If they were fully implemented they would have a drastic effect on hunger. That's what makes the problem of hunger unique in relation to other poverty problems.". . .

"My main problem in South Dakota is we have such a pride issue here," says Kay Tourney, the operating manager of Sioux Falls' Food Service Center. "We have people not going to food pantries or applying for food stamps.". . .

Part of that resistance she blames on the inevitable isolation of western, rural living; but part of it she attributes to a stubborn loyalty to the regional folk mythology.

"Really, it's a part of the country where people are used to doing the most for themselves, the most they can. In the rural areas, we really have a lot of trouble finding the people who need help."

Food Is a Right

Tourney applies some of that folksiness to her own common-sense approach to the ups and downs of food-pantry life. Some of her clients are a little tough to work with because of mental illness or just plain ornery owing to their circumstances.

"Food is a right, not a privilege. We got some people here who say, 'How can you let so-and-so in after the trouble they were last time?' or 'They didn't even say thank you.'

"I always say, 'I don't care if anybody ever thanks me here.' We ain't gonna play politics with food here. Why should someone come here and kiss my boots when they've been through hell?"

45

"Poverty is not the cause of malnutrition in America."

Hunger in America Is Not Increasing

Shawn Miller

The food stamp program provides coupons for food to those whose income is near the poverty level. Currently, 10 percent of Americans participate in the program. The fact that this figure is increasing even though the unemployment rate is relatively level has been touted as proof that hunger is rampant in America, according to Shawn Miller. In the following viewpoint, Miller disagrees and argues that no evidence exists to prove that Americans are malnourished. Instead, she suggests, the aggressive push by welfare advocates and government administrators to expand the food stamp program has merely undermined the pride and the work ethic of low-income Americans. Miller is a reporter for *Insight on the News,* a monthly publication of the Washington Times Corporation.

As you read, consider the following questions:

1. What factors, according to Miller, have recently affected the level of participation in the food stamp program?
2. What reasoning does the author offer to refute the idea that an increase in food stamp recipients proves there are more hungry people in the United States?
3. What paradox does Miller present in the picture of welfare workers trying to enhance their clients' self-esteem in order to convince them to accept food stamps?

From Shawn Miller, "Giving Free Food the Stamp of Approval," *Insight on the News,* January 18, 1993. Reprinted with permission.

Sitting in the reception room of the Floyd I. Hudson State Service Center in Newark, Del., Yvonne Pizarro fidgets nervously with her purse strings. She would rather be anywhere on this cold, gloomy December day than applying for food stamps.

"This is not something I wanted to do," Pizarro says to the carpet. Despite losing the income of her husband, who recently left her, Pizarro, a nurse who works part-time with the elderly, resisted the idea of government assistance for herself and her 6-year-old daughter. Her cousin finally convinced her that she didn't have a choice, but "it was a week before I could force myself to come here and actually do this."

Millions of Americans over the past three years have similarly overcome their qualms about receiving food stamps. In Delaware, the number of food stamp recipients has increased in that time by 75 percent. And the story is much the same across the country. The number of Americans receiving food stamps set yet another monthly record in September 1992; the Agriculture Department has announced that 26.43 million recipients were on the books that month. Even discounting the 530,000 recipients added due to hurricanes Andrew and Iniki, this figure represents an increase of more than 7 million since the end of 1989. Congress authorized $28.1 billion, also a record, for the burgeoning program in the fiscal year that began Oct. 1, 1992.

The System Is Working

Critics of the Bush administration have been quick to characterize the food stamp explosion as another "cold reminder of the human toll the recession has taken," in the words of Democratic Sen. Patrick Leahy of Vermont. But the recession doesn't come close to accounting for the magnitude of the increase, which far outstrips that during earlier and more severe economic downturns.

"The whole situation has been very unusual," says Andrew Hornsby the Agriculture Department's deputy administrator for food stamps. "In the past, food stamp participation has always tracked along with unemployment." This stands to reason: The gross monthly income of a household must be at or below 130 percent of the federal poverty level for its members to be eligible for food stamps. The poverty line for a family of four is $1,512 a month; the food stamp cutoff is $1,966. The addition or subtraction of one paycheck often will make the difference. "But unemployment leveled out two years ago," says Hornsby, "and food stamps have continued to skyrocket."

What does the end of the cause-and-effect relationship between unemployment and food stamps signify? To Hornsby, it's simple: "The system is working." More and more people who qualify are availing themselves of the program. "The most overwhelming evidence of the success of the food stamp program is the fact that one American in every 10 currently participates."

Not everyone applauds the accomplishment. Robert Rector, a policy analyst at the Heritage Foundation, says the government "has worked very hard to break down the extremely valuable work ethic of low-income Americans who wanted to be self-sufficient and didn't want to depend on welfare. It looks like they're succeeding."

The term food "stamps" is an anachronism; stamps were used only in a temporary program from 1939 to 1943. Under the Food Stamp Act of 1964, which launched the modern program, participants have received coupons, which now come in the same denominations as currency: $1, $5 and $10.

What the modern program shares with its predecessor is a dual purpose: providing food for the needy and serving as a vehicle for distributing the surpluses created by federal agriculture subsidies. Indeed, the program has been the linchpin in an enduring alliance that cuts across party lines, between big city and rural members of Congress. Since 1968, food stamps and agricultural programs have been voted on in tandem. "Throughout the sixties and seventies food stamps were basically used as a hostage to make sure urban congressmen would vote for farm subsidies," says James Bovard, author of *Farm Fiasco*.

Andrew Hornsby's measure of success—how many qualified participants can be signed up—is one widely shared by program administrators and welfare advocacy groups. "USDA [U.S. Dept. of Agriculture] will always take more criticism for not having enough people on the program than for having too many," says Maurice MacDonald, a food stamp expert who has done research for the University of Wisconsin's Institute for Research on Poverty.

Use Rises During Bad and Good Times

Unhappiness with less than full participation has prompted Congress to legislate repeated reforms, which may finally have produced the desired effect: rising rates of participation during good times and bad.

Based on USDA findings that only a third of eligible households in 1976 were receiving food stamps, the Carter administration in 1977 proposed the first thoroughgoing reform of the program. The chief goal was to make food stamps "free." Previously, recipients had been required to spend their own cash to buy coupons of higher value from the government. (The purchase requirement was aimed at combating fraud; in theory, people who paid cash for the tickets were more likely to use them for food, not resell them illegally for cash.)

The 1977 reform achieved its aim: The Agriculture Department estimates that elimination of the purchase requirement added as many as 4.7 million food stamp recipients by 1980. Adjusted for inflation, spending on the food stamp program went from $4.4 billion in fiscal 1977 to $9.7 billion in fiscal 1980.

Poor Americans Are Not Malnourished

Rich and poor Americans typically eat rich diets in comparison to the rest of the world. The item most associated with an expensive diet is the level of meat consumption. . . . There is very little difference in meat consumption between high and low income Americans, but the differences between poor Americans and the average population in the rest of the world are dramatic. Low income Americans eat 75 percent more meat than the average Briton and 61 percent more than the average Italian. In a nation allegedly afflicted with a "hunger crisis," low income Americans eat twice as much meat as the average Portuguese, and two and a half times as much meat as the average Mexican, and nearly four times as much meat as the average Brazilian.

Malnutrition and hunger caused by poverty are virtually nonexistent in the U.S. Protein and overall caloric intake are the most expensive factors of any diet. Nevertheless, in its extensive surveys the U.S. government has found no evidence of significant caloric or protein deficiencies among the poor. Indeed, being overweight is the number one dietary problem of both rich and poor Americans.

Robert Rector, Kate Walsh O'Beirne, and Michael McLaughlin, Heritage Foundation *Backgrounder*, September 21, 1990.

Having found a blueprint for success, Congress would use it again. Participation in the food stamp program began to drop in the mid-1980s; the Reagan economic boom had driven down unemployment, and as in the past, food stamp use also fell. A Congressional Budget Office study requested by Rep. Leon E. Panetta of California (then chairman of the Agriculture subcommittee on nutrition and now budget director for the Clinton White House) found that in 1984 only 51 percent of those eligible were on the program. Panetta was distressed, commenting, "When people slip through the cracks of one of the nation's key hunger prevention programs, we need to find out why."

A slew of government researchers went to work finding a sealant for the cracks. Their consensus was that USDA was failing to advertise its services sufficiently; too many people who qualified for food stamps were claiming to be unaware of the fact. Congress provided a number of legislative nudges in the mid- to late eighties intended to increase participation.

As detailed in a 1990 study by the USDA's Food and Nutrition Services agency, which oversees the program, these included:

• The 1985 Food Security Act, which extended automatic food stamp benefits to households already receiving welfare payments from the Aid to Families with Dependent Children or Supplemental Security Income programs.

• The 1987 McKinney Homeless Act, which funded outreach efforts to help homeless people obtain food stamps.

• The 1988 Immigration Reform and Control Act, which by providing amnesty to illegal aliens allowed them to become eligible for food stamps.

More significant than all of these, however, may have been the expansion of the Medicaid program in the late 1980s. By extending the reach of the welfare state, Medicaid brought new clients into seemingly unrelated programs such as food stamps, noted Sheena McConnell of Mathematica Policy Research in a 1991 USDA-funded report to Congress. McConnell estimates that a fourth of the increase in food stamp participation from 1989 to 1990 can be explained by the growth of Medicaid. She points out that once people enter the labyrinth of federal entitlement programs, they are more likely to be told they qualify for food stamps. In fact, some states have passed laws requiring social service workers to inform Medicaid recipients if they qualify for food stamps.

Coupled with the recession, the cumulative effect of all these efforts has been striking. Maurice MacDonald doesn't think Congress expected its actions to result in the dramatic increase in food stamp use over the past three years. "What we have to watch for now," he warns, "is that food stamp participation drops as the economy strengthens. If it does not, then we have to start asking new questions about the structure of the economy and the effectiveness of the food stamp programs."

Solution Is Proof of Hunger?

While the growth in food stamp participation is driven in large part by a political and bureaucratic imperative to sign up as many recipients as possible, the higher numbers this produces are almost invariably presented as proof that hunger is running rampant in the U.S.

When the USDA on Dec. 1, 1992, released the figures showing record participation for the month of September, it produced a flurry of warnings from Capitol Hill. "Food stamps are a last resort," said Ohio Democratic Rep. Tony P. Hall, chairman of the House Select Committee on Hunger. "It's a bad sign when 26 million Americans are so desperate that they need them to eat."

Besides pointing to the numbers as representing the human toll of the recession, Vermont's Leahy, chairman of the Senate agriculture committee, urged the Clinton administration not to forget those who "are struggling to put food on the table for their families."

The hunger-is-rampant interpretation of the food stamp numbers has been assiduously promoted in recent years by an advocacy group called the Food Research and Action Committee, which has repeatedly criticized the food stamp program for being stingy and insufficient. With lawsuits and the threat of legal action, the group works to pressure USDA into more aggressive outreach efforts to find those who are eligible and not on the program. Its lobbying played a large role in a 3 percent across-the-board increase in food stamp benefits passed by Congress in 1988.

The group takes no public satisfaction in the fact that one in 10 Americans now uses food stamps. It believes the aid is insufficient: "We have the television cameras showing us the starving children in Somalia, but we have to start thinking about those who are hungry in our own country," says Carrie Lewis, a food stamp specialist in the group's legal department.

A Flawed Report

The committee is a prime source for almost every report on hunger in the major media, sometimes the only source. Most influential in this regard is its 1991 Community Childhood Hunger Identification Project, which reported, among other findings, that one out of every eight of the nation's children go to bed hungry at least once a year. Minus the "once a year," the "one in eight" sound bite was amplified by the *New York Times*, the *Washington Post* and *USA Today*, not to mention television commentators.

Not everyone was as impressed with the group's efforts as the national media. George Graham, a retired Johns Hopkins University professor of nutrition and pediatrics, calls the hunger identification study "asinine" and "as unscientific a project as you're ever going to find." The problem, he says, is that it depended on the impressions of people answering "totally unscientific" survey questions. These included: "Do your children ever say they are hungry because there is not enough food in your house?"—the sort of comment that middle- or upper-class parents of teenagers might hear on a regular basis.

Graham prefers to speak of "malnutrition" rather than "hunger," since the latter term is subjective—most people, in fact, feel hungry every day before meals, but malnutrition can be measured objectively. And, he says, poverty is not the cause of malnutrition in America. Among other studies, he points to the *Nutrition Monitoring Update*, a 1989 joint research report by the USDA and Department of Health and Human Services that he says found "no evidence of health problems associated with

51

deficiency or excess [of protein]" that could be traced to poverty.

"I don't think the general public takes these charges of hunger seriously anymore," says MacDonald. "We understand that there are isolated pockets of malnutrition in this country, but they don't exist because public assistance is not readily available."

Nutrition, rather than hunger, is in fact the chief selling point for food stamps on Capitol Hill. After helping to appropriate $29 billion for food stamps, Republican Sen. Thad Cochran of Mississippi declared that "what once was an agricultural appropriations bill has now become a nutrition bill."

One of the arguments for food stamps, as opposed to cash transfers, has always been that recipients, given money and the choice of how to spend it, would not eat as well. Interestingly, notes USDA critic Bovard, government dietary studies dating to the mid-1950s show, if anything, a slight decline in the overall nutritional value of the American diet since the food stamp program started in the early sixties. Bovard notes that a 1979 USDA study showed almost no difference in diet between those who were eligible for and using food stamps and those who were eligible and not participating.

"There is this paternalistic attitude that poor people are by nature untrustworthy, and that if you give them money they will blow it all on cigarettes and booze instead of buying food for their children," says Vita Rose, head nutritionist at Marin Maternity Services in San Francisco. But "there are certainly no nutritional reasons to give them coupons instead of cash."

Maybe not, but there are political reasons. Despite the fact that printing and distribution of food stamps costs about $100 million a year, the coupons themselves may be one reason the program has flourished.

Food Stamps Seem Less Like Welfare

"Food stamps have an aura of protection around them," says the Heritage Foundation's Rector. "There is a public misconception that giving free food doesn't have the same deleterious welfare effect as does giving cash."

Lewis of the Food Research and Action Committee admits that food stamps are "a little patronizing" toward the poor, but favors them because "cash programs are much more likely to get cut." Despite efforts to cut other welfare programs, the food stamp program has not faced a significant legislative attack since the early Reagan years.

Ironically, those who most adamantly denounce the idea of a straight cash transfer seem to be recipients. Yvonne Pizarro says that though she would use the money to buy food, "too many other people would spend it on themselves instead of their kids."

Linda Weaver, another food stamp recipient at the Hudson center in Newark, echoes Pizarro. "Personally, I think a lot of the people would waste it," she says.

Both, however, would appreciate the cash themselves for a simple reason: it would eliminate some of the stigma that comes with using food stamps. Weaver, who has been in the program off and on for two years, says, "At first you have a complex about it, but after a while the stares stop bothering you.". . .

Pride, says Joan Rossi, a food stamp administrator in Delaware, is a greater obstacle to expanding the food stamp rolls than embarrassment in supermarket lines is. Potential recipients "are already experiencing extreme self-esteem problems," says Rossi, "and we have to convince them that they are not doing something wrong by getting help from the government in a time of need."

To that end, the Delaware Department of Social Services has been training its social workers to "minimize the discomfort" of food stamp applicants by enhancing their self-esteem. Workers are taught to emphasize to recipients the areas of their lives where they are "succeeding and not failing." Known as "The Vision," the training materials read somewhat like a New Age manifesto: "We affirm the value and dignity of all individuals. We create hope and optimism by empowering the clients to achieve their maximum potential."

To welfare critics such as Bovard, the "pride" that looks like an obstacle to social service workers trying to sign up clients is a healthy instinct that keeps people self-sufficient, not dependent on government transfers. "There are lots of folks who see food stamps as another way to change the distribution of income," he says. "And they regard almost any increase in participation as a moral triumph. There is an entire industry built around making food stamps as attractive as possible, and that is simply the wrong thing to do."

"Homelessness makes it clear that . . . equality of opportunity remains out of our reach."

Homelessness Is a Serious Problem

Ann Braden Johnson

Ann Braden Johnson is a social worker who works primarily with the chronically mentally ill. In studying the problems of her "deinstitutionalized" patients who are supposedly "returned to the community," Johnson was drawn into a study of the causes of homelessness. In the following viewpoint she examines the web of government policies and economic circumstances that have increased homelessness in America. Entwined in those policies, she contends, are political reasons for systematically undercounting the homeless. Johnson is the author of *Out of Bedlam: The Truth About Deinstitutionalization*, from which this viewpoint is excerpted.

As you read, consider the following questions:

1. Why might a homeless person find it difficult to rent an apartment, even if he or she had a job, according to Johnson?
2. Johnson suggests that those who are counting the homeless have a political and financial stake in the numbers that may make it difficult to get an unbiased count. What is at stake? How does this affect the pressure to find high or low numbers of homeless, according to the author?

Everyone, it seems, has a theory about the homeless—who they are and how they got that way. . . . What is it about homelessness that commands the attention so forcefully? There are, after all, other poignant and dramatic social problems. None other—not even AIDS—has caught the public attention and imagination quite so consistently over so long a time. . . .

Whatever else homelessness in the latter part of twentieth-century America is, it is not a simple problem, although it is one that probably could have been prevented. . . . Causes identified by students of the phenomenon are unemployment, a chronic scarcity of low-cost housing, cutbacks in public assistance of various kinds, and, of course, deinstitutionalization.

Homelessness and Unemployment

When the federal government counts the unemployed, they count those who collect unemployment insurance. They do not count those who have never worked, who used to work but have given up looking, or those who are underemployed, meaning that they work at unskilled, low-paying jobs. They also do not count those who have used up their unemployment benefits without finding new jobs, or those whose skills have been rendered obsolete by changes in the labor market. Any way you look at it, the national figures for unemployment are misleading and deceptive; and it should go without saying that the unemployed homeless are squarely among those who go uncounted.

Homeless people found in public shelters across the country are predominately black or Hispanic males, whose median age is thirty-four; and fully 40 percent of them attribute their homelessness to job loss. . . .

Perhaps least appreciated of all as a group at great risk for homelessness, however, are the so-called underemployed. . . . These are people who work yet who earn too little to afford more than their own subsistence, people whose resources are inadequate to enable them to survive a blow like an illness or a rent increase. The U.S. Conference of Mayors estimated that 22 percent of the homeless served by their cities in 1987 were people with full- or part-time jobs, and they predicted that the percentage, already up from 19 percent the year before, would continue to rise. The jobs the underemployed are likely to hold are not, of course, either particularly lucrative or very desirable; typical examples include hotel maid, security guard, dishwasher, or low-level assembly worker. These are all jobs that pay at or close to the minimum wage. . . .

It should be easy to see how difficult it must be to manage on so little money, and how impossible it would be to weather a crisis. For example, one man living for two months with his fourteen-year-old son in shelters, on the street, or with relatives, earned the minimum wage and had been just able to pay the rent on a small apartment in a building that burned down. As he pointed out, starting over would require a month's security deposit and the purchase of furniture plus equipment, none of it within the reach of one with so small an income. It is entirely possible that the city shelter in which he lived was one of those demanding as much as 75 percent of the income of its employed residents, to pay for services rendered and to "encourage those who can afford their own housing to get it rather than linger in the shelter system." It is hard to see how anyone can hope to escape the shelter system if all he or she has to work with is one-quarter of the minimum wage.

The Housing Shortage

Even if a homeless person has a job and can save the amount needed to rent an apartment, he has to confront the other big social problem behind homelessness—the chronic shortage of low-cost housing. There are many reasons for the shortage, none of them particularly admirable. For one thing, federal subsidies for low-income housing have been on the decline—the Reagan administration was proud to announce a $30 billion cut in housing assistance provided by the Department of Housing and Urban Development between 1981 and 1983—and from the outset of their years in office, the Reagan administration intended that the number of households receiving housing assistance was to be held to an absolute maximum of 3.8 million. Before the Reagan era, housing assistance had been available to all who qualified for help, so this represented a major change in U.S. housing assistance policy, one whose immediate effect was to make housing assistance a limited entitlement program.

The loss of housing assistance for all but a limited portion of the needy was thus no accident but part of a calculated shift of government priorities away from the poor, "a fundamental redirection in U.S. housing policy" as it had stood since the 1930s [according to researchers Raymond Struyk, John Tuccillo, and James Zais]. In 1985, for example, a deputy assistant secretary of HUD said at a National Urban League Conference, "We're getting out of the housing business. Period." And since the federal government considers the taxes that homeowners do not pay because they are entitled to deduct mortgage interest—$44,000,000,000 in 1985—from their federal income tax to be part of the money it "spends" on housing, it is clear that federal housing policy, as reflected in expenditure, greatly benefits middle- and upper-income families even as it provides a convincing fiscal excuse for not providing more housing assistance to the needy. Any way you look at it, U.S. housing policy in the late twentieth century is not geared to address the needs of the people at risk for homelessness.

There is more bad news. Each year about 2.5 million people are involuntarily displaced from their homes by gentrification, economic development schemes, eviction, or inflated rents. Another half-million housing units of low-rent dwellings are lost each year to arson, co-op or condo conversion, abandonment, demolition, and inflation. . . .

Wiley, for the *San Francisco Examiner*. Reprinted with permission.

[An] interesting example of governmental indifference to the part of its citizenry that exists at the outer limits of respectability can be found in the death of the single room occupancy (SRO) hotel, where for years marginal isolates could find shelter that was often quite decent. These hotels were located on side streets in undesirable neighborhoods and were often assumed to be a source of criminal activity. In fact, the SROs performed a useful social function: they tolerated a variety of residents who had in common that they were alone, socially marginal, and for one reason or another, chronically dependent on the dole—the old, the mentally ill, the blind, the permanently disabled, the addicted. Joan Hatch Shapiro, the lone scholar of the SRO phenomenon, observed in 1971:

> There simply is no alternative housing available to [the SROs'] single clients. A series of discriminatory practices in public and private housing severely limit choices for "undesirable" people. Public housing regulations specify twenty-one per-

sonal characteristics which are considered disqualifying. SRO tenants rarely are acceptable.

Shapiro believed that the SRO hotel was not necessarily as awful an environment as most of its critics assumed, because it offered some social support to its residents and made very few demands on them. The hotels also housed a lot of less-than-desirable tenants, including ex-mental patients, when no one else would. . . .

SRO hotels, unhappily, were (and are) unattractive, and their residents were anything but desirable as neighbors, so municipal governments came under fairly steady pressure from angry neighborhoods and ambitious real estate developers to get rid of them. According to an information paper prepared for the U.S. Senate's Special Committee on Aging, "It was the urban renewal efforts of the sixties that brought the existence of SRO hotels to public attention. The gutting of old hotels in favor of condominiums and high-rent apartments sent thousands of residents into the streets to search for other low-rent accommodations.". . .

Welfare Cuts and Soaring Rents

The United States changed its working definition of poverty in the early 1980s and made fewer people eligible for various kinds of aid, reducing the total Aid to Families with Dependent Children (AFDC) caseload by some 3 percent even as the percentage of people below the poverty line rose by as much as 10 percent, depending on where in the country they lived. One million food stamp recipients have been cut from that program since 1981, while the average recipient lucky enough to be kept on the program has had his or her benefits reduced by about 14 percent. Far from being the profligate handout Reagan's people would have had the public believe, the average stipend . . . in 1984 worked out to forty-seven cents per person per meal. . . .

This decline in welfare income to families was accompanied by a huge increase in rents. At the same time, the federal government made it a virtual certainty that poor people would be unable to afford housing, by requiring each state to set a maximum rent allowance for its welfare recipients, a uniform national standard that unfortunately did not specify how to adjust rental allowances to market conditions. In places where housing costs tend to be especially high, like New York City, this meant that for the first time the state *could not* help its welfare recipients pay their rent if it went higher than the new maximum, even if it wanted to. What happened was all too predictable: rents rose by 100 percent between 1975 and 1984 in New York City, while the maximum rent for New York State stayed at 1975 levels until it was finally raised in 1984—by 25 percent. The 1984 maximum rent allowance of $270 per month was clearly

58

not adequate in a city where the median rent was $330—where
. . . some 2,000 units of low- and moderate-income housing were
being lost to the market altogether each month. . . .

The Census Bureau Missed Most of the Homeless

What transpired on a single evening in March 1990—the 1990
Street and Shelter Night (or "S-Night" in the parlance of the Census Bureau)—shows that the traditional head-count approach is
woefully inadequate when it comes to enumerating hard-to-count
persons such as minorities and the homeless.

The S-Night results were often ludicrous. Are there really 75
times as many homeless on the street in Birmingham, Ala., as
there are in Richmond, Va.? Are there really no homeless persons
in Wichita, Kan., and only one in Rochester, N.Y.? . . .

Studies have repeatedly shown that two-thirds of the homeless
sleep concealed to avoid victimization. The bureau was fully
aware of this. Yet, in localities where the bureau did count, it
made a deliberate decision to exclude from its head count all of
the hidden homeless—those sleeping in automobiles, abandoned
buildings, bushes, dumpsters, roofs, caves, or those concealed by
tarps, cardboard boxes, or shanty structures. . . .

Most of the homeless were missed.

Bruce J. Casino, *Christian Science Monitor*, September 24, 1991.

Welfare recipients and low-income workers alike wind up paying far too large a portion of their income for rent and can all
too easily fall behind if they need to buy food *and* pay the light
bill. Since their income is so small to begin with, people living
at the margin are never able to catch up. To a great extent, the
first remedy sought by families unable to pay their rent has
been to double up with relatives and friends: 52 percent of the
families in New York City shelters reported in a 1986 Human
Resources Administration study that they had come from shared
households. In general, the issue of doubled-up families has
been most controversial: advocates insist there are millions of
people in this precarious position, teetering on the verge of
homelessness; but governmental bureaucrats have so far refused to accept any of the advocates' predictions of more homelessness to come. The doubling up was even noticeable on the
1980 U.S. Census: the census takers found the first rise since
1950 in the number of housing units shared by two or more unrelated families, from 1.2 to 1.9 million.

Nor is all this just a New York City problem. In some places, some people have managed to hold on to their homes by using soup kitchens and taking advantage of the increasingly infrequent federal handouts of surplus cheese and peanut butter. Cleveland and Detroit, for example, are both home to laid-off blue-collar workers and have seen business at their soup kitchens rise by as much as 32 percent in one year. Other families have lost their homes and have had to turn to public shelters. In Chicago, where the rate of mortgage foreclosure is the highest in the country (1.6 percent), city-run shelters opened for the first time in 1983 and have operated at more than 100 percent capacity from the very first night. Fully 80 percent of Chicago's homeless families reported becoming homeless after being evicted when their AFDC or other government entitlement was cut. In Tulsa, Milwaukee, and Denver, unemployment doubled during the early 1980s, which led to an increase in homelessness as businesses went bankrupt; skilled workers took day laborers' jobs, forcing the unskilled into unwanted unemployment; and migrants moved into these cities looking for work. Homelessness is by no means exclusively an urban problem, for there are more and more farm foreclosures, currently at a post-Depression high. Unquestionably, as Dan Salerno, Kim Hopper, and Ellen Baxter write in *Hardship in the Heartland*,

> in the past few years, homelessness has changed radically from a comparatively rare phenomenon of the deteriorated inner-city regions, to the increasingly common lot of the desperately poor everywhere. . . . The only thing it can be asserted with confidence they all share is the one thing they all lack: a home. . . .

Counting the Homeless

In 1984, the Reagan administration issued its official document on homelessness, a report by HUD. The report represented an attempt on the part of the federal government to achieve a legitimate and useful goal: an accurate count of the homeless. Ostensibly, knowing this number would enable planners to come up with realistic responses to actual need, and services could thus be targeted appropriately, to use the language of the bureaucracy. This noble aim was in fact subverted by the political agenda that has plagued homelessness from the very first; and the HUD estimate came in *so* much too low, in the view of the advocates and agencies who were actually trying to cope directly with the problem, that it was dismissed by them as transparently political. The battle between advocates and service providers on the one hand, with HUD and the Reagan White House on the other hand, was not so much concerned with learning once and for all the dimensions of the homeless population as it was with establishing accountability and thus fiscal responsibility. A high estimate—three million is tops so far, and even the U.S. Department of Health and Human Services guessed two million for the 1983-84 fiscal year—suggests that homelessness stems from a profound failure of the Reagan administration's social and economic policies, one that will require a massive deployment of federal resources to put right. But a low estimate—HUD came up with 250,000 to 300,000—suggests the problem is not a national one but one that can be dealt with on the local level. In the end, the HUD report was widely criticized for serious methodological weaknesses by many of the experts brought in to testify about it before Congress, and it wound up being further discredited by evidence that its consultants had been pressured by HUD to keep their estimates low.

Counting and recounting the homeless has proved to be a great distraction from the much more difficult task of figuring out what to do about the conditions that create homelessness, and we have become very creative in our counting techniques and our debating tactics when needed to defend those techniques or to rebut others' counts. . . . We have focused on determining who is homeless, how many of them there are, where they came from, and especially, whose fault, responsibility, and/or problem homelessness is, with a great deal more dedication and interest than we have so far shown in facing up to the obvious: we do not have enough low-income housing in the United States, nor do we have anywhere near the quantity of specialized housing we need to care for the disabled and dependent. . . .

How the Mentally Ill Homeless Got That Way

Conveniently, we have been able to distract ourselves from the magnitude of the problem of homelessness, and the profound implications thereof, with the idea that the homeless were on the streets because mental hospitals put them there. . . .

Although some of the homeless are indeed crazy, it is more precisely the case that they have been a group easily made homeless by circumstances over which they have even less control than the rest of us. . . . The mentally ill, like the children of poverty, are among the people most likely to become homeless. To have stretched this simple fact into a causal relationship has . . . encouraged all of us to avoid looking at the serious weaknesses in our larger housing and welfare policies.

Something that has not been studied to any appreciable degree, surprisingly, is the relationship between life without a home and mental status. Living on the street or in a shelter, as many homeless people do, cannot possibly have a positive effect on one's self-esteem or provide much in the way of gratifying experience; and homelessness itself is a state of such unremitting crisis that one would expect it to provoke some kind of emotional or mental disorder, in and of itself. . . . The detachment prized by science has allowed researchers to look at specimen homeless people so objectively that the possibility of their having been driven mad by worry, fear, grief, guilt, or shame has not seriously entered the observers' minds. . . .

For all the time and money that have gone into studying the homeless in order to decide how many are mentally ill, we do not know much more than what should have been obvious from the outset: some are, some are not; and the mere fact of being homeless cannot be ruled out as a factor in the creation of the condition. . . .

To the apparent surprise of onlookers, many of the homeless mentally ill have made it clear that they prefer life on the streets to life in an institution. Take the example of Rebecca Smith, who died at the age of sixty-one in a cardboard box in New York City in 1982, described by Madeleine R. Stoner in *Housing the Homeless:*

> She froze to death in the home she had constructed for herself inside a cardboard box. She preferred it, she said, to any other home. Rebecca Smith had spent much of her life in a state psychiatric hospital under treatment for schizophrenia. Life in the box was preferable.

This should not be taken to mean that the homeless mentally ill should be living on the streets, but rather that they do not necessarily regard it as helpful to be offered the alternative of involuntary mental health care. Agencies whose workers visit their homeless clients on the street are adamant that what homeless people, mentally ill or not, need and want is homes and money. . . .

The American Dream Is Not Working

Homelessness . . . throws the cold water of reality on the fantastic idea that the Reagan revolution in social programming has been a success. No wonder then-Attorney General Edwin Meese felt it necessary to bluster about reports of hunger among Americans as being "purely political" and to make the preposterous charge that people who eat at soup kitchens do so "because the food is free and that's easier than paying for it." How much more reassuring to the conservative sensibility to continue to believe that the homeless are mentally ill persons for whom [as Thomas Main writes] "institutions already exist" and that "the people in the shelters have not been helped yet." More than any other single public problem, homelessness makes it clear that the American dream of ever-increasing affluence and conspicuous consumption is not for everyone, that "the system" is not evenhanded, and that equality of opportunity remains out of our reach.

"The truth is that many of the homeless are responsible for their own plight."

The Homeless Problem Is Exaggerated

Rush H. Limbaugh III

There are homeless people who need a helping hand in America, acknowledges well-known conservative media personality Rush H. Limbaugh III, but their numbers are far smaller than liberal activists would like to believe. In the following viewpoint, Limbaugh maintains that many of those who are homeless prefer living on the streets to assuming the responsibilities of being a human being. He argues that homeless advocates exaggerate the problem of homelessness in order to blame Republicans for the problem and to increase federal spending. Limbaugh is the author of *The Way Things Ought to Be*, from which this viewpoint is excerpted.

As you read, consider the following questions:

1. What are the root causes of homelessness, according to Limbaugh?
2. What evidence does the author offer to prove that liberals want the homeless to remain homeless? What evidence does he use to show that some of the homeless prefer to remain on the streets?
3. How would the author solve the problem of the homeless mentally ill?

Ronald Reagan and his policies created America's homeless. That's the message homeless advocates and the liberal media have been pumping out for the last decade. The very word *homeless* hardly existed before Ronald Reagan became President. It became a household word—excuse the pun—because some way had to be found to discredit Reagan's policies and shift attention from the economic recovery he helped bring about.

Until 1985, I was unaware of the extent to which the homeless were being exploited for propaganda purposes. I was living in Sacramento then, and was at home one Thanksgiving quietly watching the half-time show of a football game on television. Suddenly, some local reporterette interrupted the show with a report on how the homeless were spending Thanksgiving in the shelters. She interviewed an unshaven, unkempt, bedraggled homeless guy stuffing food into his mouth as if he hadn't eaten for years and might never again. The implied message of her report was that while the television audience might be prosperous and warm at home, they dare not enjoy it as long as there were people living in conditions of such squalor.

That burned me up. The homeless man on my TV screen wasn't in that condition because of anything I had done or because I didn't care. I hadn't done anything to cause his homelessness. The fact that I had a home and a turkey wasn't the reason he was in a shelter, any more than cleaning my dinner plate as a child would feed the starving Chinese. But why was this homeless man in that shelter? Could he perhaps have been even partially responsible for his plight? It would have been totally unthinkable to this reporterette to pose that question.

Now, you people should understand that I am not some bastion of noncompassion, without any concern for my fellow man. But what galls me is something many people have learned when trying to help the homeless, even though such experiences are never reported in the media. When you try to help them, they often refuse. I've been accosted on the streets of New York City by homeless people asking for money. I sometimes have offered to take them to a diner and buy them a cheeseburger. They've refused. Why? Because many of these "starving" people have other plans for the money they want from me and you. . . .

It was at about this time that I first realized the hidden agenda behind much of the homeless advocacy efforts. Homeless advocates enjoyed having a problem that provided them a platform to point the finger of blame at Ronald Reagan, the achievers of America, and the free enterprise system. And at the same time, they could peddle the guilt generated by their activities to get federal funding to set up their own version of the "poverty Pentagon" that black conservative Robert Woodson talks about.

Oh, how they relished blaming Reagan administration policies, including the mythical reductions in HUD's [Housing and Urban Development] budget for public housing, for creating all of the homeless! Budget cuts? There were no budget cuts! The budget figures show that actual construction of public housing INCREASED during the Reagan years. The only reductions in HUD's budget occurred under Jimmy Carter's administration, despite his grandiose plans to pour yet more money into failed housing projects.

Many Have Chosen to Be Homeless

Many of the homeless have willingly chosen to be homeless and chosen to steal, take drugs, and abandon their families for a life free of ties and responsibilities. . . .

Street people who mind their own business, keep out of trouble, and stay out of the way can be ignored. Their decision to drop out of society should be respected, but it should not be subsidized by the state. However, those who harass the public, create health and safety hazards, and become an aesthetic drain on the community should be placed into whatever facility is most appropriate—jail, a drug treatment center, or a mental institution.

Theodore Pappas, *Main Street Memorandum*, December 1991.

But there is a deeper motive at work in the constant attention focused on the homeless and the plethora of misinformation disseminated about them. The homeless are being used as a prop by liberals for the resurrection of class envy in America. The media folks have fallen for this completely. It fits in with their desire to always display their good intentions and their genuine concern for the downtrodden. So long as something makes them look good and imbued with an empty well of compassion, to hell with the facts—and with anyone who dares to defy them by exposing those facts.

When I left Sacramento to move to New York for my national show, I resolved to do a bit on how the homeless were being exploited in furtherance of a liberal agenda. . . . In my Homeless Updates I have pounded home three themes, which I'd like to share with you. The first is that most of what you hear about the homeless is fraudulent. Second, the so-called solutions to the homeless problem advanced by liberals usually involve nothing more than the liberals' age-old solution for all problems: throw federal money at it. Their proposed solutions do not remotely alleviate the problem, but are offered by liberals simply to assuage their unbounded feelings of guilt and to build support for their big-government agenda. Third, we must examine why people end up on the streets. Real solutions to the homelessness problem can only be found by understanding its root causes, most of which are tied to a lack of personal responsibility and a generation-long decline in respect for the traditional American values of hard work, self-reliance, and respect for the law. We should strive to help these people put their lives back together, to begin to take responsibility for their actions, and to assimilate into society. But we must also recognize that there are different types of homeless people. Some of them are mentally ill. These people are best helped by getting them into an institution.

Fraud, Lies, and Deceit

One of the main targets of my Homeless Updates over the years was Mitch Snyder, the nation's premier homeless advocate. You remember Mitch. He's the guy who went on a hunger strike until President Reagan coughed up several million dollars for his shelter so he wouldn't die on network news. He finally assumed room temperature in the spring of 1990, by means that only Dr. Jack "Jack the Dripper" Kevorkian would endorse. But during his last years Mitch committed more mischief, spread more outrageous propaganda, and simply *made up* more "facts" than almost anyone else I know in America.

What really frosts and frustrates me—a condition I call frostrating—is the ease with which the media will believe almost any "fact" about the homeless. Mitch Snyder claimed early in the Reagan years that there were three million homeless in America. This figure was accepted on faith by almost everyone in the media. You heard that number bandied about everywhere. "This country can't be doing well. We have three million homeless." All of our homeless policies were supposed to be based on this number drawn from Mitch Snyder's fevered imagination.

But in 1990 the Census Bureau decided to settle the controversy by a special census with which they planned to count the number of homeless on a given night. You would have thought that Mitch and company would have welcomed this effort. But noooo. They told the homeless not to participate. They told them that the government was only going to use the information to harass them and that they dare not participate. Who knows how many people chose not to cooperate with the Census Bureau because of that.

When the night of the Homeless Census rolled around, it took only hours for the media and others to declare it a failure. Television reporters would stand in out-of-the-way corners where a few homeless were hiding and report that no Census worker had visited them.

The final Census Bureau count of the homeless was 272,000

people. In fairness, I believe the number of homeless is actually higher—closer to the Urban Institute's estimate of 600,000—but the Census Bureau's effort was helpful in dispelling the grossly exaggerated numbers of Snyder and his disciples. The reaction of the homeless advocates who had counseled the homeless not to cooperate was sputtering rage. . . . They ranted and complained about the inaccuracy of the count. Just for the sake of it, let's give them that. Let's say the number was grossly undercounted . . . say by 100 percent. If we missed 100 percent of the number of homeless and arrived at 272,000, then the actual number would be 544,000. Still less than the Urban Institute number and far less than the 3 million claimed. Still not satisfied? Okay, let's say the census missed 500 percent. We are still below 1.5 million. The point is that there is absolutely no way we have, or ever did have, 3 million homeless people in this country.

The Majority of the Homeless Are Bums

With the exception of the flocks of mental patients released from their psycho wards in response to suits brought by civil-rights activists, the majority of the sainted "homeless" are simply misfits, drunks, and crackheads—what even in the Great Depression were known as "bums" and "hobos."

Chilton Williamson Jr., *Chronicles*, March 1992.

Now wouldn't you think a bunch of people who claim to want to end homelessness, who claim to really care about these people and their plight, would be ecstatic about the fact that there were far fewer homeless than was thought? Uh-uh. The truth threatened their power base. Not having 3 million homeless would mean less funding for their programs and would expose as fraudulent their claims that America would have 15 million homeless by the end of the century. They didn't want to hear any good news about the homeless, or anything to the effect that the problem wasn't as bad as they claimed. After all, if it wasn't that bad, their own meal ticket was in jeopardy.

There is nothing the homeless advocates won't say to make Americans feel guilty. Before he assumed room temperature, Mitch Snyder gave a speech at Lehigh University in Pennsylvania in which he stated—and I'm not making this up—that 45 homeless people die every second. When I saw this report, I couldn't believe it. I ran the numbers and found that for that to be true, some 23 million homeless people would die in America every year. This is a classic example of how the media doesn't check the statements of the "good intentions" crowd. Mitch Snyder was trying to "help" people, so why embarrass him with the facts. Why point out his checkered past: that he ran out on his wife and kids and was prone to telling outrageous lies about almost everything.

But distortions about the homeless aren't limited to homeless advocates such as Mitch Snyder. Some members of the New York clergy recently took out ads in the *New York Times* warning people that not doing everything possible for the homeless was the equivalent of denying Mary and Joseph a room at the inn. What unmitigated gall! Imagine comparing the Virgin Mary and Joseph, a gainfully employed carpenter, with some street people. Let's not forget why Mary and Joseph were traveling that night. They were going to register to pay their taxes. They were taxpayers! . . .

Liberal Feel-Good Solutions

Liberals delight in proposing solutions to problems such as homelessness that make them look good, but they do *nothing* to solve the problem. . . . Take Project Dignity, a community organization in Orange County, California. The homeless in Orange County like to drag all their worldly possessions with them in shopping carts, which they "liberate" from supermarket parking lots. Now, supermarket owners are naturally unhappy about losing their carts, which cost an average of $120 apiece.

Every so often they would ask the police to round up shopping carts that had been stolen from them. The folks at Project Dignity were outraged. How dare the police take away their residence of choice! "That's all they have," they bleated. "How insensitive and callous!" Project Dignity set out to end this injustice. They raised money to buy the homeless their own shopping carts. They spared no effort in this project. Once the shopping carts were purchased they were color-coded so that each homeless person would know which cart was his. . . .

This whole affair boggled my mind. How is it, I asked, that it is compassionate for one human being to say to another, "I love you, I really care for you, so here's a shopping cart"? What kind of compassion is that? The solution is to find some way to address the problems that made this person homeless, help him clean up his life, and teach him to access opportunity. It is a total insult to think that giving a homeless person a shopping cart is contributing to the solution to the problem.

But I guess once you have a worthless concept of help and assistance, most of your ideas will be skewed. Again, Project Dignity. Early in 1992, *Newsweek* reported that Project Dignity had produced a video they dubbed "Dumpster Dining." This video is shown at homeless shelters because most homeless people do not have VCRs hooked up in their shopping carts (unless they live in South Central Los Angeles). It actually demonstrates what should and should not be eaten out of trash dumpsters! Do you get that, folks? A group which claims to have more compassion than you do produces a video on dumpster nutrition. And with typical liberal logic: they advise the homeless not to get food from dumpsters—"but if you must, here's what not to eat."

Well, heck, why bother telling them not to do it? It's the same as saying, "Don't steal a shopping cart from the supermarket. But if you do, make sure nobody sees you." The next thing you know Project Dignity will be demanding that we install incline ramps and handlebars so that the disabled homeless will have easier access to dumpsters. How else are they going to get in and out of the things? Oh, and there should be a flag or some other warning device on dumpsters so that the guys in the garbage trucks will know a homeless person is rummaging around in the dumpster. Otherwise the homeless will be dumped and compacted. This of course would not be a hazard had they not designed auto-dumping during the Reagan years.

But you see, the liberals don't want the homeless to hold a job that has any real promise. They prefer to accommodate and humor them by making it easier for them to stay in their present condition. That's why they vigorously advocate a constitutional right to beg. And Judge Leonard Sand so ruled when he declared that the homeless should be allowed to accost subway riders as a First Amendment right of free speech. I simply refuse to believe that this nation's Founding Fathers, who were all achievers and believed in encouraging rather than deterring the achievements of others, meant to write into that sacred document that bums have a right to invade public property and harass people for money.

When he was mayor of New York, Ed Koch would sometimes try to offer the homeless a life outside of begging. His aides would go down to City Hall Park and offer them jobs, bus them to interviews, hold jobs open for them. All to no avail. The simple fact is that some—not all—of the homeless consciously choose their plight. They don't want to work. It's a hard fact to swallow, but some fellow members of our species just refuse to accept the responsibility of being human beings. Why should we romanticize what they are doing? . . .

The Real Homeless Agenda

I want you to pay attention. This section is important. . . . Notice that . . . the so-called homeless crisis is used by the left to drag down the American way of life. That is the common theme. . . . The message is that the American people are at fault, and the downtrodden—whether they are drug abusers or homeless people—can't be at fault. You're never supposed to blame the downtrodden. Who, then, should we blame? It's true that some of the homeless have lost their homes. But the government's disastrous policies of urban renewal are responsible for destroying many of the single-room-occupancy hotels they used to live in. And many of the homeless have only themselves to blame. They either aren't willing to assume the responsibilities that go with being a citizen or they are mentally ill or abusing drugs or alcohol. Of course, we have to find some way to help them, but is it necessary to lie to them or ourselves about their own contribution to their condition? Their actions often are responsible for their problems. Unless we recognize and are honest about that, we aren't going to be able to clean up our streets and help repair these wrecked lives. . . .

A Program to Deal with the Homeless

Here is my Five-Point Program to deal with the homeless.

One, we must first have an *honest* count of how many people we're talking about. It's more than the Census Bureau's 272,000 counted in 1990, but it's certainly nowhere near the 3 million figure drawn from Mitch Snyder's fevered imagination. . . .

Two, we need to make a cold-eyed assessment of the reasons why people are homeless, realize that there are different categories of homeless people, and fashion separate solutions for the various categories. Analyst Peter Rossi estimates that some 40 percent of the homeless are alcohol or drug abusers. Another 25 percent or so are people with serious mental problems. Others, and this will be controversial, *CHOOSE* to be homeless. Mark my words, people would be surprised how many people choose to be on the streets and won't go into shelters or other places of refuge regardless of how much people beg them. We're told that "no one would choose that lifestyle." Well, I'm here to tell you that some do.

You don't believe me that some homeless people choose to live that way? Take the case of Richard Kreimer, a homeless man in Morristown, New Jersey, who liked to frequent the public library there. He would stare at patrons, and many had to leave the library because of the strong stench he gave off. He refused to bathe, and would wander about the library as if it were his living room. The library passed a rule barring the homeless from disrupting its activities. Mr. Kreimer sued, and won not only the right to permanently reside in the library during open hours but a $150,000 settlement! It is an outrageous decline in civil standards when a library has to kowtow to the likes of Mr. Kreimer, but library officials must have at least expected that $150,000 would rid them of his presence. After all, he could now afford an apartment! But no, Mr. Kreimer is still haunting the streets of Morristown and still visiting the library. He says the money isn't enough to let him buy a house, and he has a right to live any way he chooses. I rest my case.

Three, for those who are drug or alcohol abusers, we have to find some way to get them into rehabilitation clinics. I'm talking about using tough love here. Telling the homeless they are responsible for at least part of their plight and that they can't forever blame the rest of society might be a start at forcing them to confront the misery caused largely by their own behavior.

Four, those that are mentally unbalanced or ill should be institutionalized. People say we don't have enough beds for them. Well, we could. There are a lot of military bases and hospitals that will be closing down and they could be used to house some of the homeless. Some of the mentally ill homeless can function in society if they take their medication. But many don't, and the ACLU blocks those who would force them, as a condition of their being allowed to remain in society, to take the medicine that separates them from paranoia, schizophrenia, or deep depression.

Five, the able-bodied homeless who are not mentally ill must be educated in how to access the boundless opportunities in the American economy. I'm convinced that a lot of people simply don't know what's available out there and how it is possible to find a job and work your way up if you are willing to accept responsibility for your life. I know what it's like to be on the bottom. I've been broke. I've been fired seven times from jobs. And I don't even have a college degree. But I didn't blame anyone else for my problems. I knew that if I didn't try to solve them on my own or with the help of friends or family members, no one else was going to take care of me. . . .

What is our greatest obstacle to solving the homeless problem? It is simple, but it will shock you. Simply put, the liberals don't want the problem solved. They are interested in power, and the way they maintain their power is to build up a giant network of government programs that employ their friends; a welfare state that constantly lobbies for its own expansion. The Poverty Pimps don't want solutions to these problems. . . .

The leaders of the alms race and the hate-America left will continue to focus their homeless efforts on blame rather than solutions. Their primary scapegoats are, of course, capitalism, the decade of greed (the 1980s), and the wealthy. Topping their list of villains will always be Ronald Reagan. But the truth is that many of the homeless are responsible for their own plight. That doesn't mean we should abandon them; real efforts aimed at helping them clean up their lives will do a lot more than false compassion. But if homeless advocates are so intent on assessing blame and if they really want to know who is most guilty of prolonging the suffering of the homeless, they need do no more than look in the mirror.

Periodical Bibliography

The following articles have been selected to supplement the diverse views presented in this chapter.

Felicity Barringer	"Whether It's Hunger or 'Misnourishment,' It's a National Problem," *The New York Times*, December 12, 1992.
Ken Boettcher	"Poverty and Hunger on the Rise for U.S. Children," *The People*, July 24, 1993. Available from the Socialist Labor Party, 914 Industrial Ave., Palo Alto, CA 94304.
Dollars & Sense	Interview with Kip Tiernan, "Justice, Not Charity," September 1992.
Farmline	"Poverty a Persistent Problem in Rural America," March 1993. Available from U.S. Department of Agriculture, 1301 New York Ave. NW, Washington, DC 20005-4789.
Jim Genova	"Housing for People, Not for Profits," *People's Weekly World*, August 28, 1993. Available from Long View Publishing Co., Inc., 235 W. 23d St., New York, NY 10011.
Nancy Gibbs	"Answers at Last," *Time*, December 17, 1990.
James B. Goodno	"Fields of Misfortune," *Dollars & Sense*, March 1992.
Guy Gugliotta	"Drawing the Line on Poverty," *The Washington Post National Weekly Edition*, May 24-30, 1993.
Robert Haveman	"Who Are the Nation's 'Truly Poor'?" *The Brookings Review*, Winter 1993. Available from 1775 Massachusetts Ave. NW, Washington, DC 20036.
Carl F. Horowitz	"Inventing Homelessness," *National Review*, August 31, 1992.
Irving Howe	"In Honor of Mike," *Dissent*, Summer 1993.
David L. Kirp	"A Sedan Is Not a Home," *Commonweal*, February 12, 1993.
John Leonard	"Listen to the Dispossessed," *The Nation*, February 1, 1993.
Jerome D. Simpson	"Turning a Blind Eye to the Homeless," *The Christian Century*, October 16, 1991.
Denise M. Topolnicki	"The American Dream: Economic Myths and Realities," *Current*, May 1993.
Kris Zawisza	"Rural Homelessness: The National Picture," *The World & I*, December 1991.

What Are the Causes of Poverty?

POVERTY

Chapter Preface

Poverty in America is not caused by a lack of material resources. The United States has for decades produced more than its people need. In fact, as Robert Adams, secretary of the Smithsonian Institution, points out, "During and after World War II it was commonly said that we could feed the whole world." But the abundance of goods available in the United States is produced by employing only part of the work force; the unemployment rate stubbornly remains high. Nancy Folbre warns in *A Field Guide to the U.S. Economy*, "Unemployment rates move like a roller coaster, going up when economic growth slows, back down again when economic growth picks up. But overall . . . the roller coaster has been heading up."

During previous periods of high unemployment, as during the Great Depression of the 1930s, companies as well as individuals suffered—and then the nation as a whole recovered. In contrast, today much of corporate America is experiencing what economists call "a jobless recovery": Many corporations are achieving high levels of profitability by "downsizing"—reducing the size of the work force—and by increasing productivity through new technology or the use of cheaper labor in other countries. Economist Robert J. Samuelson elaborates:

> The "good corporation" was supposed to provide stable jobs and generous fringe benefits . . . for more and more Americans. Instead, the process is sliding into reverse. As companies strive to stay competitive, they are shedding workers. . . . No company, regardless of how prosperous, now seems permanently safe from upheaval. We . . . underestimated the disruptive power of market changes, from new technologies to foreign competitors.

These changes in the economic environment are among the causes of the current sustained high level of unemployment—and of an increase in poverty among many who never expected to face long periods without work. The authors of the following viewpoints provide a range of perspectives on these and other causes of poverty in the United States today.

"New technologies almost always destroy more jobs than they create."

New Technologies Cause Poverty

Richard Douthwaite

It has been widely assumed that the steady introduction of new technologies into the workplace is a salient factor in the socio-economic growth of nations. In the following viewpoint, British economist and journalist Richard Douthwaite rejects this premise. He contends that in the majority of cases new technologies have profoundly weakened the economic well-being of a society. Using Great Britain as his point of reference, Douthwaite stresses that technological advances in industry contribute to joblessness and ultimately promote poverty. Douthwaite's book *The Growth Illusion* (Tulsa: Council Oak Books, 1993) depicts the interrelationship of technology and social change in the modern world.

As you read, consider the following questions:

1. According to Douthwaite, why did Adam Smith delay the publication of *The Wealth of Nations?*
2. In the author's opinion, to what extent did obtaining a college education in Great Britain benefit those who attended?

Richard Douthwaite, "The Growth Illusion." In *Buying America Back*, Jonathan Greenberg and William Kistler, editors. Tulsa: Council Oak Books, 1992. Reprinted with permission.

In 1989 when I began to write my book on green economics, which eventually appeared as *The Growth Illusion*, my views were fairly conventional. I believed that economic growth was responsible for the comfortable life most people have in industrialized countries. It was a pity that the Earth's carrying capacity was not sufficiently great to allow the same techniques to be used to make things better for the Third World, too, but perhaps we could clean up those techniques to make them more widely applicable. I believed that growth did not conflict with full employment and that the introduction of new technologies, despite their teething problems, usually led to an improvement in the general quality of life. If I wanted to see growth continue so that capitalism could survive, it was not that I had any admiration for the latter. It was that I could not see any alternative economic system being introduced before irreparable damage was done to the environment.

The Opposite Opinion

I still cannot, but that apart, I now take up the exact opposite of most of these positions and, so commonsensical do my new views seem, I am surprised and ashamed it took me so long to reach them. Yet I have moved so far from the ideas most people hold that I am likely to be thought cranky or extreme. Instead of my old belief that new technologies are generally beneficial, I now think that in most cases they are positively damaging and that society needs to be extremely cautious about which ones it allows to be used. In other words, I think we need a control system akin to that used in the Middle Ages when craft guilds specified the materials and methods their members could use and workshops had to be open to the street to facilitate inspection. If an inventor develops a machine which enables 10 people to do the work of a thousand, few will condemn the firm which puts it to work and costs 990 people their livelihoods. Most of us accept Adam Smith's argument that an "invisible hand" will ensure that the workers so released will be redeployed in a way which ultimately benefits us all. In any case, even if the company had moral scruples about causing unemployment and did not use the invention, another firm would take it up and the workers' jobs would be lost anyway.

Because I had never questioned this type of thinking, it came as a surprise to me when my research revealed that Smith, a moral philosopher, was so unhappy about the invisible hand concept that he delayed the publication of *The Wealth of Nations* for several years in an effort to disprove his own argument. While he pondered, several significant labour-displacing inventions appeared, including James Hargreaves' spinning jenny, Sir Richard Arkwright's water-frame and James Watt's steam engine. Eventually, of course, he gave up. His book appeared in

1776 and, by overturning the conventional wisdom of the day, it provided the prime minister, Lord Liverpool, with the moral and intellectual backing he needed to send thousands of troops into Nottinghamshire and the surrounding counties in 1811-12 to prevent the Luddites, who were mainly starving textile workers, from destroying the knitting frames which had put them out of jobs.

Toles. © 1993 *The Buffalo News*. Reprinted by permission of Universal Press Syndicate. All rights reserved.

New technologies almost always destroy more jobs than they create. It has taken 180 years for the evidence that this is so to become apparent because, until very recently, the jobs which were lost were in the Third World, where growing poverty and underemployment were blamed on the laziness and stupidity of the natives. For example, British textile exports damaged the handweavers of India and eliminated those in Africa but enabled a high level of work to be maintained at home. The Third World was gradually sucked dry. The start of the debt crisis in 1982 marked the point at which it could be drained no more and, since then, the industrial nations have been unable to maintain full internal employment at the expense of jobs overseas. They have been forced instead to compete amongst themselves for a shrinking pool of available work. Only those industrial nations with balance of payments surpluses can now aspire to full employment and, if a member of this privileged group fails to increase its national income by around 3% a year, it sees its joblessness grow, so rapidly are new technologies eliminating the need for human labour.

Economic Growth and Human Welfare

The introduction of new technology powers the growth process by generating its profits. However, our unthinking reliance on the invisible hand has meant we have failed to develop any mechanism to ensure that the overall gains from a new invention exceed the overall losses and that the winners compensate the losers. This is despite the fact that while a new process generally benefits those who introduce it, there is no guarantee that it will lead to gains for the community as a whole. As a result, economic growth can often mean a net loss of human welfare.

Economic growth was adopted as the paramount national goal surprisingly recently. The first official British national income figures are for 1938 and were only released in 1941, when people had other things on their minds. Consequently, the mid-1950s were the first time in which there was a consistent series of government figures to show how the economy was growing year by year which were unaffected by the Second World War and its immediate aftermath. The availability of this data enabled R. A. Butler to make a speech as Chancellor of the Exchequer to the Conservative Party conference in 1954 pointing out that if the country was able to grow at 3% per annum, national income per head would double by 1980. Each man and woman would then be twice as rich as his and her father was at the same age, Butler said. It was a marvelous yet thoroughly realistic goal.

His speech marks a turning point in British life. Hitherto, governments had set themselves specific, finite targets, such as establishing the National Health Service or building 300,000 houses a year. Afterwards, only the rate of growth which the economy achieved was important. The ideological struggle between Conservative and Labour was largely left behind. What mattered now was which party's policies could achieve the fastest growth rate, not how a finite national cake was shared out. For the Left, economic growth meant more resources to spend on health, education and social services. For the Right, it meant bigger corporate profits. Unfortunately, nobody bothered to look very hard to see if the benefits of growth were actually coming through. It seemed as if they were—people had more cars and better houses. Why question the obvious?

Because Britain did not grow at quite 3% and the population grew, it was 1988 before national income per head had doubled. In other words, Lord Butler's experiment had just ended and the results were coming in exactly at the time I was planning my book. It seemed the perfect moment to establish the nature and extent of the benefits of the growth process.

Initially, I had no doubt at all that the gains had been considerable: problems only arose when I attempted to identify what they were, especially as it quickly became apparent that almost every social indicator had worsened over the third of a century the experiment had taken. Chronic disease had increased, crime had gone up eight-fold, unemployment had soared and many more marriages were ending in divorce. Almost frantically I looked for gains to set against these losses which, in most cases I felt, had to be blamed on growth. True, the housing stock had improved, but this could have been achieved without growth taking place because more houses had been built in 1955 than in most years since. It was the same with consumer durables: the mid-1950s economy had the capacity to produce all the washing machines, fridges and videos Britain had in 1988 without requiring extra resources at all. Only the huge expansion in road transport would have been impossible without growth, and whether this was actually a benefit seemed very dubious indeed.

When Innovation Eliminates Jobs

While more corporate executives recognize that employees are their most important assets, the strategies they use to produce leaner corporations also eliminate jobs. It is hard to sponsor a convincing social contract in which employees innovate when the next money-saving innovation eliminates their own jobs.

There is a paradox here. When one company becomes more competitive by doing more with less, the result is greater productivity. But when the entire economy competes that way, the income lost to displaced workers may outweigh the gains to productivity. Unless we devise complementary strategies to yield jobs for the displaced, the "competitiveness" craze is likely to worsen this problem.

Robert Kuttner, *San Diego Union-Tribune*, August 3, 1993.

The other obvious change by 1988 was that many more people were getting a third level [college or university] education but, here again, the extent to which this was a real, personal benefit seemed open to question. It could just have been that a more technologically complex economy required people to receive more training if it was to function and that the increased competition for jobs had pushed up entry requirements all round. However, even if the extra education was a Good Thing, it could have been provided out of 1954 resources. National Service, under which every fit 18-year-old youth was given an expensive military training, was still in operation in the mid-50s. If society had wished, it could have switched those resources to educate young people in other things and, had it done so, many more people would have been in further education in 1988 than was the case.

"If I don't find at least one significant benefit, people will think that I'm hopelessly biased and reject what I have to say," I told myself as my enquiries went on but, eventually, like Adam Smith, I gave up. The weight of evidence was overwhelming: the unquestioning quest for growth had been an unmitigated social and environmental disaster. Almost all of the extra resources the process had created had been used to keep the system functioning in an increasingly inefficient way. The new wealth had been squandered on producing pallets and corrugated cardboard, non-returnable bottles and ring-pull drink cans. It had built airports, supertankers and heavy goods lorries [trucks], motorways, flyovers [overpasses] and car parks with many floors. It had enabled the banking, insurance, stock-broking, tax-collecting and accountancy sector to expand from 493,000 to 2,475,000 employees during the 33 years. It had financed the recruitment of over 3 million people to the "reserve army of the unemployed." Very little was left for more positive achievements when all these had taken their share. Moreover, growth in the [Prime Minister Margaret] Thatcher years had become particularly damaging after some of the taxes which had ensured that those who benefitted from the process helped those who did not were lightened in an effort to speed expansion up.

Society Shapes the Market

I hope that this perception will open people's eyes to the nature of undirected economic growth, just as it did mine, and convince readers that we cannot rely on the invisible hand to ensure that self-interest will serve the general good. When enough people think along these lines, a new path will open up and, instead of striving for constant expansion in order to stave off collapse, nations will be able to aim to build stable economies in which resource consumption is kept at a sustainable level. Instead of the market shaping society, as it does at present, society will be able to shape the market by ensuring that profits accrue only to those businesses which deliver what it wants, such as lower fossil energy use. We will be able to use the undoubted power and flexibility of the capitalist system for society's ends, rather than letting it look after its own.

At present, governments like to see a high proportion of national income invested because it leads to high growth. This is a dangerous game because, if growth falters, investment drops and unemployment soars. A stable economy would be very different from the high-consumption model we know today and heavy investment will be needed to get us there. The current level of investment represents resources we can divert to this end. We need growth, but only in a particular direction. Over the years, as we get nearer and nearer our ideal society, investment and interest rates can be allowed to fall so that the need for growth withers away. As St. Augustine said about chastity, "Oh Lord, give me zero growth, but not yet."

What the Future Holds

If my thinking has changed have I changed too? Well, I no longer think that the future will be more prosperous than the past, which is one of the distinctive features of the growth age: for most of their time on the planet, people have not expected even a century-over-century gain. I disbelieve the life assurance companies' claims that they will pay me out several times more, in real terms, than I put in. Where will those extra resources come from, I ask myself, and at whose expense will they be made? I've given up running a car, finding that, even though I earn appreciably less, I'm better off physically and socially using a bicycle and, after allowing for the absence of fuel, repair, road tax, insurance and depreciation bills, I might be better off financially too. Certainly, my attitude these days is that it is easier and pleasanter to find a way of managing on less than trying to earn more.

More fundamentally, though, in spite of the fact that I no longer believe in a more prosperous future, I do believe that there might be a future, which was something I was beginning to doubt. Although I'm naturally biased, I think that I have identified the flaw which makes our economic system so voracious and the way it can be surgically taken out. If I'm correct, then the size of the current conflicts between rich and poor over resources and between people and the planet over scale—conflicts which cloud the future of us all—can be cut down considerably.

"The hidden costs of corporate takeovers are much larger than most Americans realize."

Corporate Takeovers Cause Poverty

Jonathan Greenberg

In the 1980s, a large number of corporate takeovers occurred in the United States. Usually hostile in nature, these takeovers often resulted in the dismantlement of a corporation. In some cases management, in an effort to stave off a takeover, would buy back all existing stock at inflated prices, forcing the company to borrow heavily to finance the buyback. In the following viewpoint, Jonathan Greenberg argues that these corporate takeovers gravely damaged the American economy. He contends that not only did millions lose their jobs or suffer severe pay cuts, but also that the economic consequences of the takeovers can still be felt today. Jonathan Greenberg is an investigative financial journalist and a contributor to the *New York Times*, the *Washington Post*, *Forbes*, and numerous other publications.

As you read, consider the following questions:

1. What does the author believe was the ultimate effect on the Safeway Corporation of the leveraged buyout by its management?
2. Which presidential administration(s) does Greenberg blame for the success of the corporate takeovers of the 1980s?

From Jonathan Greenberg, "The Hidden Costs of Corporate Takeovers." In *Buying America Back*, Jonathan Greenberg and William Kistler, editors. Tulsa: Council Oak Books, 1992. Reprinted with permission.

In 1982, I completed a year-long assignment as the chief researcher for the first *Forbes* magazine listing of the 400 wealthiest Americans. At that time, we placed 19 people on the list who had made their $100 million-plus net worth from the business of "finance." Just five years later, the 1987 Forbes 400 listing had a minimum worth requirement of $225 million. Of the 400 wealthiest Americans, 69 of them had made their fortunes from finance.

How did these financiers—whom *New York* magazine during the eighties dubbed the "rock stars of this decade"—acquire their newfound wealth? Most of them cashed in on the wave of corporate takeovers that had swept the nation. Fueled by the Ronald Reagan administration's anti-antitrust and anti-labor policies, clever stock market manipulators found that they could take over publicly traded companies by borrowing huge sums of money, paying premiums for the stock, then demanding wage concessions from the companies' workers with the excuse that money was needed to pay back the new debt. In addition, the manipulators knew that our corporate tax structure would subsidize their purchases. Because the interest on all the money they borrowed to take over the company could be deducted from profits, the money that once went for federal taxes could now go toward financing these takeovers. So while a few ruthless number crunchers were earning hundreds of millions of dollars taking control of huge companies and reducing the wages of—or firing—tens of thousands of workers, we, the taxpayers, were making up the difference in the federal budget through cutbacks, increased taxes, and a larger budget deficit.

The hidden costs of corporate takeovers are much larger than most Americans realize. Between the "hostile takeovers" of "corporate raiders," the leveraged buyouts of companies buying up their own stock to ward off the raiders, and the "friendly" acquisitions of corporations, such unproductive economic activity became the main focus of the nation's businesses during the eighties. This was money that did not go into building new plants, creating new products, or hiring new workers. It was siphoned out of the economy to inflate the value of stock, pay exorbitant fees, and make a few people extremely rich.

Statistics on Takeovers

In 1988 alone, approximately $500 billion was spent on corporate takeovers. That's greater than 20 times as much as had been spent on takeovers just eight years earlier, and more than double that year's combined profits for the nation's 500 most profitable companies. Almost all this money had to be borrowed. Every dollar that went to pay off debt service amounted to 50 cents or so that otherwise would have gone into the federal treasury to pay corporate taxes.

The most thorough analysis of how corporate taxes were affected by the takeover wave was written in late 1991 by Donald L. Barlett and James B. Steele, two Pulitzer Prize-winning journalists for the *Philadelphia Inquirer*. In one section of their investigative series (entitled "America: What Went Wrong?"), Barlett and Steele revealed that throughout the eighties, corporations paid a total of $675 billion in income taxes, and $2.2 trillion in interest on borrowed money. At least half of this debt expense probably could be attributed to corporate takeovers, which means that well over $500 billion that would have gone to federal taxes instead went to fund the takeover binge. During the 1950s, the writers explained, corporate America paid $4 in taxes for every $1 it paid in interest. Through the 1980s, however, this ratio had reversed itself: corporations paid out $3 in interest for every $1 they paid to Uncle Sam.

According to Barlett and Steele, because of the interest deduction on debt, throughout the 1980s corporations paid $67.5 billion per year in taxes, *and avoided paying $92 billion per year!* Their analysis left no room for doubt over who has been making up for the shortfall. During the 1950s corporations paid a 39% share of all taxes collected in the U.S. During the 1980s, that corporate share had dropped to 17%, and the share paid by individuals had risen to 83%.

Even *Forbes* magazine, generally a booster of corporate takeovers, acknowledged that taxpayers have been subsidizing them. In late 1988, a *Forbes* cover story analyzed some of the largest takeovers of the eighties. It estimated that the $26 billion leveraged buyout of RJR Nabisco would result in a tax shortfall to the federal treasury of $7 billion. That's because the company, which had been paying $682 million per year on $2.6 billion of operating profit, had taken on so much debt that it would pay no taxes at all for the foreseeable future—*and would probably even collect a $2 billion tax refund from the federal treasury for taxes it had paid during the three previous years!*

The Cost to America

The same story held true for each and every company that was saddled in debt so that one manipulator or another could take it over. Macy's paid $206 million in taxes the last year before it underwent a leveraged buyout. In 1988, the company collected a $32 million tax refund from the federal government. All of these tax deductions, and all this debt, might somehow he justifiable if they improved the financial well-being of the corporations that were being taken over and their workers. But it has had the opposite effect. During the past few years, millions of Americans have been waking up to a terrible hangover because

84

the corporate takeover phenomenon required even more money than the hundreds of billions of dollars in tax deductions. To pay down all that debt, and pay all the lucrative fees for those who engineered the takeovers, hundreds of thousands of employees of those companies that were taken over were fired, while millions of others were forced to accept wage concessions that would have been considered unconscionable just a decade earlier. The AFL-CIO Executive Council called the takeover frenzy "a waste of scarce resources" resulting in employees being "traded and bartered like chattel." In some cases, the council noted, new owners were buying companies "for the sole purpose of reaping whatever gains can be achieved from breaching contractual commitments."

Leveraged Buyouts: An Evil Game

The leveraged-buyout binge of the 1980s was exciting while it lasted, but more than two-thirds of U.S. chief executives believe that the economy has suffered as a result. Among the most serious consequences, they say: LBOs sapped R&D [research and development] spending and capital expenditures by diverting the money to debt repayment and investment banking fees. Management's attention was squandered on short-term financial concerns, and long-term planning languished. Any good that may have come from the takeovers was outweighed by the extremes to which Wall Street pushed the trend. . . .

Says Ryal Poppa, CEO of Storage Technology: "It was raw foolishness. We bought the self-righteous and self-serving arguments that justified a raider strategy to pursue wealth." Adds Richard A. Bernstein, CEO of Western Publishing Group: "To me, it was the worst disaster since the Great Depression. It became an evil game in and of itself, inhabited by people who added nothing to the economy."

Richard S. Teitelbaum, *Fortune*, August 26, 1991.

Under the Reagan administration, the National Labor Relations Board took a stiff anti-union stand while all this was going on. Because the union contracts of a company's labor force could be renegotiated if the ownership of a company changed hands, many corporate raiders used this loophole to borrow money, buy out the stock, then force down wages. Other "financiers" went so far as to buy out companies, then use "excess" money from workers' pension funds to pay off the crippling interest on their debt. According to Barlett and Steele, of the *Philadelphia Inquirer*, nearly 2,000 businesses dipped into their pension funds and removed $21 billion during the 1980s.

Far from protecting workers from this new form of economic piracy, the "government of the people" encouraged it. The enormous growth in the number of takeovers during the 1980s coincided with a drop in the number of attorneys employed by the Antitrust Department of the Justice Division, from 429 in 1980 to 240 in 1986. In 1982, the division's guidelines were relaxed to make takeovers easier. Whereas 11 civil monopoly cases were brought by the Antitrust Division between 1976 and 1980, from 1981 to 1985 only two were filed. Charles Rule, the assistant attorney general who headed the Antitrust Division under Reagan, made the administration's policy crystal clear during a speech to the American Bar Association on October 9, 1987. "The goal of anyone who is truly concerned about customers and shareholders should be to *reduce* costly regulation of the market for corporate control, not to increase it . . . takeovers generally increase the competitive vigor of the targets. Moreover, current merger policy implicitly promotes the social and political values upon which our nation was built."

The Safeway Story

What type of social and political values was Rule speaking of? To give an example, why not look at the corporate takeover of Safeway Supermarkets, which is widely regarded in business circles as one of the most "successful" leveraged buyouts of the eighties.

In 1986, Safeway Supermarkets owned 2,365 stores and employed 172,000 workers. Its motto to employees was "Safeway Offers Security." The company did its best to live up to this, offering good job benefits and decent union wages. The previous year, Safeway reported record profits of $231 million.

Then all the rules changed. In July 1986, after a hostile takeover bid by a group of corporate raiders, Safeway's management called in Kohlberg, Kravis, Roberts & Co. (KKR), a leveraged buyout specialist. KKR came up with $130 million of its investors' equity, then borrowed more than $4.3 billion to buy up all of the company's stock. KKR received $60 million in consulting fees for the transaction; when added to fees received by the investment bankers, junk bond financiers, lawyers, and accountants, more than $200 million went to take Safeway over.

At this point, the new owners needed to come up with more than $500 million a year to pay off interest and debt. Jane and Joe taxpayer, involuntarily, have been kicking in their share; the company immediately stopped paying $122 million a year in annual taxes and even received a U.S. treasury "refund" check for past taxes of $11 million. But that only paid off part of the debt. The rest had to come from liquidating stores, firing workers, and cutting people's pay. Eventually more than 1,200 stores were sold, putting 63,000 people out of work. According to a 1990 analysis of the closing of Safeway's Dallas area stores by the *Wall Street Journal*, one year after losing their jobs, 60% of the workers still had not found new jobs. Those lucky enough to find work for the companies which bought out the Safeway stores saw their hourly wages drop from $12 to $6.50.

These Dallas-area Safeway workers had an average of 17 years' service with the company. They had refused a $5-an-hour pay cut. Although the company was making a small profit from their stores, far more money could be made liquidating them and selling off their inventory and equipment. "There's so much debt in a leveraged buyout that you have to look at your assets in a cold and calculating way," Safeway chairman Peter Magowan explained. Employees lost all health benefits within two weeks and received a maximum severance pay of eight weeks. Magowan kept his million-dollar-a-year job and wound up with options to buy 2 million shares of Safeway stock at one-sixth its current value. This translates into a personal profit of more than $20 million—probably more than every severance check the company cut for the 9,000 Texans it put out of work. Today Safeway's headquarters sports a new corporate motto: "Targeted returns on current investment."

A Costly Buyout

In late 1990, *Forbes* magazine wrote an article entitled "The Buyout That Saved Safeway." It noted that profit margins were higher, largely because the leveraged buyout "freed" the company "from the albatross of uncompetitive stores and surly unions." The article reported that the threat of store closings forced unions to negotiate concessions. Indeed, workers in Denver took a 14% pay cut, and truck drivers now complain of being forced to work 16-hour shifts. Yet *Forbes* felt that this undermining of the American worker, subsidized with an indirect tax subsidy which will eventually exceed $500 million, was good for the economy. No mention was made of the welfare, unemployment, and health benefits which the firings have cost all Americans, nor the loss of those hundreds of millions in taxes which tens of thousands of former Safeway workers no longer pay. As for the damage done to the economy by having fewer consumers with the money to purchase products and services, that is another intangible which corporate takeover boosters would rather not address.

Boosters of corporate takeovers, like *Forbes*, speak of "saving" a company which had paid good wages and made good profits, because now it can pay people less and make even higher profits (although when calculations include debt service, Safeway nets far less than it ever did). Other apologists, like Safeway's Chairman Magowan, observe that Safeway had no choice, that if KKR had not taken it over, a worse "corporate raider" would have. But such arguments purposely avoid the most critical question of the corporate takeover phenomenon: Would America have been better off had our government stepped in to prevent the eighties takeover binge from happening in the first place? . . .

Nowadays, with the weakening of the market for junk bonds, corporate takeovers have slowed down considerably. Words like "greenmail" and "hostile takeover" don't make it into the business pages every day. But we are still paying for them. To understand the corporate takeover phenomenon is to understand how the American economy has been legally manipulated into denying workers their living wages, all to benefit a small number of financial manipulators. It is essential to unmask the hypocrisy of the Reagonomics free enterprise rhetoric that all business activity performed under the cloak of the "free market" is good activity, and that any form of financial manipulation which makes somebody rich is good for the economy. Only when the average American taxpayer and worker understands that he or she is the one who footed the bill for the get-rich-quick corporate takeover frenzy of the eighties will we compel our politicians to bring about an equitable tax structure and regulatory system. Had the government acted, by insisting that existing labor contracts needed to be enforced and limiting the tax deductions that corporations could take for their interest expense on debt to finance unproductive economic activity, the corporate takeover wave of the eighties, and much of the damage it caused, would never have happened. . . .

Need for Intervention

The free market is often the most suitable regulator of the economy. But its aberrations need to be reformed. To those who would dispute this concept, I would call attention to the child labor laws of a century ago, which sought to protect nine-year-olds from coal mines and sweat shops. It was government intervention which interfered with the ability of big business to have its way with poor children. And what limited the cruel power of the vicious monopolies during the early part of the century? It was antitrust regulation—not an appeal to the goodness of the robber barons. In the same way, a century ago union organizers who tried to strike were being shot dead by the dozen by private corporate armies. Workers' rights in the United States—whether for child labor laws, decent hours, pensions, or protection from racial or sexual discrimination—have always come from federal intervention, not corporate largesse. These "reformations" of capitalism's crueler edges are now widely accepted as "advances" in the creation of our modern society.

The United States is the only major industrialized country in the world in which the government would tolerate—and even encourage—the sort of economic behavior that allows hundreds of thousands of workers to be fired from their jobs at healthy corporations simply to enrich the pocketbooks of a small number of financial manipulators. In 1989, 42% of American households earned below $25,000: a figure that had risen from 31% a decade earlier. Unemployment rates do not tell the whole story of the millions of Americans who have seen their real wages, health benefits, and job security fly out the window. While contributing greatly to this decline in the livelihood of American workers, corporate takeovers have also slashed corporate taxes, increasing the huge federal deficit, which in 1992 reached a record $350 billion. . . .

The Taxpayers Suffer

It took two centuries for the United States to build the world's largest, most robust middle class. During the years 1980-1992, with the endorsement of the Reagan-Bush administrations, big business [was] allowed to hack away at the health care benefits, pension plans, job security, and wages of millions of Americans. All under the banner of making a "free marketplace more competitive." All to support the myth that the economy *always* functions best when left alone. But who has been paying the tens of billions in taxes that newly indebted corporations once paid? The American taxpayer. And who pays for the unemployment, hospital care, or welfare benefits for those hundreds of thousands like the Texans who lost their jobs when Safeway closed their stores? The taxpayers, again.

The twisted logic of the robber barons of the Reagan era is that the living wage of middle America has decimated our economy. Listen to the words of George Roberts, KKR's other principal partner. Like Henry Kravis, Roberts is worth more than $450 million. Roberts, Kravis and three partners put up some $2 million of their personal money to buy Safeway; their group's investment of some $2 million in Safeway stock is likely to yield more than $200 million within the next decade. In 1991, Roberts justified Safeway's mass firings and wage cuts by telling the *Wall Street Journal* that the supermarket chain's employees "are now being held accountable. . . . They have to produce up to plan, if they are going to be competitive with the rest of the world. It's high time we did that."

One of the biggest Big Lies of the Reagan-Bush era has been that what is best for the short term profits of corporate America is best for America. There once was a time when a good job with an American corporation meant security and a decent livelihood, when the rising tide of a company's fortunes lifted all boats. But that was before top management and financial manipulators, with junk bond financing, discovered a way to buy boat after boat, then increase their value by throwing the crews overboard. The legacy of this lie will haunt our nation for years through a growing disparity between the haves and have nots, through millions of shattered lives, through an increased deficit and tax burden shouldered by our paychecks and those of our children.

In fact, what's best for corporate America is simply best for the owners of corporate America. And their enrichment is coming out of everyone's pockets. Yet despite more than a decade of such abuse, the complexity of the situation has insured that most Americans still don't get it. The truth of the era of corporate takeovers has little to do with economic competitiveness. It's this simple: we've been robbed.

"Various labor market interventions of the federal government have done more to harm than to help provide job opportunities for the American worker."

Government Intervention in the Labor Market Causes Poverty

Richard K. Vedder

Historically, conservative economists have held that the law of supply and demand will largely determine both the need for labor in any industry and the amount of compensation that labor receives. Accepting this, Richard K. Vedder, author of the following viewpoint, argues that governmental interference in the labor market can severely disrupt the natural influence of market forces. In fact, beginning with President Herbert Hoover and his "high-wage" policy, he says, the government's imposition of mandatory wage guidelines on industry has had a negative impact on employment and prosperity in the United States. Vedder is Distinguished Professor of Economics at Ohio University and a research fellow at the Independent Institute, a conservative think tank in Oakland, California.

As you read, consider the following questions:

1. According to the author, what four mechanisms can reduce unemployment?
2. What lesson does Vedder draw from the transition to a peacetime economy in the United States after World War II?

From Richard K. Vedder, "Out of Work: Is Government the Major Cause of Unemployment?" *Heritage Lectures*, #445, February 3, 1993. Reprinted with permission.

Roughly two decades ago, the noted South African economist William H. Hutt told my colleague Lowell Gallaway and me that the Great Depression in the United States was caused by Herbert Hoover's intervention in the labor market. Professor Hutt said that businesses followed the requests of the President to maintain wages at a high level in order to maintain purchasing power in the wake of the October 1929 stock market crash. We were more than a little skeptical. After all, why would profit-maximizing businesses increase their labor costs and reduce profits in order to appease the President? Jawboning, we felt, was an ineffective technique to change private economic behavior.

At the same time, however, Professor Gallaway was a labor economist who believed that wage rates were important determinants of employment. I was an economic historian who knew that Hoover was a former businessman who was much revered by America's business elite. Accordingly, we began a study that has continued sporadically for two decades, culminating in our 1993 book, *Out of Work: Unemployment and Government in Twentieth-Century America*, which we wrote for the Oakland, California-based Independent Institute.

In our book, we look retrospectively over the first nine decades of the twentieth century, concluding that not only was Bill Hutt correct, but that various labor market interventions of the federal government have done more to harm than to help provide job opportunities for the American worker. Not only has the government contributed to the instability and volatility of unemployment in several important episodes in American history, but the overall long-term level of unemployment has been raised by governmental policies. Finally, we conclude that the victims of these well-intentioned government policies have been largely the poor, the unskilled, and minorities, not the more affluent educated middle classes.

Law of Demand

Let me make the unremarkable but critical observation that when something becomes more expensive, people usually buy less of it. This is the Law of Demand. Economists evoke it constantly to explain phenomena. For example, when oil prices soared in the 1970s because of the OPEC cartel, economists knew this would lead eventually to voluntary energy conservation. When stores have surpluses of unsold goods, they have clearance sales and the problem of surplus inventories disappears. Yet when it comes to dealing with surpluses of labor, which we call unemployment, a majority of economists pay relatively little attention to the price of labor (wages), despite the fact that it is an important determinant of employment.

There are four mechanisms by which the labor market can

bring about a reduction in unemployment. First, if money wages fall, employers will hire more workers, reducing joblessness. Second, if prices of goods rise, employment will likewise rise, since the dollar value of each worker's output goes up, and thereby it becomes profitable to hire more workers at any given money wage. Third, if the productivity of labor rises, the dollar value of each worker's output likewise increases, stimulating employment. Fourth, a decline in the number of workers willing to supply their labor services can reduce unemployment.

Historically, major shifts in labor supply—the willingness of individuals to work—are rare. However, changing wages, prices, and productivity often induce changes in unemployment. We can say that unemployment varies with the "adjusted real wage," which is money wages adjusted for price and productivity change. Over time, over 90 percent of the variation in joblessness in the United States can be explained by variations in the adjusted real wage and its three components—money wages, prices, and labor productivity. Put a little differently, when labor costs rise as a percent of sales revenue, profits get squeezed and employment falls. Falling relative labor costs, by contrast, reduce unemployment and increase employment.

Failure of the Federal Reserve

With this by way of background, it is interesting to look at the unemployment experience of the United States over time. Arguably the most successful period in this century was the first three decades, when the average level of unemployment was well under 5 percent. This also was the least interventionist period in the century. There was one short period of extremely high unemployment, called the Depression of 1921, when the annual unemployment rate approached 12 percent. This episode arose because of an abrupt change in the direction of prices that caught people off guard. Prices had roughly doubled during the era of World War I and its immediate aftermath, but in 1920 prices began their steepest descent in modern history, temporarily pushing up real wages and leading to reduced unemployment. This did not just happen by chance: the newly created bank, the Federal Reserve, assisted in creating the double-digit annual monetary growth that preceded the 1920 debacle, and they failed to counteract the deflationary tendencies that brought about the downturn. Rather than an example of market failure, it might be viewed as the first big failure of our new instrument of monetary policy, the Federal Reserve.

What did the government do about the rising unemployment? Was there a massive new infrastructure program, a job retraining problem, or the like? No. The government did nothing. Indeed, during most of the downturn, the President of the

United States, Woodrow Wilson, was seriously ill with a stroke, and a normally interventionist government adopted a classic laissez-faire stance not out of choice but out of necessity. In March 1921, the new president, Warren Harding, continued Woodrow Wilson's do-nothing policy out of a sense of conviction. What happened? The unemployment rate fell sharply in 1922 and by 1923 was well below 3 percent. Money wages began to fall in 1921, contributing to an end of the labor market disequilibrium situation.

Hoover High-Wage Policy

The contrast with the Great Depression is stark and tragic. An interventionist President, Herbert Hoover, began to jawbone leading industrialists within a month of the October 1929 stock market crash. They listened to Hoover, imbued by his pre-Keynesian underconsumptionist philosophy that demand could create its own supply. If we just raise wages, workers will spend money, assuring prosperity. Henry Ford said, "Wages must not come down, they must not even stay on their present level; they must go up." The nation's business elite virtually unanimously publicly stated their support of the Hoover high-wage policy.

The high-wage policy was aided by the Hawley-Smoot tariff (1930), which reduced international labor competition, thereby reducing normal wage-cutting pressures. As a consequence of both jawboning and the tariff, wages in 1930 were about 8 percent higher than they normally would have been. This squeezed profits enormously. As a consequence, companies increasingly had a cash flow problem that began to make bank loans to corporations more risky. This led to a declining real market value of bank loans to corporations. The markets acknowledged this, as bank stocks fell far more in price than stocks generally throughout 1930. By the fourth quarter of that year, stockholder concerns over bank safety had spread to depositors, beginning the banking crisis. Labor market intervention led to crisis in banking.

While financially desperate companies finally abandoned the high-wage policy in 1931, the salutary effects of wage reductions were more than offset by deflation brought on by the bank failures induced, in our opinion, in large part by the Hoover labor market interventions. Federal Reserve policy failures added to the earlier Administration errors, compounding the downturn. The labor market became the primary transmission mechanism by which the policy failures of the Fed were transmitted. . . .

While the policy sins of the era are many, a few especially stand out: the National Industrial Recovery Act of 1933 brought about an early version of the minimum wage, with that wage set at approximately the average wage prevailing in manufacturing at the time of its passage in June 1933. From June 1933 to

December 1933, wages rose by an average of more than 20 percent—at a time when the unemployment rate exceeded 20 percent. This killed the market-led recovery. The Wagner Act of 1935 provided the legal basis for the use trade union growth of early 1937, which led to another wage explosion, bringing on the 1938 downturn. The Social Security Act similarly contributed to the rise in labor costs with its new payroll taxes. . . .

Postwar Prosperity

The policy sins did not end in the 1930s. Ironically, the prosperity of the late 1940s and 1950s can be attributed to relative inactivity in labor markets. Harry Truman talked a liberal expansionist line, but followed relatively conservative non-interventionist monetary and fiscal policies. Legislation such as the Taft-Hartley Act of 1947 and the Landrum-Griffin Act of 1959 actually repaired some of the damage created by New Deal legislation.

The greatest testimony of the powers of the labor market to adjust to changing conditions came right after World War II. Think of it: from June 1945 to June 1946, the federal government reduced its own employment by 10 million—the equivalent today of about 20 million. The government went from running a budget deficit the equivalent today of over one trillion dollars to running a massive budget surplus. Monetary growth slowed abruptly. No job training problems were implemented. Keynesian economists freely predicted double-digit unemployment was around the corner. What happened? The annual unemployment rate never reached 4 percent. The post-World War II transition makes the post-Cold War transition look puny by comparison. At the very time Keynesian economics [advocating government programs to increase employment and spending] achieved statutory victory with the Employment Act of 1946, the economy and the labor market were demonstrating the inappropriateness of federal demand management policies.

The prosperity of the postwar era continued and indeed expanded in the 1960s, but in some respects it was a false prosperity in that the seeds of the 1970s decline were sowed. The Kennedy-Johnson-Nixon Administrations pursued policies of Keynesian activism. The supply-side effects of the Kennedy tax cut were very real and positive, and the deliberately inflationary policies of the government temporarily lowered real wages, boosting employment. The policy of inflation, intellectually supported by the newly discovered Phillips curve [a statistical measure of the increasing rate of inflation as employment decreases], ultimately led to disaster. The first great believer in the role of expectations in economic theory, Abraham Lincoln, said it best: "You can fool all the people some of the time, some of the people all the time, but you cannot fool all the people all the time."

Labor Supply and Demand: A Self-Regulating System

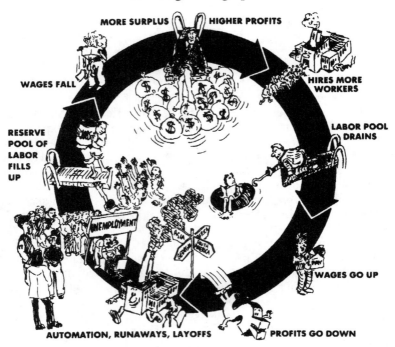

A Field Guide to the U.S. Economy, © 1987, The Center for Popular Economics. Used by permission.

Whereas in the late 1960s a 4 percent inflation rate gave the nation some economic stimulus, the same amount of inflation by the early 1970s was expected, and distinctly unfoolish workers demanded and got bigger wage increases. As for the individual in advanced stages of drug addiction, ever larger injections of stimulus seemed to provide less and less happiness. The prosperity of fiscal stimulus proved as artificial as the powdered happiness of drugs. The 1970s was the first decade in American history where we ran a deficit every single year. In half of the years, the money supply increased more than 10 percent, compared with no years in the previous decade. In spite of all this attempt to inflate the economy to keep real wages artificially low, the adjusted real wage actually rose. Incidentally, this process began even before the oil price explosion following 1973.

By 1980, the bankruptcy of interventionist macropolicies as a remedy for high unemployment was apparent to most of the

American population. In 1980, unemployment was over 7 percent, historically a high figure, while prices were rising at an annual rate of at least 10 percent. The Reagan-Volcker [Paul Volcker, Federal Reserve chairperson] approach at disinflation had the desired effect. The 1982 recession was almost inevitable, as the sharp reduction in inflation was not instantly followed by corresponding declines in money wage growth. Real wages rose for a while, leading to some reduction in the quantity of labor demanded. Within a year, however, market forces began to respond, setting the stage for the extraordinary 1980s peacetime expansion. . . .

Compromise and Accommodation

In our view, the 1990 recession reflected in part George Bush's policy of compromise and accommodation. In the late 1980s, wages rose at an annual rate of roughly 4 percent a year. Beginning in early 1990, a wage explosion occurred, with wages rising at an annual rate of over 8 percent in the second quarter. In part, this reflected rising inflationary expectations as people began to doubt that Bush and [Federal Reserve chairperson] Alan Greenspan had the same commitment to inflation reduction that Reagan and Paul Volcker had earlier. More important, however, was the 13 percent increase in the minimum wage on April 1, 1990, followed by another double-digit increase just one year later.

In addition, the minimally accepted wage for employment for those that were unemployed, what economists call the reservation wage, was pushed up by government policies. On three occasions, unemployment insurance benefits were extended, so many unemployed were on the dole for more than a year. Why push hard to get a job when the government is subsidizing you not to work? The wage-enhancing effects of these policies were aggravated by three pieces of legislation destined to lower long-term productivity growth: the Clean Air Act amendments, the new Civil Rights Act, and the Americans with Disabilities Act.

Despite these negative shocks to the adjusted real wage, the market's resiliency should not be underestimated. Money wage growth began slowing in 1991 and 1992, and productivity growth brought about by cost-reduction strategies of companies helped lower the adjusted real wage. We are on record as predicting a fairly noticeable decline in unemployment in 1993, which the Clinton Administration will no doubt take credit for, but which in reality reflects the lagged effects of falling real unit labor costs.

Government labor market intervention has not only contributed to unemployment instability, but also has added to the gradual upward drift in unemployment observed in the 1970s and 1980s. Of even greater interest, however, is the fact that the biggest victims of these policies have been disadvantaged

Americans. Let me ask a couple of questions:

1) Why was it that in the era between 1900 and 1930 the black unemployment rate was about the same as that for whites, but today the incidence of black unemployment is more than double that for whites?

2) Why is it that in the years since the beginning of the civil rights era with *Brown vs. Board of Education* in 1954 has the proportion of black Americans of working age that work actually fallen, while for whites that proportion has increased significantly?

Harming the Poor

While rising black unemployment over time reflects to a considerable extent the geographic and occupational migration of nonwhites, it also probably reflects the fact that the unemployment-creating effects of public policy tend to hurt those in lower paying jobs the most. The minimum wage is more likely to price black workers out of the market than white workers. The Davis-Bacon Act [which requires government contractors to pay "prevailing wages"—generally equal to union scale—on federally funded construction projects] was actually implemented in part to keep black construction workers out of the North in the Great Depression. The welfare programs of [President Lyndon Johnson's] Great Society and after have had the effect of creating the equivalent of very high marginal tax rates [rate that applies to an additional dollar of taxable income] on work income for low-income Americans, disproportionately black, relative to high-income ones. I would surmise that the typical marginal tax rate on work income for black Americans is much higher than for white Americans, all a consequence of government policies ostensibly designed to help the disadvantaged. The same principle holds true with unemployment insurance.

If our observation about labor markets has any generalized validity, it would seem that the unintended consequences of government policies particularly hurt the poor, the politically weak, including children, and minorities. It is also our observation that the market has great egalitarian tendencies seldom appreciated by those on the left. The income differential between the northern industrial states and the American South has dramatically narrowed over time, not because of government policies as much as because it historically has been in the self-interest of labor to move North and for capital to move South, equalizing considerably the capital resources available per worker. . . .

We are not saying that the path to progress is through lower wages. What we are saying, however, is that higher employment and a higher standard of living are both possible only if labor productivity rises sufficiently to keep labor from becoming relatively more costly. The key to having both job opportunities and material prosperity is an increase in the productivity of American labor. . . .

Reteaching the Lesson

The message is simple. Let markets do their job. Markets are efficient and they are fair. They do not discriminate against blacks or gays or even liberals. The stifling of markets leads to less efficiency, more injustice and a reduction in the standard of living. With regards to labor markets, that lesson was pointed out two generations ago by economists such as A.C. Pigou, Ludwig von Mises, Bill Hutt, and Lionel Robbins. One generation ago, Murray Rothbard repeated the lesson, showing how Hoover's labor market interference contributed to the Great Depression. Every generation, it seems, needs to be retaught. We hope that our work will make a modest contribution in educating the present generation into the pitfalls of intervening in market forces.

"Government has always taken responsibility for creating the material and legal conditions that allow families to coordinate their personal reproduction with the prevailing system of socioeconomic production."

Inadequate Government Assistance Causes Poverty

Stephanie Coontz

Stephanie Coontz is the author of *The Social Origins of Private Life*. In the following viewpoint, excerpted from her testimony before the House Select Committee on Children, Youth, and Families, she challenges traditional views of the philosophy of welfare—namely that welfare is a recent socioeconomic phenomenon, that it creates a dependent class of citizens, and that it is destructive to society. Coontz instead contends that throughout America's history, government assistance has played an active and constructive role in economic progress. Therefore, she concludes, government should recognize its historic role and broaden its assistance programs. The question, she believes, is not *"whether* to intervene, but *how."*

As you read, consider the following questions:

1. According to the author, what approach did the government take in the late 19th century with regard to family assistance?
2. What economic assistance did the government provide to pioneer families a century ago, according to Coontz?

From Stephanie Coontz's testimony before the House Select Committee on Children, Youth, and Families, July 23, 1992.

Despite the extraordinary amount of change that there has been in families, some positive and some very negative, one of the constants is, families have always required government assistance and no family form, structure, or set of values provides a magic bullet for avoiding that.

The first point I want to make today is that the common conception of some natural family existing prior to government and, until recently at least, free of state intervention is a myth. Families have never existed independently of the legislative, judicial, and social-support services set up by governing authorities, whether those governing authorities were the clan elders of native American societies, the city officials of colonial New England, or the judicial and legislative bodies established by the American Constitution. Government has always set the conditions that allow families to function in the prevailing economic and cultural climate. And these conditions have included regulation of the way that employers and civic bodies must relate to families, as well as investment in the infrastructure required to provide families with jobs, mobility, education, and security.

Necessity of Outside Aid

The second point I want to make is that there has never been a natural family economy or perfect family structure that was able to fully provide for all the personal dependencies and changing fortunes of its members. Families have always required outside aid. Elders, for example, had the highest poverty rate in our nation prior to the advent of such government initiatives as Social Security and Medicare. Today, as we know, it is children who have the highest poverty rates. This is not something that government can rely on family structure or values alone to solve, as we can see by the doubling of the poverty rate among intact, married-couple young families since 1973.

Now, I'm not here to advise you on current policies for the family, but I can tell you that you're not setting any dangerous new precedent when you do adopt legislation assisting families, or requiring other institutions, either public or private, to accommodate them in some way.

In colonial days, contrary to myth, government created a legal and political framework that required other individuals, households, and economic institutions to share the functions of education, socialization, work training, welfare, and other material assistance with nuclear families. This changed during the antebellum era when judges and legislatures limited those family-like rights and responsibilities of people outside the nuclear family. The result was that the new isolation of families, combined with changing economic conditions, created a crisis that forced local governments to build poorhouses, to provide direct

101

outdoor relief, and to acquiesce in the development of the huge institutions that were founded in this period to warehouse individuals whose families could not shoulder their newly private functions, or handle the changing economy.

Tie Benefits to Citizenship, Not to Jobs

The ruthless corporate downsizing of recent years has demonstrated that the economy cannot bootstrap its way to good jobs for all simply by running individual companies more efficiently.

If all of the new productivity is to add up to broadly shared prosperity, the human workers shed in corporate restructurings need the availability of other work. This reality requires national policies for:

Full employment: Technological change is broadly beneficial only when other jobs replace the ones lost.

Socialized fringe benefits: If more people work as independent contractors, then health insurance, pensions, retraining opportunities, child care and the like had better become perquisites of citizenship rather than benefits tied to a particular job.

Better buffers: To humanize the new corporate turbulence, society needs to devise something better for workers between jobs than unemployment compensation and "temp" stints. Paid sabbaticals for retraining, parenting or public service could keep millions of workers productively occupied as corporate America downsizes.

Our workplaces are indisputably in a brave new world, but not one that is a simple blessing. It will take broader innovations to make these shifts economically beneficial and socially bearable.

Robert Kuttner, *San Diego Union-Tribune*, August 3, 1993.

Even at the height of laissez-faire ideology, in the later 19th century, government never took a hands-off approach to families, though in this period government spent more of its resources and energy regulating gender roles and sexual morality than it did in assisting needy families. In fact, laissez-faire government sanctioned a policy of breaking up poor families that did not meet reformers' religious or moral criteria for how a proper family should operate. Fortunately, this policy was abandoned in the early 20th century, when reformers concluded that the moralistic interventions of the previous 40 years had failed and that families required material assistance and government social services in order to survive the rapid changes induced by transition to a mass production economy.

In consequence, they attempted to institute a family wage system, to strengthen the ability of a male breadwinner to support his family without having his wife or children work. But this family wage system, again contrary to myth, was not a natural outgrowth of the market. It was a political response to what had been the natural outgrowths of the market: child labor, intensive poverty, employment insecurity, recurring depressions, and an earning structure in which 45 percent of industrial workers fell below the poverty line, and another 40 percent hovered just barely above it. State policies involved in the family wage system included abolishing child labor, pressuring industrialists to negotiate with unions, Federal arbitration, expansion of compulsory schooling, adoption of Mothers' Pensions, and legislation discriminating against women workers.

Even if we tried to reinstate the male breadwinner system today by reversing the rights that women have won in the public arena, it's important to realize that the family wage system never worked for millions in America. Men continued to earn less than many needed to support a family, a trend that accelerated, of course, during the Great Depression. Unfortunately, we have seen this trend rising again since 1973. Under these conditions, I would suggest that contemporary political initiatives to create a more favorable environment for working mothers are a different but not a new expression of government's long established practice of regulating the economy and adjusting its political programs to respond to changing family needs.

There's an equally long tradition of not just regulating but providing material assistance to families. Not only have working people always needed help in periods of economic and ecological change, but the condition of existence for successful middle-class families has historically been generous government funding of a large supportive infrastructure.

Federal Help to Pioneers

Pioneer families, for example, depended on huge federal land grants, government-funded military mobilizations, and state-sponsored economic investment. The Homestead Act of 1872, for example, allowed settlers to buy 160 acres for $10.00, far below the actual cost to the government of acquiring the land. Westward settlement depended on continuous federal funding of exploration, development, transportation, communication systems, and construction of dams or other federally subsidized irrigation projects. During the 1930s, it was government electrification projects that brought pumps, refrigeration, and household technology to farm families, allowing them, for the first time, to participate in the market economy in a meaningful way. The well-known strengths of western families, I submit, depended in large part, and emerged out of, their access to such non-stigmatized aid.

This is similarly true of the other oft-cited example of familial self-reliance, the 1950s suburban family, which, in fact, was extraordinarily dependent on government assistance. Federal GI benefits, available to 40 percent of the male population between the ages of 20 and 24, were one of the main reasons that a whole generation of men could expand their education and improve their job prospects without foregoing marriage and childbearing. Suburban home ownership depended on an unprecedented enlargement of federal regulation and financing. The Federal Housing Authority transformed traditional banking practice by ceasing to require 50 percent down payments on homes, allowing down payments of only 5 to 10 percent, and guaranteeing mortgages of up to 30 years at interest rates just 2 to 3 percent on the balance. The VA [Veterans Administration] asked a mere $1.00 down from veterans.

Almost half the housing in suburbia during the 1950s depended on such federal programs. And I think it's worth noting that such government aid to suburban residents during the 1950s and 1960s encouraged family formation, residential stability, upward occupational mobility, and high educational aspirations among youth. There is thus no intrinsic tendency of government help to induce dependence, undermine self-esteem, or break down family ties.

I was also asked to address changing family values but I must confess, I had some difficulty in defining precisely what those were. . . .

An older generation of Americans, however, such as my grandparents, would in many cases have defined family values as raising children who felt an obligation to the less fortunate and made a contribution to the community. Our founding fathers placed the values of civic engagement and public commitment ahead of private interests and private emotions. Prior to the second half of the 19th century, for example, the word "virtue" was not a sexual but a political word. It referred to a person's willingness to fulfill civic obligations, not to a person's personal sexual behavior. When documents from past times mention family values, they often mean the importance of treating others like family, or taking them into your family if they're on hard times.

A Slippery Concept

So, I think family values is a very slippery concept, once we get beyond the kind of basic values of human decency that probably everyone in this room would agree on. It's not at all clear, considered historically, that one set of values about sexuality, marriage, and parenthood is so sound that it should be made a pre-condition for government aid. I recently taught for six months in Hawaii. I found that modern mainland America's assumptions about the necessity to raise a child exclusively by his own parents sounded extremely alienating to traditional Hawaiian culture, which has always stressed child exchange as a way of cementing social ties and building larger kinship networks. Many other cultures and religions have similar beliefs.

Even the Christian tradition, from St. Augustine to the Puritans, has often urged people not to put the ties of marriage, sex, and parenting above the fellowship that is owed to the entire community. Conversely, we all know that strong values in favor of chastity, sanctions against divorce, and tight generational bonds can occur in families that are extremely disruptive or antisocial. The example of organized crime families springs to mind.

Of course we know that some relationships and values have a healthy dynamic in our society, and that some don't. But that's very different from saying that one particular family form or value system is always likely to create healthy relationships, and therefore deserves unique prerogatives or special government sanctions, while others should be penalized.

Even the issue of family structure is, I think, much more complicated. . . . The 1960s rise in welfare, for example, had much to do with the effect of the civil rights movement in opening up access to welfare for people who previously wouldn't have applied. Changes in family structure in recent years are often result, rather than cause, of economic breakdown. . . . There are plenty of experts doing research on this topic. . . .

In conclusion, government has always taken responsibility for creating the material and legal conditions that allow families to coordinate their personal reproduction with the prevailing system of socioeconomic production. The historical debate over government policy toward families has never been over whether to intervene, but how: to rescue or to warehouse, to prevent or to punish, to mobilize resources to help families, or to moralize? The historical record suggests that government action is more helpful to families when it provides a general and generous support system of infrastructure, allowing families to work out their own values and interpersonal arrangements, than when it tries to impose a unitary value system and set of gender roles inside the family.

*"Poverty is a reflection of social system
pathology, not family pathology. "*

America's Unfair
Socioeconomic System
Causes Poverty

Holly Sklar

For several decades a debate has endured over whether poverty
is caused by inequities inherent in America's socioeconomic
structure or by dysfunctional behavioral patterns and nonpro-
ductive personal habits prevalent among poor families themselves. In the following viewpoint, Holly Sklar maintains that
the system, not the people, is responsible for poverty. She
contends that the increase in the number of poor working families has been caused by a sharp decline in real wages over the
past two decades and exacerbated by inequalities in pay scale
between men and women. Sklar, who resides in Boston, is the
author of several books, including *Trilateralism: The Trilateral
Commission and Elite Planning for World Management* and *Poverty
in the American Dream*.

As you read, consider the following questions:

1. What objections does Sklar raise about the "wedfare" system,
   which penalizes women for not being married?
2. According to the Children's Defense Fund as quoted by the
   author, what measures must many poor families take in order
   to survive?

From Holly Sklar, "Reaffirmative Action," *Z Magazine*, May 1992. Reprinted with permission.

Why are more and more working families poor? Because average real wages have crashed 19 percent since 1973 and the average wages of young families with children have plummeted 26 percent. Minimum wage no longer fulfills even the official definition of minimum subsistence.

One out of four people surveyed by *Time*/CNN "said they had been unemployed, not by their own choice, at some point during 1991." About nine million Americans are unemployed according to official statistics. Another six million are involuntarily working part-time because they are on partial layoff or unable to find a full-time job. On average one-third of the unemployed received benefits from 1984 to 1989, down from over 50 percent a decade ago. A report by the Boston-based Dudley Street Neighborhood Initiative points out that in 1985, during the "Massachusetts Miracle," 44 percent of Boston's young people of color 16-19 years old, and 11 percent of those 20-24 years old were unemployed. The respective figures for whites were 6 percent and 3 percent.

Even in an era of high unemployment, two-thirds of poor families with children have at least one worker (full or part time). In 1990, says the Children's Defense Fund, "Poor families with children received twice as much income from work as from welfare."

Just as a full-time, year-round job is not sufficient to avoid poverty, neither is being married. According to the 1990 census, the poverty rates are 5.1 percent for white married-couple families, 12.6 percent for Black married-couple families, and 17.5 percent for Hispanics. More than two in five poor children live in families where the father is present. For female-householder families, no husbands present, the poverty rate is 26.8 percent for whites, 48.1 percent for Blacks, and 48.3 percent for Hispanics.

As Andrew Hacker points out in *Two Nations: Black and White, Separate, Hostile and Unequal*, while the numbers of Black female-headed households are rising, so are white. The ratio of white to Black female-headed households has remained rather constant over 40 years. In 1950, 17.2 percent of Black households were headed by women compared with 5.3 percent of whites, a multiple of 3.2. In 1990, 56.2 percent of Black households were headed by women compared with 17.3 percent of whites, again a multiple of 3.2. Approximately half of all Black single mothers, says Hacker, are fully self-supporting.

Worse for Working Women

It's no surprise that many female single-parent households are poor since many mothers who want to work cannot find affordable child care, and women who do work earn much less than men. Sixty-seven percent of all workers who earn the minimum wage are women. "Equal pay for comparable work" is still a slogan, not reality.

A 1977 government study found that if working women were paid what similarly qualified men earn, the number of poor families would decrease by half. In 1983, women working full time earned on average only 59 cents for every dollar earned by men—down from nearly 64 cents in 1955. In 1986, they were back to 64 cents. In 1988, writes Susan Faludi in *Backlash*, "women with a college diploma could still wear the famous 59-cent buttons."

A Sharp Decline in Real Wages

Change in Average Real Hourly and Weekly Wages, 1970-90 (in Constant 1990 Dollars).

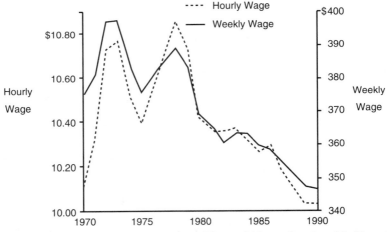

Source: U.S. Congress, House Committee on Ways and Means, *Overview of Entitlement Programs: Green Book, 1991.*

The welfare system has penalized women for being married, denying benefits if able-bodied men were present, whether or not they could find employment. Today's "wedfare" penalizes mothers for not being married. The rhetoric assumes that all women are better off getting married and staying married, and that all mothers are heterosexual or should be. There's no acknowledgment that divorce can be a good choice for women of all incomes, nor that some women leave men who physically abuse them and their children. As Susan Faludi points out, between 1976 and 1984, a period when the homicide rate actually declined, sex-related murders rose 160 percent: "At least one-third of the women were killed by their husbands or boyfriends, and the majority of that group were murdered just after declaring their independence in the most intimate manner—by filing for divorce and leaving home." Society blandly calls that domestic violence, not savagery.

The average welfare recipient stays on welfare less than two years. Welfare is not a free ride, but a test of how to subsist on too little. According to U.S. Department of Agriculture estimates, a low-income family of three (a mother with children ages seven and ten) needed $309 a month to purchase a nutritionally adequate diet in 1989. The Department of Housing and Urban Development estimated nationally that rent and utilities for a modest two-bedroom apartment cost $482 a month. That left $33 for all other expenses from health care to child care to clothes and school supplies if a family had the official poverty line annual income of $9,885 for a family of three in 1989. As the Children's Defense Fund points out, the average poor family with children has an income below—often far below—the official poverty threshold. In 1990, the average poor family with children had a monthly income of $615—$7,380 annually—far short of the $9,009 poverty line for a family of two, or $10,419 for a family of three.

Declining Standards

"Many poor families," says the Children's Defense Fund, "manage by cutting back on food, jeopardizing their health and the development of their children, or by living in substandard and sometimes dangerous housing. Some do without heat, electricity, telephone service, or plumbing for months or years. Many do without health insurance, health care, safe child care, or reliable transportation to take them to or from work. Some borrow money if they can. Some beg. Some have small amounts of unreported income or feel compelled to engage in illegal activities."

According to a 1991 U.S. House Committee on Ways and Means report, AFDC [Aid to Families with Dependent Children] benefits (for a mother and two children) steadily declined (adjusting for inflation) from $8,178 in 1972 to $4,823 in 1991. "This represents a 41 percent decrease, and when combined with food stamps yields a 26.5 percent decrease in total AFDC and food stamp benefits since 1972." The report notes further that "In 1972, all States paid AFDC benefits to a family with wages equal to 75 percent of the poverty threshold; by 1991, only 5 States paid AFDC to such a family. Average tax rates on such earnings increased from 52 to 69 percent from 1972 to 1984, and then fell to 56 percent in 1991."

Instead of higher wages and supports, single mothers get blame, stigmatization, and more cutbacks. According to the U.S.

109

House Ways and Means Committee report, "in 1979, approximately 30 percent of individuals in single-parent families were removed from poverty as the result of means-tested transfers, food and housing benefits, and Federal tax policy. By 1990, this had declined to 20 percent." The government maintains Social Security without means-testing for the elderly, and meanness for poor women with children. "The percentage of elderly individuals removed from poverty due to social insurance programs," reports the House Committee, "increased from 68 percent to 73 percent from 1979 to 1990."

Poverty is a reflection of social system pathology, not family pathology. In 1989, according to the Children's Defense Fund election-year guide, *Leave No Child Behind*, it would have cost $28 billion to raise the income of every poor family with children to the federal poverty line. "By contrast, the cost in 1991 alone of extra tax breaks for the richest 1 percent of American taxpayers added by the federal government since 1977 was $55 billion."

"Unless corporations and government reverse
[their] retrenchment policies, they will lengthen
the silent depression."

Corporate and Government Retrenchment Causes Poverty

John Miller

John Miller, a professor of economics at Wheaton College in
Illinois, posits what appears to be a contradictory situation:
Despite the economic growth and improved productivity of the
1980s and 1990s, "workers' standard of living has deteriorated
and income inequality has worsened." As a consequence, he
maintains, the general economy for the last twenty years has
fallen into an ongoing "silent depression." The reasons for this
phenomenon are explained in the following viewpoint, which
originally appeared in *Dollars & Sense*, a magazine produced by
a socialist collective of which Professor Miller is a member.

As you read, consider the following questions:

1. Why does the author believe that the economy's financial
   institutions are more fragile today than at any time since the
   depression of the 1930s?
2. According to Miller, why has the corporate response to
   slower growth made things worse for most workers?
3. What does the author maintain the government can do to end
   the current recession and bring the silent depression to a close?

From John Miller, "Silent Depression," *Dollars & Sense*, April 1992. *Dollars & Sense* is a
progressive economics magazine published ten times a year. First-year subscriptions cost
$16.95 and may be ordered by writing *Dollars & Sense*, One Summer St., Somerville, MA
02143 or calling 617-628-2025. Reprinted with permission.

Since 1973, argues Wallace Peterson, a Keynesian macroeconomist at the University of Nebraska, a "silent depression" has haunted the U.S. economy, unrecorded in the economic log books that chart the recessions and expansions of the traditional business cycle. The 1980s, and now the 1990s, have shown that economic growth and improved productivity do not automatically translate into improved living conditions and purchasing power for most workers and families. Despite economic growth in the last decade, workers' standard of living has deteriorated and income inequality has worsened. . . .

Stagnation—slow growth and deteriorating living standards—may well be the hallmark of the 1990s economy. . . .

Unconventional Recession

Unlike previous recessions, this recession has hit service and white-collar workers, including middle-level managers, in sizable numbers. For instance, more than half a million sales workers have lost their jobs. In contrast, during the 1981-82 slump, the economy actually added more than three-quarters of a million white-collar jobs.

Because this recession follows an equally long period of slow growth, output measures also mislead us. The back-to-back years of recession and slow growth paint an alarming picture of stagnating output. From 1988 to 1991, the economy [grew] an average of less than 1% per year—the second slowest period of growth sustained over any three-year period since World War II. Only the back-to-back recessions of 1980 and 1981-82 registered a worse growth record.

And the economy's financial institutions are more fragile today than at any time since the Great Depression. Record levels of debt and bankruptcy propel this recession. A decade of corporate mergers and buyouts, the overbuilding of commercial real estate, households struggling to maintain their spending, and persistent budget deficits have pushed the economy deeper in debt. Outstanding non-financial corporate debt grew from 30% of GNP in 1980 to 39% of GNP in 1990. The typical consumer now carries over 90 cents of debt for every dollar of after-tax income, a postwar high. Despite repeated promises from the Ronald Reagan and George Bush administrations to balance the federal government's budget, the gross federal debt practically quadrupled from 1980 to 1991.

Record debt has meant record bankruptcies—well beyond even 1982 levels. Business failures in the 1980s doubled compared with earlier in the postwar period. The agency in charge of insuring bank deposits, the Federal Deposit Insurance Corporation, [predicted] between 200 and 240 banks [would] fail in 1992. That's more than five times the number in 1982. And more than one million families declared bankruptcy [in 1990 and 1991], about twice the number who went belly-up in the 1982 recession.

Even the architects of the policies that led to the financial excesses of the 1980s now recognize the serious problems of today's economy. "A national day of reckoning for a decade of deficit drenched excess is upon us," warns David Stockman, Ronald Reagan's first budget director, "bringing a painful retrenchment that could burden the economy through the mid-1990s."

An Unnoticed Divorce

But according to economist Peterson, economic growth and prosperity parted company [around 1973]. The real income of the average worker or family is no greater today than in 1973, even though the economy grew in all but six of the intervening years. And for Peterson, when real income stops growing, the economy is depressed, even if the official figures indicate otherwise.

In the boom years from 1947 through 1973, real weekly earnings and real median family income grew along with the economy. From 1973, the peak of postwar prosperity, to 1982, real weekly earnings improved somewhat, then fell. They dropped sharply in the 1982 recession, and continued falling during the 1980s expansion. Today [1992], real weekly earnings are some 19% below the 1973 level. . . . Median family income, corrected for inflation, is no higher than it was two decades ago, even though almost 20% more families rely on two incomes instead of one. The expansions have not reduced poverty rates to the same degree either. While the 1960s expansion made the poverty rate fall 7.4 percentage points, the 1980s expansion made it decline by only 2.4 points.

Slower growth and greater income inequality launched this silent depression. Slower growth begins with smaller productivity gains, says Peterson. Slower productivity growth means less competitive U.S. corporations and less generous pay checks for U.S. workers. He points to overblown military spending that ate up 60% of federally funded research over the last two decades, leaving few research funds to work directly toward improving the productivity of the domestic economy. Since the mid-1970s, the United States has ranked last in productivity growth among the major industrialized countries.

The deindustrialization of the United States helped to increase inequality. Since World War II, manufacturing employment— jobs with more organized workers and higher wages—fell from over one-third of U.S. non-farm jobs to less than one-fifth. The service-sector jobs replacing them paid less well. Added to this, productivity in service industries grew at only one-quarter the rate of manufacturing during the 1980s. Higher wage disparity within service industries has also contributed to income inequality. Altogether, nearly 90% of the new jobs created during the 1960s and 1970s paid middle-income wages. During the 1980s, just over one of every three new jobs did.

A New Infrastructure of—and for—the Next Century

There is widespread agreement that much of the nation's networks for transportation, power, sewage, water, and communications are eroding and need to be rebuilt. Anyone who has operated a business where the infrastructure is lousy—say, the phone networks in Eastern Europe—knows the damage it wreaks on efficiency. Providing modern infrastructure would stimulate not only productivity but also innovations, from low-maintenance structural concretes to optical networks, to take advantage of the new infrastructure.

The additional opportunity here would be to fashion new infrastructure that uses emerging critical technologies of the next century—new materials, visual systems with flat-panel displays, real-time electronic controls—and then to support the development of commercial, domestic capabilities in them through nationwide procurement. . . .

These long-term needs are likely to provide the next frontiers of American technological innovation. More than technological pre-eminence is at stake. Historically high growth rates, competitive wages, and a growing standard of living—all depend on regaining leadership in commercial technological innovation. For twelve debilitating years [1980-1992], the government has refused to invest in America's commercial technology position. It's high time to revive public support and set it to the task.

Michael Borrus, *The American Prospect*, Fall 1992.

These employment trends kept middle- and low-income wages in check, and, along with tax cuts for the well-to-do, combined to redistribute income and wealth toward those at the top during the 1980s. Almost 80% of families—those who depend almost exclusively on wage income—saw their real income fall while their taxes increased. For the top one percent, after-tax income more than doubled.

The corporate response to slower growth hasn't helped. It's only made things worse for most workers. The 1982 recession initiated an era of corporate restructuring that profoundly shifted the balance of class power in the United States against labor. Anti-worker public policy allowed employers to slash wages, canceling out workers' share of subsequent productivity increases during the latter half of the 1980s. Real wages stagnated through 93 months of economic growth.

Restructuring has intensified again during the current downturn. General Motors, IBM, and Digital Equipment Corporation alone will sack more than 100,000 workers [by 1995] and close plants across the nation. These retrenchment programs aim to return corporate profitability by keeping labor costs down. To meet their retrenchment target, several blue-chip corporations, like Digital and IBM, have abandoned long-standing no-layoff policies.

Good News for Whom?

The *Wall St. Journal* regards the cost control wrought by these retrenchment programs as the "good news" of the recession. As the *Journal* sees it, lower labor costs should boost the international competitiveness of U.S. corporations. U.S. labor costs have in fact declined. Among the 14 leading industrial countries, only the United States showed a decline in labor costs per unit of output from 1985 to 1990. By 1990 the average hourly compensation for U.S. production workers had fallen from highest to sixth. Norway, Germany, Italy, Canada, and France all paid their production workers more.

Several political economists, like Massachusetts Institute of Technology's Paul Osterman, regard corporate retrenchment policies as the most alarming news of the recession. These policies violate the innovative industrial relations adopted by some high-tech corporations. Applying a middle-management salary model to all workers, these corporations promised lifetime employment in exchange for workers' relinquishing some prerogatives around work rules and embracing rapid innovation in their work. Retrenchment and massive layoffs have ended this Japanese-style collaboration.

According to Osterman, while retrenchment will cut costs, it will also slow innovation in U.S. corporations and compromise their international competitiveness. One especially despondent political economist dubbed these retrenchment policies the "Haitian road to development."

Those who would stay the course have plenty to be despondent about. Unless corporations and government reverse these retrenchment policies, they will lengthen the silent depression. . . . Even when service industries revive, the overexpansion and slow productivity growth of the last decade will still take their toll. The Bureau of Labor Statistics projects that service companies will create jobs at only half the 1980s rate. Nonetheless, these industries will produce practically the only new jobs in the 1990s, according to labor experts. Unemployment rates will likely hover above 6% for years, long after the recovery begins.

The [Federal Reserve System] hasn't pulled a magic cure out of its old bag of tricks either. The current recession has showcased the limits of monetary policy as a cure for economic stagnation. Since the recession began, the Fed has lowered the discount rate—the rate of interest it charges commercial banks to borrow money—an unprecedented 15 times [by early 1992]. . . . But the mountain of debt accumulated in the 1980s and record levels of bankruptcies have blocked the Fed's ability to revive economic growth through these channels.

Conventional wisdom claims that changes in monetary policy take about six months to work their magic. Lowering the discount rate should bring down long-term interest rates (such as the rates on 30-year Treasury bonds) and inject more money into the economy, thus stimulating investment and pumping up consumer spending. . . . But monetary policy has not worked so far. Despite the Fed's interest rate cuts, as of January 1992, the money supply has barely grown. Since the beginning of this recession one standard of the money supply—M2, the sum of all currency, checking accounts, and some savings and money-market funds—has grown more slowly than in any recession in the past three decades.

Hangovers from the 1980s

Another nasty hangover of the 1980s excesses, bank failures, has absorbed much of the increased money supply. When the Federal Deposit Insurance Corporation (FDIC) closes a bank and bails out depositors, depositors at healthy banks withdraw money to buy the Treasury securities or to pay the taxes needed to fund the bailout, shrinking the money supply. As the FDIC bails out more failed banks, this drag on the economy will increase.

The credit crunch, brought on by nervous lenders, has also stymied the Fed's loose money policy. Even though banks can now acquire money at a lower cost, they are reluctant to lend. . . . But banks, at least those still standing, have good reasons to hesitate: debt and bankruptcy. Banks still carry loads of bad loans on their books, particularly from commercial real estate. Nearly half of the banks' $77 billion in past-due loans in 1990 were real-estate loans. Declining property values have shrunk the collateral insuring their still current loans.

Nor have lower interest rates spurred corporations to invest in new projects. Corporations are balking at new investments. According to the Commerce Department, manufacturers [planned] to reduce capital spending by 0.5% in 1992—the first drop since 1986.

Nor are consumers spending more. Homeowners have profited from lower interest rates by refinancing home mortgages at lower rates or from automatic decreases in monthly payments on adjustable-rate mortgages. But this has not stoked spending. Consumption, which accounts for about two-thirds of spending in the economy, has already fallen in real terms further during this recession than during the early 1980s. Consumers who have spare cash are paying off their debt rather than buying.

Some still maintain the Fed is not acting boldly enough. Interest rates corrected for inflation, the rates that matter to borrowers, are still higher than in 1989 and than at the recession troughs of other postwar business cycles. At the same time interest rates have fallen, so has inflation. In fact, real interest rates are three percentage points higher than during the 1960s and early 1970s—the last period of real prosperity.

Many economists and most politicians believe that even a bolder monetary policy will not by itself revive economic growth. Most say more government spending and taxing is necessary to promote growth. That economists and politicians have rediscovered public spending as an economic tool is hopeful. Their actual policies, however, are insufficient to counteract stagnation. . . .

A Loud Answer to the Silent Depression

But government is not powerless. It could lay the groundwork for a cure to the current recession and bring the silent depression to a close. A dose of old-fashioned public investment and genuinely progressive taxation is the best strategy for reviving economic growth and recoupling it with improved living conditions.

Public investment needn't be a make-work proposition. We need to repair our crumbling infrastructure, from roads and bridges to water and sewer systems. . . . Governments at all levels vastly underfund human services. National health care could safeguard workers' physical health while better funded education could augment their skills. These changes would also improve the lot of most workers and families.

Public investment would also improve economic productivity over the long term. Economist David Aschauer says in a report written for the Washington-based Economic Policy Institute that restoring public investment to the levels of the 1950s and 1960s would do more to increase private-sector profits and productivity than an equal amount of private investment.

But improving productivity won't mean fuller pay checks and better lives for most workers unless corporate America abandons its anti-worker retrenchment policies. If we are to restore the U.S. economy's competitiveness, companies will have to experiment with cooperative industrial relations that genuinely empower workers, push innovation, and increase productivity, experiments they have not tried to date. Improving workers' wages and work life is the better hope for sustaining economic growth.

While these programs might get the economy going again, the

federal government must use tax policy to spread widely the gains of renewed growth. . . . For instance, merely increasing the top U.S. income tax bracket from 31% to the international average of 47% would generate well over $15 billion in tax revenues. At the same time, lowering payroll taxes on wages would make sure that these tax changes were not a drag on the economy. Both changes would go a long way to giving more people a piece of the benefits of economic growth.

A sweeping program of public investment funded by the rich will help counteract the current recession. In the long run, such a change has the promise of both righting the economy and undoing social wrongs. With those changes, the 1990s could witness the return of prosperous growth. Without them, economic stagnation will continue and workers and families will suffer through the third decade of silent depression.

Periodical Bibliography

The following articles have been selected to supplement the diverse views presented in this chapter.

Daryl Anderson	"On the Dole in the 'Burbs," *In These Times*, July 26, 1993.
Paul Bass	"Meet the 'Employables,'" *In These Times*, April 5, 1993.
Janice Castro	"Disposable Workers," *Time*, March 29, 1993.
Barbara Dority	"The Right to a Decent Life," *The Humanist*, May/June 1993.
James E. Ellis	"Where Troop Cuts Will Be Cruelest," *Business Week*, June 8, 1992.
Nancy Fraser and Linda Gordon	"Contract Versus Charity," *Socialist Review*, vol. 22, no. 3, July/September 1992.
Lawrence E. Harrison	"Those Huddled, Unskilled Masses: Is Our Immigration Policy Contributing to Our Economic Undoing?" *The Washington Post*, January 12, 1992.
Kenneth Labich	"The New Unemployment," *Fortune*, March 8, 1993.
New Unionist	"Bogus Recovery: More Americans Fall into Poverty," no. 191, June 1993. Available from the New Union Party, 621 Lake St., Minneapolis, MN 55408.
Mary E. O'Connell	"Coming Unfringed: The Unraveling of Job-Bases Entitlements," *The American Prospect*, Spring 1993. Available from New Prospect, Inc., PO Box 383080, Cambridge, MA 02238.
The People	"Widespread Unemployment Leaves No Room for Workforce," August 28, 1993. Available from the Socialist Labor Party, 914 Industrial Ave., Palo Alto, CA 94303.
Robert J. Samuelson	"R.I.P.: The Good Corporation," *Newsweek*, July 5, 1993.

Why Does Poverty Disproportionately Affect Certain Groups?

POVERTY

Chapter Preface

Statistics show that poverty rates in the United States are much higher among certain groups than for the population as a whole. They reveal that one in five American children (one in four under the age of six) lives in poverty, usually with a single mother. While the general unemployment rate has gone up and down, for more than thirty years unemployment levels for blacks have held fairly steady at twice the rate for whites. Many Native American tribes suffer devastating rates of poverty; for instance, the poorest county in the country—Shannon County, South Dakota—is home to the Oglala Sioux.

However, being a single mother, Native American, black, or a member of any other minority in the United States is not in itself a sentence of poverty: All of these groups are represented in the wealthy and middle classes. Statistics can only suggest a correlation between poverty and certain demographic characteristics. They do not show whether being a member of a given group brings into play external factors, such as racial discrimination, or internal factors, such as lack of self-esteem or a solid work ethic; they do not show causes. And those causes are the subject of often heated debate, as the following viewpoints demonstrate.

Perhaps in considering these causes, we should heed Christopher Jencks, author of *Rethinking Social Policy: Race, Poverty, and the Underclass*, who ventured this opinion on the effects of racism on poverty: "Isn't it obvious that both sides are right? Whenever we talk about race, it almost always boils down to either-or: a matter of justice or a matter of effort. It's time to start thinking in terms of both-and."

121

"Marriage is a significant buffer against poverty for children and their mothers."

The Breakdown of the Family Forces Women and Children into Poverty

Family Research Council

A collapse of social morality, evidenced by increased divorce and out-of-wedlock births and a decrease in payment of child support, has led to financial devastation for many women and their children, the Family Research Council maintains in the following viewpoint. Changes in the federal welfare system, originally designed as social insurance for widows and abandoned mothers, have exacerbated the problem by decreasing or ending benefits for those who marry. The government should instead offer incentives for marriage, the council believes, and make divorce more difficult to obtain when children are involved. The Family Research Council, a nonprofit advocacy organization promoting traditional family values, is located in Washington, D.C.

As you read, consider the following questions:

1. What changes in the divorce laws are cited by the council to illustrate a change in the concept of marriage?
2. Define the phrase "shotgun marriage." Does the council seem to be in favor of shotgun marriages? How can you tell?
3. What suggestions does the council offer for decreasing poverty among women and children?

The family in America today is undeniably weaker than at any point in our nation's history. One child in four today is born out of wedlock. One child in two spends at least part of his childhood in a single-parent household. One child in five lives in a family receiving some form of public assistance.

Still, some experts argue that these trends suggest that the family is not "declining" per se, only "changing." This view ignores the devastating social consequences—such as higher crime and suicide rates and lower educational achievement—associated with family breakdown. Moreover, it turns a deaf ear to the growing number of people (particularly children) who have been the victims of more than a quarter-century of domestic upheaval. . . .

Breakdown of the Family: Single Parenthood

Despite the persistence of traditional family structure, the increasing signs of family breakdown should be alarming. A prime indicator of that decline is the rapidly rising number of children being raised in single-parent homes:

• 27.1 percent of our nation's children are born into single-parent homes;

• In the black community it is an astounding 68 percent;

• The number of children in single, female-headed homes has increased 170 percent, rising from 5.1 million in 1960 to 13.7 million in 1989.

The trend is ominous. In 1960, only 9.1 percent of children under 18 were living with only their mothers; in the black community 21.9 percent were. Although approximately 10 percent of the population has been widowed, that number remains relatively constant—the skyrocketing rates of divorce and out-of-wedlock birth are the real factors driving the increase in single parenthood.

In the 1960s, a wave of change in divorce law swept the United States and Western Europe. Whereas divorce law during the formative decades of our nation had formerly assumed that the marriage contract could not be voided without a showing of fault, the new "no-fault" rule was that nothing more is required than an affirmation, by one party, that the marriage is in a state of "irretrievable breakdown.". . .

Underlying the change, of course, is a change in the concept of marriage. It is no longer viewed as creating a new entity that is more than the sum of its parts and that society has an interest in protecting. In place of that view, our culture has adopted a view of marriage as a partnership of autonomous individuals, to be dissolved as soon as it no longer coincides with the desires of one or both partners. This view may be congenial to notions of lifestyle-liberty that are widely cherished today, but it runs counter to other values that we hold dear: stability, the home—even romantic love itself, whose natural orientation is a desire for permanence. . . .

The Feminist Critique on Divorce

While most feminists in the 1960s saw liberal divorce as an escape from domesticity, some feminists in the 1980s began arguing that it worked a tremendous shift of wealth and social power from women to men. In particular, Lenore Weitzman argued in *The Divorce Revolution:* "[D]ivorced men experience an average 42 percent rise in their standard of living in the first year after divorce, while divorced women (and their children) experience a 73 percent decline."

Weitzman's figures are hotly contested, both by the pro-divorce feminists and by non-feminist critics of divorce. After all, "standard of living" is inherently difficult to quantify. Nevertheless, few challenge the proposition that divorce is implicated in the impoverishment of vast numbers of women and children whose husbands and fathers abandoned them with the help of modern divorce law. Weitzman's book was seized upon by women with a genuine grievance: they must live with the realization that, while their husbands have not yet abandoned them, the legal system virtually invites them to do so. The current debate over what motivates women to enter the paid workforce concentrates on the dichotomy of necessity and desire; but given the effects of liberal divorce law, policy analysts ought to consider a third explanation: insurance—that is, self-protection against future desertion. . . .

Some male critics of divorce point out that women initiate more divorces than men do. As the generation of women for whom this is true mature, so too do the results of their decision. Free-lance writer Kay Ebeling wrote a piece in *Newsweek* that attracted a good deal of comment. In it, she reminisced:

> In 1973 I left what could have been a perfectly good marriage, taking with me a child in diapers, a 10-year-old Plymouth and Volume 1, Number One of *Ms.* magazine. I was convinced I could make it on my own. In the last 15 years my ex has married or lived with a succession of women. As he gets older, his women stay in their 20s. Meanwhile, I've stayed unattached. He drives a BMW. I ride buses.

Though Ms. Ebeling probably must shoulder at least partial responsibility for the failure of her marriage, she is a casualty of liberal divorce law; so, too, is her "ex"—who, though wealthier, is probably just as unhappy. Ultimately, the battle of the sexes over who is more hurt by permissive divorce law is really collateral to the main point, which is the havoc that these laws have wrought. Expectations of permanence, or the absence of such expectations, have an impact on whether permanence in fact occurs. Professor William Catton, Jr., of Washington State University notes: "[W]ithin families the occurrence of divorce tends to raise the probability of divorce in the next generation."

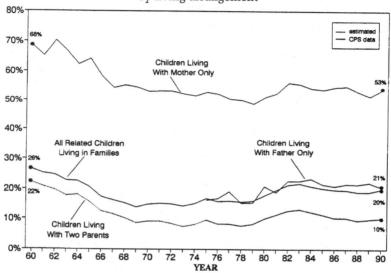

Poverty Rate of Children
by living arrangement

Source: U.S. Bureau of the Census, *Current Population Reports*, series P-60, No. 175 and earlier reports.

The easier divorce is to obtain, the less effort many couples put into making a marriage work. As Professor Norval Glenn of the University of Texas at Austin puts it in a paper published in *The Retreat from Marriage: Causes and Consequences:* "[M]erely contemplating alternatives to one's marriage may engender marital discontent." Thus, a regime of easy divorce fuels its own demand. . . .

Furthermore, the pace at which this phenomenon plays itself out may be accelerating. A generation ago, there were far fewer divorces; what Catton calls the "background divorce pressure" is increasing. "We are living in a society that seems to be undergoing a transformation—from one that defines permanent and monogamous pairing to one that accepts ephemeral pairings as its norm.". . .

Unwed parenthood is the second reason for the increase in children being raised by single parents. Nineteen percent of all births among white women were nonmarital in 1989. Among black women it was 68 percent. The increase from 1940 has been dramatic: a mere 1.8 percent of all births among whites were nonmarital then and among blacks it was 13.7 percent.

Although the percentage of nonmarital births is lower in the white community, the number of children affected is actually higher than in the black community. In the white community the increase was from 40,000 children born to single mothers in 1940 to 594,000 in 1989. In the black community, the number grew from 59,200 in 1940 to 500,000 in 1989.

As a subset of nonmarital motherhood, teenage pregnancies have garnered much public attention and discussion. . . . Births among unmarried teenagers have been steadily increasing. Since 1950, nonmarital teenage births have increased 490 percent. This trend has held steady since the late '60s and shows little sign of abatement. . . .

Single parenthood has a strong correlation with many negative effects also seen with family breakdown: poverty, infant mortality, child abuse and neglect, violence and educational failure. All of these problems are national concerns, and are the subject of much public debate and hand-wringing. Frequently missing from these public discussions, however, is the acknowledgment of the central role single parenthood often plays in the genesis of these difficulties. . . .

It does not benefit the many single parents who are struggling heroically to raise their children alone, through no fault of their own, to ignore the root cause of their difficulties.

And ignoring it we are. Unwed parenthood is taking hold in our culture. The messages being sent through the media—music, radio, film, advertising—are subtly promoting nonmarital and extramarital sexual activity and undermining marriage and family. It has become common for Hollywood superstars to bear children out-of-wedlock proudly, making it a more acceptable standard. American culture, once characterized as "motherhood and apple pie," is becoming increasingly hostile to traditional values. Unfortunately, while millionaire entertainers can afford financially to support a child out-of-wedlock, the majority of men in our culture cannot. . . .

Financial Consequences of Family Breakdown

The biggest threat to the material well-being of children is the insecurity of the modern family. Family breakdown deprives a child not only of security, stability and happy home life, but it also threatens the economic support and well-being of the child. In some instances, the child may have to suffer only a decline in living standards, but far more often, single parenthood means a plunge into poverty.

A huge gap exists between the poverty levels of children living with two parents and children in single-parent homes. Over half of the children in single-parent homes live in poverty—this is five times the rate for other children. The financial devastation of single parenthood holds true whether one enters through divorce or unwed parenthood. Both usually cause serious economic hardship for the mother and her children. Simply put, marriage is a significant buffer against poverty for children and their mothers.

The connection between single parenthood and poverty for children is clear and irrefutable. Children, as a whole, are better off now than they were in 1960, but worse than in 1970. Since 1980 the poverty rate of children in two-parent homes went up and came back down again to approximately the 1980 level, but children in single-parent homes are still worse off than in 1980. However, children in two-parent homes have always been less likely to live in poverty The poverty rate for children in single-parent homes, even at its lowest, has never been as low as the rate for children in two-parent homes, even at its highest.

As the single-parenthood trend continues upward, the poverty rate of children will accompany it. Poverty for the children living with both parents can be helped through an improved economy; indeed their poverty level fluctuates with movement in the economy. But for the children in single-parent homes, poverty is persistent.

Child-Support Enforcement

Of course, no child is the offspring of a single parent. And, there are very few American children who are being raised in a single-parent home as a result of the death of one of their parents. As we've already seen, the vast majority of children in single-parent homes today are there as a result of divorce or illegitimacy. This means that most of the poverty-stricken children in single-parent homes are there because their fathers have failed to support them. In 1989, 5 million women were supposed to receive child support payments: only half received the full amount they were due. The rest were equally divided between those who received some money and those who received none. Of the women below the poverty level who were awarded child support, 377,000 received no payments.

However, to understand the full picture, the 58 percent of single mothers who were not awarded child support at all must be recognized as well. Twenty-two percent did not want child support; 64 percent wanted it but could not get it (among poor women the percentage rose to 71.6 percent). This points out a significant fact: even the availability of court-awarded child support does not negate the importance of marriage. Only 23.9 percent of women who have never married the fathers of their children receive child support awards, compared to 72 percent of formerly married women. . . .

Despite the clear need for better child-support collection, the real problem must remain in focus: children need their fathers. Even if child support collection was 100 percent effective, would children really be supported in the way they should? *Even among those receiving child support*, 21.8 percent of women trying to raise children alone remained in poverty. Child-support payments are a very poor substitute, financially and in every other way.

Secretary Louis Sullivan, in addressing the first national leadership conference of the National Commission on Interstate Child Support, made these remarks:

> The core of child support must be the stabilization and strengthening of families. The relationship between family strength and childhood well-being is clear and unequivocal. . . . We must address the sources of increasing need for child support enforcement and the non-economic dimensions of the child support issue. Our perspective on child support must encompass the wide-ranging and multi-faceted losses a child endures when its family is torn apart or the loss from the failure of the family to form in the first place.

> The dimensions of the problem we are addressing are enormous and their implications for American culture are sobering. Our country, unique in its time and unprecedented in history, is producing a whole generation of children who lack the influence of a father in their lives. . . .

> At this point, let me say—clearly and unequivocally—our children will not thrive until we reverse today's cultural trends. Numerous research studies are substantiating what we have known, but have not protected—strong, stable, loving, nurturing two-parent families provide the best environment for child-rearing.

Reforming Aid to Families with Dependent Children

Despite the basic truth about the connection between family structure and the poverty of children, our approach to combatting child poverty on the federal level does nothing to encourage marriage. If anything it discourages marriage through a system of perverse incentives—thereby exacerbating the very problem it was created to solve.

The federal welfare system—and its primary cash transfer component, Aid to Families with Dependent Children—began in the 1930s as a project to undergird "social morality, family and tradition." As Allan Carlson, president of the Rockford Institute, has pointed out, the origins of Aid to Families with Dependent Children (or ADC as it was originally termed) were explicitly family-oriented. The program was designed as social insurance, conceived as aid to widows and abandoned mothers, means-tested, and focused, according to one report to President [Franklin D.] Roosevelt, on fostering fulfillment of the maternal role.

For a time, as nonmarital pregnancy and childbearing rates held relatively steady, the program worked basically as envisioned, with no evidence to suggest that its existence or structure exerted significant influence on decisions to marry or form families. But all that soon (in historical terms) changed. As the pace of family dissolution accelerated after 1965 and AFDC participation rates lost their historic link with the business cycle and unemployment rates, argument ensued over whether, and to what extent, welfare policy drives or reinforces family breakdown. . . .

The Maternalization of Poverty

Family instability and poverty are inextricably linked. The persistent rise in the number of children in AFDC-supported families is due almost entirely to the breakup or nonformation of intact families among poorer Americans. In effect, the U.S. is experiencing the "maternalization" of poverty. Nearly half of America's poor live in families with no husband present, even though such families are only 16 percent of the population. In 1987, two-parent families had a 6 percent poverty rate, in sharp contrast to 34 percent for female-headed families.

Stuart M. Butler, in *Mandate for Leadership III: Policy Strategies for the 1990s*, 1989.

Marian Wright Edelman of the Children's Defense Fund has even argued that, to the extent that AFDC and other programs relieve women of economic dependency on the father of the child, they may make women "less likely to enter into bad marriages, or more apt to leave ones that have turned bad"—a not "universally undesirable" outcome.

Clearly, the structure of AFDC makes marriage less attractive, by the simple method of making it unprofitable. Married couples are typically excluded from coverage under AFDC even if they have the same level of economic need as a household headed by a single parent. For the single parent already on AFDC, a decision to marry could cost her nearly 30 percent of the combined income she and a cohabiting partner could receive if they do not marry. The less stable the relationship, the higher—temporarily in all likelihood—the household income.

Undoubtedly, all would not be well today if every single mother had merely chosen to marry the father of her child. But if welfare payments are averting some or even many bad marriages, they are obviously not a particularly efficient means of achieving this relatively benign social result: failure of nearly half of contemporary marriages suggests that, somehow, quite a few bad marriages are still "getting through." It seems more plausible to suggest that the configuration of benefits in AFDC does nothing to inhibit the tragic flight from marriage (the same argument applies to such tax benefits as the Earned Income Tax Credit).

A Matter of Social Morality

Marital flight, clearly occurring across ethnic and economic lines, is in itself a matter of social morality. What has collapsed is the sense of obligation, of a socially defined and reinforced system of duties and personal responsibilities. In testimony before a Senate Finance Committee hearing on middle-income tax relief, Robert Reischauer, director of the Congressional Budget Office, told how his own children had never heard of, and were unable to define, the phrase "shotgun marriage." Today the notion of a "duty" to marry seems transparently quaint; but so too, for less obvious reasons, does a duty to *consider* marriage. This is especially troubling given the overwhelming evidence of harm to the children of fractured families under even the best economic conditions. . . .

If the recent convergence on family policy means anything, it should mean redoubled efforts to devise welfare and tax policies that encourage the formation and retention of stable family units. For liberals, this will mean abandoning the vitriolic attacks on marriage and family favored by many within their ranks; for conservatives, it will mean a willingness to rely less on "sink or swim" alternatives and to experiment with ideas that risk short-term costs for long-term gains. But restoring the cultural and legal norm of the marital family is a prize worth the effort.

"Improving women's earnings is the family issue of the 1990s."

Economic Conditions Impoverish Women and Children

Roberta Spalter-Roth and Heidi Hartmann with Deborah Clearwaters

The economic status of men is viewed in terms of their work and the condition of the economy, while women's status is often discussed in terms of their family relationships and roles, charge Roberta Spalter-Roth and Heidi Hartmann in the following viewpoint. They maintain that this sex-segregated analysis ignores the real reasons many women and their children are impoverished: gender and age discrimination and a decline in working conditions that affects women more than men. Improving earnings and benefits policies will help women and children more than attempts to encourage marriage or to reform welfare, they assert. Spalter-Roth, Hartmann, and Deborah Clearwaters are members of the Institute for Women's Policy Research in Washington, D.C.

As you read, consider the following questions:

1. How have the conditions of work deteriorated since 1980, according to the authors? Why does this deterioration affect women more than men?
2. What evidence of race, gender, and age discrimination do the authors cite?

From "Raising Women's Earnings: The Family Issue of the 1990s" by Roberta Spalter-Roth and Heidi Hartmann with the assistance of Deborah Clearwaters. In *Buying America Back*, Jonathan Greenberg and William Kistler, editors. Tulsa: Council Oak Books, 1992. Reprinted with permission.

Two trends that significantly affect the lives of women and their children have intensified since the 1970s. Unless public policies intervene, these two trends will produce increasing economic victimization among women of all races and classes, and an increasing number of women and children will find themselves among the growing ranks of the permanently poor. The first trend is the increase in women's economic responsibility for their families and their children. Between 1970 and 1990 the labor force participation of mothers increased from about 40% to 67%. By 1990, 22 million mothers were in the labor force and the traditional male breadwinner/female housewife family dropped to less than 20% of all families with children.

The second trend is the increase of women and children living in poverty. The proportion of poor families that are maintained by women grew throughout the 1970s and 1980s. Poverty rates for minority women and their children are especially high. In 1990, 56% of families headed by black women with children under 18, and 58% of Hispanic, single-mother families were poor.

Many researchers fail to connect these two trends: the increase in women's poverty and the increase in women's work. Instead they attribute women's and children's poverty solely to the decline in life-long marriage to a higher-income breadwinner and to the increased number of children living with mothers who are responsible for their support. Such an analysis implicitly assumes that marriage should be the major anti-poverty program for women and their children. It ignores the role played by low earnings in the poverty of families maintained by women, especially families maintained by women of color. It assumes that women's economic status (and that of their children) is determined solely by changes in family relationships and is not significantly affected by factors such as technology, international trade, industrial growth, levels of unionization, occupational segregation, level of training, or race and gender discrimination. Such an analysis ignores the impact of these factors on women's earnings.

In contrast to other researchers, we at the Institute for Women's Policy Research connect women's increasing economic responsibility for their families' well-being with the factors that result in their low earnings and suggest that improving women's earnings is the family issue of the 1990s.

The Misuse of a Sex-Segregated Model

Those who assume that lifelong marriage is the sole solution to women's and children's poverty employ a sex-segregated model of economic analysis. A sex-segregated model views women's economic status in terms of their relations to the family and their supposed willingness to forgo higher wages in order to fulfill traditional family roles. In contrast, this model views men's

132

economic status in terms of the paid work they do, the condition of their work, and the general health of the economy.

An example of the use of a sex-segregated model can be seen in the "Myth of the Drop Out Mom," where a 1.2% drop from January 1990 to January 1991 in the labor force participation of

all women between the ages of 25 and 34 was interpreted on the front page of major newspapers as indicating that mothers are scurrying home to care for husbands and children. In fact, the labor force participation of mothers with children under age three (as opposed to all women between the ages of 24 and 35) rose from 54.2% in the fourth quarter of 1990 to 54.5% in the fourth quarter of 1991, and labor force participation by women with children under age 18 also rose from 67.1% to 67.2%, despite a 0.8% decline in labor force participation by men. While the decline in the labor force participation rate of some women is misinterpreted as women dropping out of the work force to care for their families, the declining labor participation of men during this same period is attributed to such factors as recession, regional restructuring, and the export of jobs.

Throwing off the blinders of a sex-segregated model, we focus on two major factors that have affected women's economic status during the 1980s and that will continue to influence their families' well-being in the 1990s. These factors are deteriorating working conditions and continued race and gender discrimination.

Deteriorating Conditions of Work

A major workplace trend during the 1980s and 1990s is the deterioration in the conditions of work, especially in the relationships between workers and employers. Contingent work (on-call arrangements between employers and employees, use of consultants and contract employees, limited duration direct hires, and use of the temporary-help service industries) is growing much faster than total employment and may be developing into a permanent arrangement with many employers. Involuntary part-time and low-wage work is also growing.

Working women are more affected by these conditions than are working men. Women are two-thirds of all part-time workers, the majority of involuntary part-time workers, two-thirds of the temporary workers, and the majority of low-wage workers. The percentage of women employed in low-wage jobs increased from 15% to 21% from the mid-1970s to the mid-1980s. Thirty-eight percent of all women workers earn low wages compared to 19% of all male workers. Women are also the majority of all minimum wage workers (about two-thirds), and moonlighting among women increased five times between 1970 and 1991, while moonlighting among men increased less than 20%.

Women are more likely to be employed in low-wage, non-unionized service sector jobs and, as a result of these conditions, are less likely to have employer-provided health insurance (55% of women compared to 70% of men have this benefit). When they leave or lose low-wage jobs, women are less likely than men to move on to a higher-wage job (21% compared to

47%, respectively) and are more likely to experience unemployment, continued low-wage work, or to rely on means-tested welfare benefits. These conditions are especially serious for women workers whose earnings are increasingly responsible for maintaining their families' living standards.

Race, Gender, and Age Discrimination

Beginning in the mid-1970s, the United States witnessed declines in the real wages of African-American men relative to white men after many years of steady improvement. And the earnings gap between black and white women working year-round, full-time began to increase slightly during the late 1980s after closing for several decades. Between 1988 and 1990 black women's earnings fell from 92.8 cents to 90 cents for each $1 earned by year-round, full-time white women workers, and the earnings of Hispanic women fell from 83.3 cents to 78.2 cents for every $1 earned by white women. Throughout the 1980s, the United States also witnessed declines in the real wages of low-wage workers whereas high-wage workers experienced modest improvements. About half of these gross earnings disparities can be explained by race and gender discrimination.

In a recent study we found that neither human capital variables (work experience, education, and training) nor the structural characteristics of jobs, firms, and industries fully account for the lower wage levels of women, especially for the lower wages of women of color. Even when human capital and job characteristics are the same, these women workers have a greater risk of low-wage work. Women of color are four times as likely to be low-wage workers as white men with comparable skills and experience, and white women are more than three times as likely as white men to be low-wage workers.

The wage gap is much larger between older women and men than between younger women and men. Women's median earnings peak at age 40-44, when they are earning about the same as men aged 25-29; men who are just starting out. This illustrates the "glass ceiling" faced by all women workers, not only women in management. A mature woman worker with substantial years of work experience, working full-time, year-round earns just $22,000 per year on average. Although women benefit from additional years of work experience, they receive lower premiums for staying in the work force than men do. The glass ceiling is perhaps better thought of as a continuous maze, a set of barriers that holds back women's earnings at every step of the way.

Deteriorating working conditions and continued race and gender segregation, along with women's increased economic responsibility for their children, result in a high rate of poverty for these families—about 4 out of 10 single, working-mother

135

families are poor. The majority of black and Hispanic women workers (and close to a majority of white women workers) do not earn wages that are high enough to provide a family with a minimally adequate living standard. A minimally adequate living standard is defined as $6.30 per hour (in 1990 dollars). This wage, if earned full-time, full-year equals the poverty threshold for a family of three, plus an estimated $2105 per year in day care expenses, the average spent by poor working mothers according to a United States Bureau of the Census study. About 20% of white women, 50% of black women, and 36% of Hispanic women who are earning below such minimally adequate wages are the main breadwinners for their families.

What factors are most likely to increase working mothers' wages so that they can earn a wage that supports their children at a minimally adequate level? . . . We examined the returns in wages to working mothers for a wide variety of factors. . . .

Where are the family relationships that many pundits assume are so important in predicting women's labor force status? We found marital status, presence of a full-time earning spouse, and number and ages of children to be insignificant in predicting working mothers' wages. The lack of significance of these factors in affecting hourly wages suggests that these mothers do not choose to trade off lower wage rates for more time to fulfill their family responsibilities. Their wages are too important for their families' well-being.

In general three types of policies have been suggested to increase the economic well-being of women and their children. These strategies can be labeled marriage policies, income-support policies, and earnings and benefits policies. We examine each of these in turn.

Suggested Policies

Marriage Policies. It is a long-standing assumption that women can and should marry their way to financial security. Public policy can attempt to encourage marriage through favorable tax rates, by returning to "fault" divorce, by providing publicly funded counseling for married couples with children who are considering divorce, or by continuing such public policies as social security benefits that favor the non-employed wives of higher-earning men. Maintaining a policy vacuum with respect to job discrimination, occupational segregation, and pay inequities can keep women's wages low and reinforce their economic dependence on men.

Marriage as a poverty prevention strategy for women succeeds only as long as a pool of higher-wage marriageable partners exists. From our perspective, marriage policies are unacceptable ways to increase women's economic status because they assume the economic dependence of women on higher-earning partners and because they do nothing to increase the wages of unemployed, underemployed, and low-wage men or women.

A "pseudo-marriage" policy, child-support enforcement, attempts to redistribute the earnings from non-custodial fathers to their children. This approach has wide support among policy makers, who are attempting to improve the setting and collection of child support awards, especially for women receiving Aid to Families with Dependent Children (AFDC). Child support enforcement, while it does have positive redistributional effects, of course, does nothing to increase the pool of higher paid workers.

Income-Support Policies. A second policy strategy is to supplement the earnings of single working mothers through government income-support programs such as AFDC. Current welfare reforms, such as the Family Support Act of 1988, are based on the assumption that employment, even at a low-paid job, is a substitute for AFDC and will result in economic self-sufficiency. Our findings show, however, that only a small minority of welfare recipients (about 12%) were able to use low-wage work as a bridge to better-paid employment. Rather than making a permanent transition from welfare to work, we found that about 40% of AFDC recipients combine paid work and AFDC benefits in order to increase the economic well-being of their families.

In the absence of public policies to increase wages directly, we suggest that paid work and receipt of welfare benefits should be viewed as complementary activities, not as mutually exclusive approaches to policy. We suggest returning to the level of income disregards (the maximum amount that can be earned before losing AFDC benefits) prior to the 1981 Omnibus Budget Reconciliation Act and the 1988 Family Support Act. This change in regulations would likely increase the work effort of single mothers receiving AFDC and increase the economic well-being of their families.

The Most Effective Policies

Earnings and Benefits Policies. We suggest that the policies that will have the greatest long-term impact on working mothers and their families are those that increase their earnings and benefits, rather than those that attempt to increase marriage or government benefits. In a recent study, we examined the impact of a wide variety of potential public policy strategies on mothers' earnings.

We found that the most effective policy measure for moving working mothers' wages above a minimum sufficiency level ($6.30 in 1990 dollars) for all race/ethnic groups is the three-pronged strategy to maximize years of work experience, to reward work experience at the level enjoyed by white male workers, and to increase the percentage of working mothers employed full-time, year-round to the same rate as ever-married men. The second most effective strategy is a two-pronged strategy to maximize years of work experience with the same returns enjoyed by white male workers. Maximizing women's work experience alone is a less effective strategy. Raising working mothers' returns for work experience to the same level as those of white men is the most effective single strategy for all groups of mothers. This strategy brings half of all low-wage mothers up to the minimum sufficiency standard.

The Vulnerability of Female-Headed Households

What creates the widespread *vulnerability* of the female-headed household to poverty? Although many people can point to examples of women who have risen to the top of the corporate pay scale, of husbands who are left destitute by divorce, and of couples who care jointly and equitably for children, these examples do not represent the norm for women as a group. Female-headed households are vulnerable to poverty due to the sexual and racial divisions of labor which continue to give women a secondary place in the socioeconomic structure of the United States. In addition, due to child custody and support practices, female-headed households usually carry heavier economic and emotional responsibilities for children than do male-headed households but have access to fewer economic resources. Furthermore, women in female-headed households are less able to compete for higher places in the economic structure because their responsibilities for children conflict with their availability for economic competition. Finally, the macroeconomic processes of advanced capitalism have depleted the communities where female-headed households are most concentrated, particularly in the inner city.

Pamela D. Couture, *Blessed Are the Poor?* 1991.

Another important single-pronged strategy is to decrease regional wage disparities. It clearly helps low-wage black and Hispanic mothers, who lose the most when employed in the low-wage Southern region of the country. Earning a high school diploma is an especially effective measure for Hispanic working mothers, and earning a high school diploma and completing some years of college is an effective measure for all working mothers. These findings suggest that public policy should focus not only on increasing a working mother's education level and work experience, but also on ensuring that working mothers receive returns equal to those received by white males for their work efforts, and on collective bargaining and/or other strategies that would decrease regional wage disparities.

The way to raise women's incomes is not necessarily, as a sex-segregated analysis would suggest, for women to remain single and/or childless, or alternately to depend on the earnings of a male breadwinner. Instead, our findings suggest that the same factors that can be expected to raise men's wages—increasing the returns to work experience, increasing skills, improving the quality of jobs and the conditions of work—also appear to be the most important in raising the wages of working mothers.

Treat Women Equitably

Although these suggested earnings policies represent long-term goals, none of them is impossible to achieve. Each can be reached, albeit in incremental steps, using specific available remedies such as financial aid for education, comparable worth policies, pay equity adjustments, glass ceiling initiatives designed to increase women's job mobility to higher level jobs, increases in the minimum wage, labor law reform to increase the ability to bargain collectively, and increased enforcement of anti-discrimination laws.

In addition to implementing policies that will directly increase working mothers' earnings, we suggest replacing those anachronistic workplace and public policies that continue despite women's increased responsibility for their families' economic well-being. Much workplace and public policy assumes that women workers will be provided for through private arrangements with male breadwinners who have stable employment with socially responsible employers who provide generous fringe benefits. These assumptions result in large gaps in coverage for basic benefits such as family and medical leave, health insurance, and unemployment compensation, as well as a general lack of equitable pay for women.

For the earnings and benefit policies we recommend to be implemented, however, policy makers and employers must make a commitment to overcoming cultural stereotypes and to viewing working mothers as having an equal and legitimate need and right to employment in jobs paying wages sufficient to support themselves and their families. The widespread view of women as dependent on men must give way to a new understanding of women as breadwinners, with or without co-earning men. Continued economic inequality based on gender and race is not acceptable in a society that prides itself on equal opportunity and upward mobility. Such inequality breeds waste, misery and alienation—the costs of which are borne by all of us. It's time for a new egalitarian vision for working women (and their children) and for public policies which help make that vision real.

"When America is in recession, Black America is in a Depression."

Inadequate Government Spending Results in Poverty Among Blacks

John E. Jacob

John E. Jacob is president and chief executive officer of the National Urban League, which works to eliminate racial segregation and discrimination and to achieve parity for blacks and other minorities in all facets of American life. In the following viewpoint, excerpted from a speech delivered at Medgar Evers College in Brooklyn, New York, Jacob advocates a Marshall Plan for America. Just as the United States spent billions of dollars to rebuild Europe after World War II to stop the spread of communism and rebuild export markets, so should it now invest in both the physical and human infrastructure of this country to make it more competitive and productive. This investment would serve the twin goals of arresting America's competitive decline and helping disadvantaged minorities achieve parity, he maintains.

As you read, consider the following questions:

1. How does Jacob define parity?
2. Why does the author believe that barriers to black advances are more difficult and complex today than they were in the past?
3. Why does Jacob believe that progress toward parity cannot be made by African Americans working in isolation from the rest of the American economy?

From John E. Jacob, "The State of Black America: Excellence, Perseverance, and Preparation," a speech delivered March 17, 1992, at Medgar Evers College, Brooklyn, New York. Reprinted with permission.

It is a great pleasure to join you today to discuss the State of Black America—where we've been, where we are going, and how to get to where we want to be. In January 1992, the National Urban League released its annual State of Black America report—a volume of documentation and analysis by leading black scholars.

The picture that emerges from their studies is bleak.

I'm not going to deliver a statistics-filled lecture this morning, but allow me to mention some of the more urgent findings in our report, concentrating on . . . areas of the utmost importance to African Americans.

An Ugly Economic Picture

One area is economics. That is the leading indicator of the status of African Americans today, because economic realities are a factor in all other aspects of our lives—from health to housing to crime.

The economic picture is ugly. The nation is in a recession these days, and when America is in recession, Black America is in a Depression. We start from a weaker base and are far more vulnerable to downturns. Here are some of State of Black America 1992's findings about the black economy:

• The median net worth for blacks is less than ten percent of the median net worth for whites in America.

• Blacks own about 424,000 businesses out of a total of 17.5 million businesses in America.

• Total income per black person in America in 1990 was about $9,000, versus well over $15,000 for whites.

• Median black family income was only 58 percent of that for whites—$21,423 versus $36,915.

• About 25 percent of black families earn under $10,000 a year, compared to about 7 percent of white families. Put another way, African American families are three-and-a-half times as likely as whites to be making less than $10,000 a year. Twenty years ago, the likelihood was less than three times, so there's been a deterioration in our relative position over the past two decades.

• One reason for that is our higher unemployment—two-and-a-half times the white rate. Another is that we are disproportionately employed in the jobs and the industries most vulnerable to decline in a changing economy. . . .

Some Gains in the Political Arena

Moving on to the political arena—we have made great gains in terms of the numbers of elected officials, in the numbers of black congresspersons, and in the stature of the appointed positions we hold. It is particularly telling to discuss this in a school named for a black man who was killed for his role in the struggle to secure such basic civil rights as the right to vote.

• It is a sign of how far we've come to realize that a black man, Congressman Mike Espy, was elected by black and white voters to represent Mississippi in the Congress. The same state of Mississippi that cheered the assassination of Medgar Evers now has more blacks in its state legislature than any other state in the Union.

• A black man born and raised in the Bronx and a graduate of City College, General Colin Powell, is Chairman of the Joint Chiefs of Staff. . . .

• And like it or not, a black man, Clarence Thomas, sits on the Supreme Court of the United States, where he is demonstrating that he is no Thurgood Marshall. But while he appears to have forgotten where he came from in his rush to get where he wanted to go, the fact remains that a Supreme Court that once upheld segregation is now an integrated institution.

• The black vote continues to be a potential swing factor in close elections. . . .

• A complicating factor is diversity—other ethnic groups that have traditionally been excluded are now using their political muscle to win office. In many instances African Americans are the "in" group that is being challenged. . . .

• Finally, black political power is a victim of historical timing. We have come to occupy the City Halls of some of America's largest cities at a time of urban decline and economic changes that result in an inability to wield true power. . . .

The heart of the problem lies in economics. Raise taxes and revenues to meet social needs, and business and the middle class move away. That cuts revenues, reduces jobs, and increases the need for more social services. It's a vicious cycle that no single city can prevent, because all states and cities are competing for business and for job-creating industry. So if we look at the state of black America in those three critical areas, we see a very troubling situation.

Answering the Critics

The reaction to our State of Black America report was very interesting. Some black people criticized us for it, and they essentially made three major points.

One—that it paints a picture that is far too grim and neglects the enormous progress that has been made. In fact, the report does mention many of the bright spots in the picture, and acknowledges the progress made over the decades.

Almost half of all blacks now earn middle-class incomes and we are a growing number of managers in corporations that once would only hire us to sweep up.

But the true measure should not be how far we've come but how far we must go to achieve parity. And I define parity as a situation of rough equality in all aspects of life that count. That doesn't mean playing by the numbers, but it does mean that roughly the same percentage of whites as blacks are in good jobs, have good educations, enjoy comparable health and housing. It also means equitably sharing the pain—with roughly the same percentages of whites as blacks suffering from unemployment, poverty, and other indicators of disadvantage. We can't get to where we want to be without knowing where we are—and doing something about it.

A second criticism was that our report harmed the image that the white community has of blacks. I wrote back to someone who said that and asked him if he really believed that white decision makers are ignorant about the gross disadvantage faced by African Americans today. They know what's going on because they provide the figures we use. Our statistics are derived from government reports—from the Census Bureau, from the Labor Department, from a hundred other sources and studies that the federal government makes available.

It Is Policymakers Who Should Be Ashamed

It's no secret that we're in trouble today, and it is known to anyone who reads a newspaper or watches the news on television. We can't hide those facts as if they were shameful reflections on black people. We should advertise them as the shameful reflections on our national policymakers that they are. And we need to leverage that information for positive changes in our communities.

That leads me to the third criticism we got: you're only telling about our troubles, not doing anything to solve them.

That's the most absurd of all. It reflects gross ignorance about what organizations like the Urban League can do. We are not General Motors or AT&T. We can't hire people, pay them, produce goods and services, build highways, or directly do the other things that will solve the problems of African Americans.

What we can do is to mobilize the community to demand the programs and actions that can create jobs and incomes.

And we can offer America solutions, not only to the problems facing African Americans, but to problems facing all Americans. We do that in our State of Black America 1992, where we propose a Marshall Plan for America—a bold, imaginative new nationwide thrust.

First let me expand on the "you don't have solutions" critique, because it can subvert our civil rights and community-based organizations. I'll tell you a little story about how such critiques are based on ignorance, and also on ill-will. If you recall, that was the old Ronald Reagan excuse too—he accused civil rights groups of singing the same tunes, while he went back to the old reverse Robin Hood tune of soaking the poor to give to the rich.

A couple of years ago I first proposed the Marshall Plan idea, and a prominent black columnist wrote an article in which he said it's the same old story—looking to the government to do something. A few months ago, I picked up his column and read his advocacy for new government programs to rebuild the infrastructure, invest in human resources, and create new jobs. I wrote to remind him that he was now backing what he criticized me for supporting. I'm not surprised that he hasn't answered. I hope he's embarrassed. He ought to be. Because black community-based organizations are about the only places in America where you do find new ideas to get the country out of recession and to provide equal opportunities for all.

Complex Barriers to Black Advancement

But we haven't been able to make much headway. It is frustrating that in the 1960s we were able to win great gains, but in the 1990s, we are virtually ignored. To understand why, we must realize that today we face barriers to black advancement that are more difficult and more complex than in the past. After all, in the 1960s, there was national shame about segregation. Our targets were fairly simple—open housing, the right to vote, the right to public access, and others that could not be denied.

Today, it's a lot harder. We face difficult, intractable problems like drugs, crime, family breakup, inferior schools, a changing economy that's destroying low-skill jobs, and a host of others. And compounding those problems is the persistence of discrimination and racial stereotyping.

America has come a long way, but the terrible truth of the matter is that America has not come as far as she thinks. I am reminded of that whenever I see how we respond to the hardships of recession. Just look at the way the poor are being scapegoated lately. We're hearing a lot more talk about people sponging off the welfare system than there is about providing jobs and training to help people become independent and productive.

There's a meanness about that kind of talk, and a hidden racism, too. Poverty is seen as a "black" problem or an "urban" problem, when more whites than blacks are on welfare and when poverty rates are higher in rural areas than in metropolitan areas. But when states are hard-pressed for money, it's popular to cut welfare and social programs and to balance their budgets on the backs of the poor. . . .

We're told the middle class is angry about being taxed to help support the poor. But their taxes are going to bail out banks and

144

to build bombs, not to bail out the poor or to build new opportunities for the people shut out of our society.

I can understand some of the anger attributed to the middle class today. But I have to ask how much angrier African Americans ought to be, when so many of us are denied the opportunities to become middle class. Sure, we have made strong strides. But parity is still a distant goal, and too many of us are in a state of permanent economic depression.

And I can understand the attractiveness of tax-cutting as a way to try to get us out of the recession. But there's a better, faster way to do that—by investing in programs that put people back to work and lay the foundations of future economic growth.

That's why the Urban League has come up with a Marshall Plan for America.

Not simply a short-term plan to end the recession, but a long-term plan to develop all of our people's skills so we can compete in a changing world economy.

We're in a whole new ball game today.

America used to be the undisputed world economic leader. Today Japan, Germany and others are surging ahead. Our heavy industries, and even some of our newer ones, are on the ropes. . . . Millions of jobs—the kinds of jobs that helped people to enter the middle class—are being wiped out today. But better jobs are being created—jobs that require new and higher skills. They're better because they add more value to products and services so they pay more. You get a higher salary for designing an automobile than for assembling it on the shop floor.

An Integrated World Economy

Today, a dollar spent on a typical product might be split many ways—to the designer in Italy, the parts-makers in Brazil and Singapore, the assemblers in Mexico, the marketing people in the U.S., and the advertising people in England. We are competing in one integrated world economy, and that is why achieving parity for African Americans will depend on three fundamental assumptions:

First: Black parity can only be achieved if African Americans play a productive role in a competitive economy.

Second: To become competitive in a global economy, America must make massive investments in its physical and human infrastructure.

Third: America's competitiveness and its future economic growth depend on improving the productivity of its workforce.

Like it or not, our progress toward parity depends on solutions to America's economic problems. Our economic future cannot be changed in isolation from America's economic future.

Some may think we can separate ourselves, and that has always been an appealing, if not a viable, prospect.

Others may insist on reparations, pointing to the great wrongs and exploitation we have suffered. To them, I offer this piece of advice—don't spend the check till it comes.

The Mismatch Problems

One underlying factor that has had a strongly negative impact on the quality of city life is what social scientists refer to as *mismatch problems*. There are two debilitating geoeconomic mismatches in U.S. urban areas. The first is the restriction (through discrimination and zoning) of the poor, especially minorities, to the city, while many jobs are located in the suburbs and exurbs. . . . The second mismatch is internal to the city: the lack of correspondence between the low educational levels of inner-city poor people, especially younger African Americans, and the high-education job opportunities available to them. . . .

What is to be done about these mismatches? The following social policy initiatives are ways to create decent-paying jobs in the city and to increase the mobility of poor minorities to the suburbs: (1) public works programs for needed urban projects, such as new schools and mass transit, which would include substantial job-training and skill-upgrading components; (2) migration regulation of business, including mandatory payment of relocation or re-training expenses for workers; and (3) breaking down suburban class and race barriers through the strong enforcement of civil rights laws and the creation of more public housing in the suburbs.

George T. Martin Jr., *Social Policy in the Welfare State*, 1990.

Like it or not, African Americans are Americans, sharing the future of this land. And understanding the direction in which America is moving, it is important that we seize this new window of opportunity for ourselves and try to jumpstart the black drive for parity.

Changing demographics mean that the nation's workforce will grow more slowly. And it is becoming blacker and browner. Some 85 percent of all net new workers in the 1990s will be women, blacks, immigrants and other minorities. That's our window of opportunity—if we can get the education and the skills this new economy requires, we have a shot at overcoming society's latent racism to win parity.

One of the vehicles to move toward parity can be the Urban League's Marshall Plan for America. It's an outgrowth of our history and our mission. Back in the 1960s the then head of the National Urban League, Whitney M. Young, Jr., called for a Domestic Marshall Plan of investments in social and economic programs to help black people overcome centuries of oppression and disadvantage. His model was the Marshall Plan of the late 1940s, when the U.S. sent billions to rebuild Europe after World War II.

That wasn't done out of altruism, by the way. We did it to stop the spread of communism and to rebuild our export markets.

That Marshall Plan worked—but America never implemented Whitney's domestic Marshall Plan. If it had, many of today's problems would not exist. But it's not too late to learn from the mistakes of the past.

In the climate of the 1960s, Whitney could call for a program focused on the black poor. In the 1990s, such a program would never reach first base. But what can work today is a program of investing in building a growth economy. African Americans would be the prime beneficiaries of a national consensus behind a program that targets the disadvantaged, invests in the nation's human and physical resources, and makes all Americans productive in this postindustrial economy.

That's what the National Urban League's Marshall Plan for America does—we're proposing massive, targeted investments in the nation's physical and human infrastructure to make America more competitive and more productive. It's broad enough to win consensus support from mainstream Americans concerned about our competitive decline, and narrow enough to serve as a springboard for black parity.

Investing in Human Resources and Infrastructure

We're telling America that unless it invests in its human resources—and especially in its neglected minorities—it won't have a competitive workforce. And we're telling America that it also has to modernize its physical infrastructure of schoolhouses, transportation links, telecommunications, and all the other public works that are the foundations of a modern economy.

We're proposing that the federal government commit at least $50 billion annually—above and beyond current expenditures—to human resource development and infrastructure programs.

They would include such vital elements as Head Start for all disadvantaged children and guaranteed educational help that lets all disadvantaged students qualify for college or a good job.

On the physical infrastructure side, we would invest in public works projects that mandate aggressive hiring and skills training programs targeted to the disadvantaged.

And the whole program would be run by a Marshall Plan "czar" who would coordinate all the elements in the Plan and be accountable for ensuring that they get to those who need them most.

We've had strong interest in our Plan from key figures in business, labor and politics, and the reason is that they see our Mar-

147

shall Plan for America as a unified, targeted program to develop the underused resources of the disadvantaged to make our economy more productive. Not a "black" program, but an American program that nevertheless will have a profound impact on black communities. I see it as a necessary precondition to put us on the fast track to parity with white Americans. But we've got to get our own act together, as well. Even if our Marshall Plan for America was enacted tomorrow, our communities would still be in deep trouble.

Community Problems Cannot Be Blamed on Racism

There are deep problems within our communities that can't be explained away or blamed on racism. The drug dealer on the corner is killing more black youngsters than the Klan ever did. The gun dealers are flooding our neighborhoods with deadly weapons. And schoolchildren who believe that studying is "white" and that failing tests is part of being black, is succeeding in doing what even the slavemasters couldn't do. . . .

It's true that the root cause of those problems lies in history and in current economic conditions. But that's theory. The reality is young children being shot by handguns in school, good minds being fried by drugs, and babies having babies. And no community can survive in those circumstances. So we have two major personal tasks today. One is to be the best that we can, to excel in whatever we choose to do. The second is to become personally involved in making our communities stronger, safer, better.

I remember seeing an interview with James Lofton, one of the all-time great wide receivers for the Buffalo Bills. The interviewer asked him what tricks he used, and James Lofton said: "One trick is to work harder than the other guy. The second trick, always hustle. Third trick, study and know what you're doing. Fourth trick, always be prepared. Fifth, never give up. Those are my tricks."

James Lofton was telling us not only how he became a great football player, but how black people have survived oppression and hardship—and how we can overcome today and in the future. Let's reach into that bag of tricks—excellence, perseverance, preparation—and use them to shape the future of ourselves, our communities, and our nation.

"In turning our backs on our great legacy of self-help, . . . our poor lost everything."

Dependence on Government Spending Causes Poverty Among Blacks

Elizabeth Wright

When "social justice" instead of "economic independence" became the focal point for black Americans, an important legacy was lost, writes Elizabeth Wright in the following viewpoint. Black leaders encouraged the masses to look to whites rather than to themselves to meet their needs, undermining both the progress blacks had made toward self-determination and their faith in the future. These members of the black elite have a vested interest in keeping those they lead dependent, she maintains, while cynical white intellectuals pursue their own agenda, promoting policies and values that destroy families and community institutions. Wright is editor of *Issues & Views*, a conservative newsletter on issues affecting the black community.

As you read, consider the following questions:

1. Describe Booker T. Washington's plan for helping the black race lift itself out of poverty, as Wright explains it.
2. What effect does Wright think the *Brown v. Board of Education* decision of 1954 had on the black community? How did this contribute to black poverty?

Elizabeth Wright, "Legacy Lost: The Road Not Taken," *Issues and Views*, Spring 1992. Reprinted with permission.

In reading Booker T. Washington's letters, speeches, personal biographies, and the many articles written about him while he lived [1856-1915], the most striking feature that one comes away with is his exceptional maturity. One can only be impressed by the clarity of this man's thinking and his objective grasp of the situation in which blacks found themselves in the late 1800s. He understood, in a way that only a son of the South could, the complicated nature of the relationship between the two races and the mutual interests they shared in the future economic development of the country.

Convinced that the progress of blacks depended first and foremost on the race establishing a firm economic foundation, he made it his mission to help his people bring this about. In Washington's lifetime he proved that it was possible for thousands of ex-slaves to prosper throughout this country as creators of a whole new set of opportunities. Not only did blacks excel beyond all expectations of the day, we did it in this land of our bondage—without set-aside contracts and without annual "civil rights" bills.

Lifting Ourselves Out of Poverty

Washington had no illusions about the shortcomings of a great many former slaves, yet he operated as though he never doubted the ability of the masses ultimately to lift themselves out of poverty. In sharp contrast to those who were to follow him as leaders of the race, he never allowed blacks to indulge in self-pity, nor did he ever look upon them or himself as victims. He came, as an ex-slave, in 1881, to the small town of Tuskegee, Alabama, called there to head a normal school for poor blacks. On his arrival, he found an old shanty on a couple of acres of land, and almost no funds to do much of anything. Daunted only momentarily, he set out to accomplish two goals: to raise money for the construction of a school building and to recruit young blacks as students.

Seven years later, the campus encompassed almost 600 acres and enrolled over 400 students. The school's buildings had been built by the students themselves, as they were taught, along with their regular academic courses, to become carpenters, electricians, plumbers and cabinetmakers. In fact, through their own labor, the students provided almost all their needs and those of the school. Washington's aim was twofold, for he wanted to teach his students "to see not only utility in labor, but beauty and dignity."

By 1901, there were 40 buildings on the Tuskegee land. Out of nothing, Washington and the dedicated poor blacks of Tuskegee had "created bricks out of straw," accomplishing what some called a miracle. Later, in *Up From Slavery*, he boasted: "Skill and knowledge are now handed down from one set of students to another in this way, until at the present time a building of any description or size can be constructed wholly by our instructors and students, from the drawing of the plans, to the putting in of the electric fixtures, without going off the grounds for a single workman."

Washington's Faith in His People

Education was part of Washington's plan for the race, but far from all. He was determined to show blacks how they might utilize their creativity and skills to establish business enterprises of their own. For it was the entrepreneurial spirit and drive, and the impulse to own land, that he wanted most to inculcate in the race. "The salvation of the black man lies in owning the soil he lives on," he often repeated.

Right from the start, he was convinced that, in terms of human resources, he had good material to work with. For, better than anyone, he knew that, as early as the 18th century, freed slaves had already begun the arduous process of building an economic foundation. John Sibley Butler of the University of Texas testifies to this in his book, *Entrepreneurship and Self-Help Among Black Americans*, by setting out in detail our early and noble history as business entrepreneurs—from 18th-century slaves who bought their freedom, to the entrepreneurial enclave of Durham, North Carolina, which, at the turn of this century, was celebrated as a hub of African-American enterprise.

Juliet Walker, of the University of Illinois, also describes in her several excellent works a "pioneering entrepreneurial spirit" among great numbers of blacks, both slave and free. She reports, "Even the absence of political freedom did not preclude the business participation of blacks as creative capitalists."

So, Washington knew what his fellow blacks were capable of achieving. Just as important, he understood the fears and insecurities of these, the poorest of blacks, and the need to inspire and encourage them. Under his direction, Tuskegee was to become the greatest single influence in enheartening blacks to begin the difficult trek toward a new future. In 1900, Washington founded the National Negro Business League, which, throughout his lifetime, was an active support mechanism for budding and established business owners, while encouraging unity and solidarity.

No Malice for Whites

Although no one was more intimately acquainted with the painful past, Washington conveyed no malice or hatred for whites. He viewed the intertwined and interdependent history of the two races as exactly that—our common history. His objective nature kept him from wasting energy on replaying the sins of the past, and he conveyed this spirit to all who came under his influence. He declared, "We should not permit our grievances to overshadow our opportunities."

He seemed to possess the ability to step outside his immediate circumstances and observe the American scene from a distance. From this vantage point, he was able to assess dispassionately how the Tuskegee experience could not only enhance the lives of blacks, but be beneficial to the country at large. This special feature of Washington's character—that is, his willingness to understand the sensibilities of whites as well as blacks—kept him in trouble with the northern black intelligentsia, most of whom were long removed from slavery.

More than almost any other goal, Washington wanted to see blacks cultivate the habit of cooperation among themselves. This he considered the crucial element needed to create the financial and material resources to continue the upward climb. His philosophy of capital development through work and thrift came to be called the "Gospel of Wealth." Under the aegis of what was known as the "Tuskegee Machine," entrepreneurial skills were honed, and over the years, a multitude of blacks founded businesses in various crafts in all parts of the country.

Washington viewed the future of the race as a series of building blocks—a slow but steady course, where the black community, intact and self-supportive, would gradually "gain knowledge, experience and wealth within our own ranks." For him, that was the key—that self-sufficiency would come within our own ranks, through our own labor and ingenuity.

Although he made it clear that "there should be no limit placed upon the development of any individual" and that "no one kind of training can safely be prescribed for any entire race," he believed that blacks should begin to build upon what they already possessed—the skills, discipline and craftsmanship that they brought with them out of slavery. As he put it, it was "training in the rudimentary elements that ultimately make for a permanently progressive civilization.". . .

Reversing Washington's Work

Washington's refusal to rebuke whites or to publicly express animosity toward them incurred the wrath of those blacks who were not about to bury the hatchet of past grievances. Festering in their resentment and envy, such people were determined to rub the white man's face in his wicked deeds and to make sure he never forgot them. Even if it meant setting back the progress of the poorest, these already privileged ones were set to do battle with the white man. These were the forerunners of today's purveyors of in-your-face politics, the so-called leadership that has kept the black masses paralyzed and unable to move forward.

Washington recognized the destructive tendencies of these opponents, and fought them at every turn. The NAACP, conceived of by this elite and their increasingly influential white supporters, was founded primarily to counter the work and philosophy of Washington. When he died in 1915, these notables quickly stepped into the breach, and began the reversal of his work that continues to this day. The leadership of the race had fallen into the hands of a class of professional povereticians.

Captives of Another Form of Slavery

"Nobody owes us anything. Not the government, nobody. What happened in the 1920s, 30s or 40s is all water under the bridge. It's up to us now to make the future. And the only way we can do that is to combine our resources." These strong words are those of Bishop Luke Edwards, who is like no black preacher you will encounter any time soon. . . .

He is a staunch believer in the potential inherent in America and the unlimited opportunities that are here for blacks. He is grateful that Jim Crow "justice" was broken in the South, so that blacks now have greater mobility and freedom to keep what they create. "The good that came out of Dr. King's movement is that we now have legal leverage against such people like those in the Klan. They are now restrained from coming in here and burning down our crops and homes and everything we've built."

He is angry that the black masses, freed from their former servitude, now find themselves captives of another form of slavery, promoted mainly by other blacks. "Welfare has made invalids out of us. After the civil rights movement there was enough money given to all these counties in Alabama and Mississippi and throughout the South to release black people from poverty, if that money had been applied correctly. Instead, blacks used their own people to undermine such efforts, and they're still doing it today."

Elizabeth Wright, *Issues & Views*, Summer 1992.

Black energy was diverted away from the drive for economic independence and turned, instead, to making whites take notice, move over, and give—all in the name of "social justice." The legacy of Washington's devotion to systematically developing what he called the "latent capacity of the Negro people" was lost to us, probably forever. Believing that opportunity was abundant and limitless, he had urged blacks to act on their own initiative. "No race that has anything to contribute to the markets of the world is long in any degree ostracized." This is the legacy we lost.

After Washington's death and the demise of Tuskegee's influence, an ambitious black middle class, via their various civil rights organizations, granted further entry into the affairs of our race to government and an eager band of white liberal crusaders. As blacks began to seek greater acceptance by whites, incentives to cooperate among ourselves diminished. Lacking a strong sense of unity and with the flight of the middle class from black neighborhoods, the stage was set for the dissolution of our families and community institutions—both of which were essentially intact while Washington lived.

Doubt and Lowered Expectations

Our tragedy began in earnest in the mid-1950s, when the psychobabble prattle of middle-class elitist Kenneth Clark was accepted as the guideline by which to judge the needs of all blacks. The demand for whites to teach our children moved on to still more and greater demands. Opting for the easy way out, the black elite began to teach that if whites would allow us access to the institutions they build and develop, we should not "bother" to create our own. Those blacks who pointed to the experiences of other groups to emphasize the importance of independent institutions were castigated as "separatists," un-American segregationists. This is the poison the black elite has fed us since the 1954 *Brown* decision, along with the gospel of salvation through politics. [In *Brown v. Board of Education*, the U.S. Supreme Court ruled that the segregation of blacks in public schools was unconstitutional, setting aside the 1896 standard that had called for "separate but equal" education.]

As our elite encouraged the masses to look to whites for all our worldly needs, such attitudes began to affect the way we viewed one other, lowering our expectations of ourselves, casting doubt on our capacity as a people to continue the upward climb, under our own steam. An increasingly dependent mindset was reinforced by a flood of government programs, severely undercutting what once had been a growing confidence that most blacks could, indeed, prosper in America. Any unwitting soul who protested the elite's perverted view of our destiny was simply blown away by the sheer force of mounting public opinion being shaped by relentless media promotion, which has not ceased to this day. . . .

In turning our backs on our great legacy of self-help, in changing course, we lost not only our chance to economically stabilize our communities, our poor lost everything. For without the power that a strong economic base brings, and without the input of middle-class resources, both financial and moral, we lost the ability to shield our neighborhoods from such outside influences as the drug trade. It is such negative influences that ultimately led to the undermining of our families and community institutions.

While the poor fell further behind, a steadily growing black middle class learned how to master the art of playing the race card, viewing an emphasis on race as their ticket to a good life in the white man's world. Having coerced preferential social programs from a cowed population, black elites now fall all over one another to reach the front of the line to be classified as "Disadvantaged"—so they may reap the rewards of social programs created especially for them.

Social Programs for the Privileged Few

Their handiwork is clearly reflected, for example, in the deformed role now played by the National Business League, initially founded to help black entrepreneurs develop healthy, stable businesses, which were to be the major force to keep blacks free of white benevolence. In Jacksonville, Florida, the once honorable League has been transformed into a set-aside welfare program for the privileged few. In 1992, the city's Mayor Ed Austin became the subject of attack by the local black gentry for publicly telling the truth, that is, minority set-asides in his city have "encouraged dependency instead of independence." A sad twist on the goal of Washington and the founders of the League.

The loss of mature and responsible leadership, as provided by our forebears, leaves our race susceptible not only to the deception of this black elite, but to the political whims and social trends of mainstream society. Our race becomes the tool of politicians and conniving interest groups as our adversities provide the fodder for a race industry created by an integrated alliance of "experts" and "specialists." As they research and analyze our foibles, grinding out reports, theses, dissertations, journal articles, discussion papers, monographs, and an endless stream of books, race hustlers of every description build careers and reputations solely on the existence of our troubles. The black poor is an industry in which throngs of black and white professionals have a vested interest.

The Betrayal of Youth

Our loss of autonomy meant the loss of control over the direction of our youth. . . . Because we turned over control of our community to outsiders, the government's school system is free to pollute the minds of our young. Since the 1950s, America's children have been the principal targets of demented educational experiments. The most recent one hypes sexual activity through phony, contrived "sex education" classes, enforcing in young minds the notion of sex as a "neutral" activity, to which no moral standards need be attached. Not content with this betrayal of

155

youth, teachers act as eager dispensers of condoms—just in case the kids fail to get the classroom message.

No American ancestor could have envisioned a society where the advocacy of abstinence for the young is denounced as "moralizing," a society ruled by timid adults who lack the will to use common sense to put restrictions on the foolhardy behavior of the young, a society that encourages its sons to put no rein on their sexual appetites (because "boys will be boys"), and thereby impels its daughters to promiscuity, because any "mistakes" can be done away with at the local abortion clinic, a society that acts as if it does not see throughout the tragic consequences of early intimacy.

When Patricia Funderburk, the black woman who heads the federal Office of Adolescent Pregnancy Programs, rejected the notion that teenagers cannot be taught to control their behavior, advocating abstinence for the young, she was hounded as a subversive and a fanatic by those who would not have youth denied "freedom of sexual expression."

Vested Interests in the Black Poor

Because our race is an open territory to manipulators of every distinction, we are subject to a cynical media that views black behavior as its primary source for filling up newspaper columns and TV soundbites. Its pseudo-serious "investigations" of our troubles are really theater and spectacle, designed to titillate an already news-numbed American audience. The 1992 Los Angeles riots provided this fatuous crew with yet another opportunity to feast on black criminality. No action was more deplorable than that of poker-faced reporters prowling amidst the ashes and debris, to locate thugs and social deviants to publicly legitimize as the latest black "leaders."

Sanctimonious editors of newspapers like the *New York Times* have long demonstrated their contempt for blacks through their condescending editorializing, that treats us like pets or mascots—a species to be protected from the slings and arrows of public criticism. These newspapers represent a class of whites for whom blacks, as "downtrodden outcasts," give vent to their need to perform "good deeds." Champions of every black cause and apologists for every black sin, such posturers have invested lifetimes in perceiving us as hapless victims and themselves as rescuers and saviors. Among our staunchest partisans, they would be devastated if the majority of blacks were ever to rise out of poverty and become their economic equals, thereby permanently removing our race from their sphere of influence.

These snakes in the grass are oblivious to their insults when, in their zeal to exonerate blacks from responsibility for our social ills, they divert discussions to the evils of "Wall Street greed" or "government neglect," which have nothing to do with why we are not adequately parenting our children.

Separate and Mutual Interests

If we ever get serious about rebuilding our families and community institutions—separate because they are uniquely ours, while still an integral part of the American fabric—we should look to the teachings of Booker T. Washington. His was the clearest exposition of the reality of the interdependence between the races, without either group sinking into dependency on the other. The races could be as separate as the fingers in most instances, he taught, yet act as one hand "in all things essential to mutual progress."

This is wisdom we would do well to keep in mind while surveying current events on the American scene, as an alliance of cynical white intellectuals climb to positions of power in academia, church institutions, and the media. Apparently bent on destabilizing American society, these crafty ones care nothing about the welfare of blacks, or the consequences of the value-free, morally neutral lifestyles they promote.

As these alienated misfits court our attention and support, mouthing sentiments of compassion and concern for our black cause, we should remember that the achievements of our ancestors were made possible through their commitment to traditional values. An America with its political institutions severely damaged, and controlled by a band of scornful ideologues, will be no place to attempt to reknit the fabric of our community.

The last 30 years of political foolery and worthless social programs have undermined most of what our ancestors sought to build. We are not helped by a leadership that benefits from the status quo, and we are certainly injured by the multitude of professionals who have vested interests in the existence of an underclass of blacks. Yet it may not be too much to hope that in some small locality, perhaps somewhere in the hinterland of America, a group of enlightened blacks, having come to grips with the folly of the recent past and possessed of the belief that they can create the future, will rekindle the fires of the Tuskegee spirit. That spirit, of course, is nothing more than the *will* to change our condition and to begin to plant again the seeds of self-help, enterprise, and solidarity that were planted long ago by people like Booker T. Washington.

"The Pine Ridge Reservation . . . the home of the Oglala branch of the Sioux Indians . . . is as poor as America gets."

Lack of Resources Keeps American Indians in Poverty

Peter T. Kilborn

Shannon County, South Dakota, home of the Oglala Sioux, is mired in bitter poverty. The land in Shannon County, as it is on most reservations, is inhospitable, but out of respect for Mother Earth, the Oglala recently refused to turn their reservation into a garbage dumping ground, which would have brought in millions of dollars in fees. Tribes on other reservations around the country have found no other income-producing options than turning their land into toxic waste dumps or promoting gambling. In the following viewpoint, Peter T. Kilborn, a writer for the *New York Times*, describes circumstances unique to Indian reservations that keep many of those who live there among the poorest people in the country.

As you read, consider the following questions:

1. Why does generosity work against the Sioux when times are hard, according to Kilborn?
2. What poverty-causing influences does Kilborn list that are similar to those in urban ghettoes?
3. Why does Gary Rowland, quoted by the author, object to the establishment of gambling casinos on the reservation?

Peter T. Kilborn, "Sad Distinction for the Sioux: Homeland Is No. 1 in Poverty," *The New York Times*, September 20, 1992. Copyright © 1992 by The New York Times Company. Reprinted by permission.

The Pine Ridge Reservation in South Dakota is the home of the Oglala branch of the Sioux Indians, descendants of the warrior heroes Crazy Horse and Red Cloud. It is as poor as America gets.

It spreads across nearly two million acres of butte-broken plains and listless creeks, and the oyster-gray cliffs and impervious clay floor of the Badlands. It is a mean and despairing place of 16,000 inhabitants ravaged by isolation, disease, political infighting, and good intentions gone bad. Fewer than 3 in 10 of the adults have jobs, and nearly all the jobs are in government agencies.

Most reservations are poor, but this one keeps sinking. The Census Bureau reports that in Shannon County, which covers most of the reservation, 63.1 percent of all residents lived in poverty in 1989—the highest rate of the nation's 3,141 counties, up from 44.7 percent (ninth poorest) a decade earlier. By comparison, the national poverty rate was 14.2 percent in 1991.

A Different Kind of Poverty

"It's a different kind of poverty here, a more bitter type," said the Rev. Joseph Daniel Sheehan, a Jesuit priest, as he stood outside his little Sacred Heart Catholic Church on a litter-blown knoll overlooking Wounded Knee, site of the United States 7th Cavalry's slaughter of Chief Big Foot and 300 Sioux men, women and children on Dec. 29, 1890.

Father Sheehan once served in India; there, he said, the attitude was "we're all in this together." Here, he went on, "they feel that anything that comes to them is what's left over. They get angry at one another. It's a kind of poverty that destroys the family. I don't know what I would be if I were an Indian. I think I would be an alcoholic."

In part, the poverty here arises from the circumstances unique to Indian tribes—their consignment to the remote and resource-poor dregs of the old frontier and the clash of their own values with a dominant white culture. All this is compounded by the arid climate and deep isolation of the Pine Ridge Reservation.

Among the Sioux, generosity is the holiest virtue, and stinginess and greed are reviled. People share their bounty with family and friends, rather than save to build a better house or start a business. In a community with wealth to spread around, everyone wins. Here everyone loses.

The conditions here also show influences that drag people down anywhere: bad nutrition, bad personal habits, high unemployment, racial discrimination, the two-decade-long erosion of American wages and Federal welfare programs that foster dependence.

"We're a fifth-going-on-sixth-generation welfare state," said Leo Vocu, a leader of the tribe. "We have, over these generations, developed some very bad habits."

But in the end, everything comes down to money. "There just ain't any money there," said James G. Abourezk, a former Democratic senator from South Dakota who practices law in Rapid City and specializes in Indian affairs. "No industry. No jobs. Not much of anything."

Families Fall Apart Under the Strain

People here routinely tell of economic stresses that match the worst of urban ghettos. Alfred Leftwich, 25 years old, married, father of three small children, is tall, agile and vigorous, a former basketball star at Pine Ridge High School.

He prepared for a career, going to college for two years to learn coaching and elementary school teaching and, not finding a job, to vocational school to learn carpentry. He has had two menial jobs off the reservation with the forest service, each lasting eight months, but they were temporary, and he has been unemployed for 18 months.

"Welfare is something I have to do," Mr. Leftwich said. "It's humiliating. I can work. I have all kinds of skills. I have two perfectly good hands." He is five months behind on his $150 monthly mortgage payments on his home, a trailer, and facing foreclosure. The power company has turned off the electricity. The pipes froze last winter and he has not been able to get them fixed. Without toilets or an outhouse, he said, "we just go to the creek."

Carmen Yellow Horse, 34, lived off the reservation, in Rapid City, for 12 years. "That's where the jobs were," she said. In February 1992 she returned with her two young daughters to the reservation hamlet of Red Shirt in the Badlands to live with her grandmother, who raised her and needed help. Recently she drove the 70 miles to Pine Ridge to look for a job.

She filled out an application for the only one for which she felt remotely qualified, as a $4.25-an-hour part-time secretary at a Federal Government welfare office. If she gets the job, the gasoline to commute in her 16-year-old Plymouth will cost about $9 a day, more than she would earn for two hours' work.

The poverty here shatters families. Mothers, not just fathers, leave spouses and children behind to try to make a living somewhere else. Many return, complaining of job discrimination and a paucity of jobs, and become alcoholics. Antoinette Wince will be among the next to try to break away.

Ms. Wince is 24, the single mother of a 7-year-old girl, a $5.50-an-hour, full-time supervisor at Big Bat's, a convenience store in Pine Ridge, and a part-time student at Oglala Lakota College, near the reservation village of Kyle.

"My major's computer science," she said. "The college will find a place for me off the reservation to do an internship. I want to leave. It's too depressing here." She said she had given her mother, a teacher, legal custody of her daughter, Stefanie— at her mother's insistence.

"My mom wants me to leave," she said. "She thinks there's nothing here for me. My mom always tells us: 'Be responsible. You're never going to make it in the white man's world if you can't behave like him. Go to work on time. Do your job.'"

Financial Windfall or Faustian Bargain?

For Native Americans, it's a modern twist on an old aphorism: Beware of white men bearing gifts. The nation's Indian tribes, most of them impoverished and ignored, suddenly find themselves being wooed with offers cumulatively amounting to hundreds of millions of dollars. There is, of course, a catch: The Indians are being asked to accept what the rest of America increasingly wants no part of—garbage, toxic waste, landfills, incinerators and nuclear-waste dumps. To some tribes, the offers represent a financial windfall and an economic development opportunity. To others, they are an ill-disguised bribe and a Faustian bargain.

Michael Satchell, *U.S. News & World Report*, January 11, 1993.

Pine Ridge, the reservation's principal settlement, is a prototype of rural poverty, the home of 5,000 people, nearly all Sioux. It is disheveled, potholed and dusty. None of the 15 miles of roads have names, and a third are unpaved.

There is no train, bus, bank, theater, clothing store, drug store, barber shop, restaurant, place to get a car fixed or home delivery of mail. A car is the only way to get around, yet a fifth of all Shannon County households don't have one. With the sole exception of Big Bat's, the new and well-lighted 24-hour store run by Bat and Pat Pourier, the few shops are fortresses against burglary, with boards or heavy metal mesh covering their windows. The sign in front of the Gospel Fellowship church in town offers "Our Only Hope Services."

In the small, white-owned Sioux Nation supermarket, a cooler displays see-through boxes of something chopped up and pink for $1.28 a pound. The label says "meat." The State Data Center at the University of South Dakota Vermillion reports that per capita income in Shannon County fell 23 percent in the 1980s, to $3,417, after adjusting for inflation.

Here, poverty kills. The Indian Health Service says that for every 1,000 children born on the reservation in the late 1980s, 29 died in infancy, almost three times the national average. Death from heart disease, pneumonia, influenza and suicide was twice

161

the national rate; from homicide, more than three times the national rate; from adult diabetes, four times; from alcoholism, 10 times. Alcoholism is showing up among newborn children, victims of fetal alcohol syndrome.

Another measure of poverty is bad and critically scarce housing. "We've got 2,000 families on our waiting list, and those are the ones who haven't given up waiting," said Carmel Richards, finance officer of the tribal housing authority that provides subsidized housing, much of it rent free. As a result, she said, "We see a lot of extended families in one unit. We've come across houses where there's 16 people in three bedrooms."

A Few Make It Against the Odds

Getting things done is difficult in part because the tribal leadership keeps changing. Tribal leaders freely acknowledge that many use their offices to put family and friends in jobs. Then other factions, having been locked out of jobs, run for office and do the same for their people. The tribe also presides over a legal system that favors individuals over businesses, discouraging investors from opening factories and providing jobs.

For a century the Federal Government wielded immense influence over the affairs of the reservation, primarily through the Bureau of Indian Affairs. In recent years it has turned over political authority to the tribe, though it does award contracts and loans to develop things like schools, hospitals and businesses. But Federal aid has not kept pace with inflation, and in the context of the reservation's poverty its contribution is minuscule.

Still, conditions at Pine Ridge could be worse. Welfare programs do provide a crutch, especially for large families. An underground cash economy of poachers, burglars, bootleggers and artisans who make quilts and beaded jewelry is another crutch.

Some people also see hope for a stronger economy. They say alcoholism, the bane and refuge of the permanently unemployed, seems to be abating. Schools are improving, too. Over 20 years, as the tribe has taken over the schools from the churches and the Bureau of Indian Affairs, tribal leaders have placed their top priority on education, and in some of the decrepit-looking villages the schools are the only large and well-kept buildings to be seen.

More young people are finishing high school and going to college than ever, and they are qualifying for the well-paid nursing, teaching and other professional jobs on the reservation that have been going to non-Indians.

John Yellow Bird Steele, chairman of the Oglala Sioux since February 1992, is planning to build up to three gambling casinos, an enterprise that has salvaged some other reservations. Uncommonly for a member of a tribe that has favored a quasi-socialist

economy based on tribe-owned business, he preaches free enterprise. "We've got to view economic development for what it is,"
he said. "It's the private entrepreneur who's going to do it."

But other tribal leaders have had new ideas, too, and are often
thrown out of office for espousing them. Tribal chairmen are
elected every two years, and none has been re-elected since the
mid-1970s. One small faction here, members of the radical
American Indian Movement, says gambling will drive Indians
deeper into alcoholism and debt. "That's genocide," said Gary
Rowland, head of the Wounded Knee chapter of A.I.M.

With or without gambling, there are people who make it even
against considerable odds. Bat Pourier, a 40-year-old, full-
blooded Oglala Sioux, was 14 when his father died. He went to
South Dakota State University to play football, injured a knee,
dropped out and started drinking. He met Pat, daughter of a
white farmer. "We became drinking buddies," Ms. Pourier said.

Living in a Dual Culture

Back on the reservation, still drinking, Mr. Pourier fell behind
in payments on his pickup truck. "I started being honest with everybody," he said. He approached Stockmens Bank for an $11,000
loan so he could keep the truck. "I'm an alcoholic, but I'm going
straight," he told the president of the bank. He got the loan.

After three years of sobriety, he was offered a job at the bank.
He became a lending officer and stayed six years. While at the
bank, he and Ms. Pourier, by then sober and a postmistress on
the reservation, made plans to open a convenience store.

They got $1.2 million in loans and a $100,000 grant from the
Bureau of Indian Affairs. It took two years to break ground.
"The white business owners did not want competition," Mr.
Pourier said. "So they contested our lease on the land. We went
to court 13 times."

Open two years now, the store is a hive of activity all day. It
has 30 employees, all Indian. The Pouriers aggressively tackled a
problem that has defeated other Indian-owned businesses on the
reservation: a cultural clash over the concept of time. In the
Lakota language there is no word for time and few people on the
reservation even wear wristwatches. "Late once, you get a written reprimand," Ms. Pourier said. "Late again and you're fired."

Still, the Pouriers have also remained loyal to Sioux traditions.
They are sharing the business, giving equal stakes in it to a
brother of Mr. Pourier, an adopted brother and a nephew.

"We have people in Washington telling us what funding we
need, what our problems are, how to solve them," Mr. Pourier
said. "Damn it, let us solve them. We can keep our values and
live in a dual culture."

"The devastating effects of collectivism, oppressive bureaucracy, and cradle-to-grave government paternalism . . . can be found . . . on almost any Indian reservation."

Government Handouts Keep American Indians in Poverty

William F. Jasper

The desperate situation of American Indians has led many liberals to believe spending more government money is necessary, both to ease suffering and to assuage guilt over past injustices, according to William F. Jasper, author of the following viewpoint. This would just make the situation worse, he contends, since dependence on government welfare programs is a major cause of the current poverty of Indian tribes. Such federal paternalism must end, the author maintains, if American Indians are to survive. Jasper is senior editor of the *New American*, a conservative biweekly newsmagazine.

As you read, consider the following questions:

1. What four areas of federal policy does Jasper believe account for the poverty of American Indians today?
2. Why does the author believe private Indian ownership of land, rather than collective tribal ownership, would improve living conditions on reservations?
3. How did Alaskan statehood change the lives of Native Americans who live there, according to Jasper?

From William F. Jasper, "Fiercely Dependent," *The New American*, August 27, 1990. Reprinted with permission.

To witness firsthand the devastating effects of collectivism, oppressive bureaucracy, and cradle-to-grave government paternalism on a people, one need not journey to Cuba, China, or the Soviet Union. And to experience the grinding poverty and despair of what has come to be called the Third World, one needn't traipse off to Africa or South America. All of these things can be found here in the United States in tragic abundance and concentration on almost any Indian reservation. There one will find the poorest of America's poor, the highest rates of unemployment and alcoholism, the worst levels of illiteracy and school dropouts, the lowest housing and health standards.

According to the 1980 Census, 14 percent of Indian households on reservations had annual incomes of under $2500, compared with 5 percent for the U.S. population at large. Only 6 percent of Indian reservation households had incomes greater than $30,000, contrasted with 20 percent for the entire U.S. The Bureau of Indian Affairs' figures show that for 1989 only 24 percent of employed reservation Indians earned over $7000 annually. These figures take on even greater significance given the fact that nearly 25 percent of reservation household income comes from welfare programs, and an even larger percentage of these earnings is derived from government jobs, or from jobs in private businesses that are subsidized by the federal government.

Unemployment on the reservations nationally has hovered at 48 percent since the late 1980s, up from its usual fluctuations in the low- to mid-40s. On some reservations. the unemployment rate is as high as 80 to 90 percent. The tiny Los Coyotes Reservation in southern California, with only 212 members, has 95 percent unemployment. And on the even smaller Augustine Reservation, with a mere five members and an eligible work force of three, unemployment is running at a perfect 100 percent! More disturbing than these figures, however, is the 25 percent of those not employed who are not even looking for work. For whatever reasons, they are not even seeking to change their unemployed status. They have accepted complete dependence on the government as a way of life. . . .

White Man's Burden?

These and other horrific statistics concerning the plight of the Indian population are breathlessly recited by liberals as conclusive evidence of the urgent need for more federal programs and massive new infusions of federal funds. Reminders of the collective guilt of the white man for past injustices against the red man are usually sufficient to secure the necessary support for passage of additional federal appropriations. "If only we had another training and education program," they say. Or another alcohol and drug treatment program, another housing program.

165

Or "X" number of additional teachers, counselors, social workers, doctors, nurses, etc. Or capitalization for another subsidized tribal business venture.

All of which is patent nonsense. It is this kind of federal program, and Washington's insistence on a collectivist approach to the "Indian problem," that is responsible for the current "plight" of Indians on the reservation today. More specifically, we can point to four areas of federal Indian policy that account for most of the tragedy on the reservations today: 1) Federal trusteeship of Indian lands, which prevents individual Indians from reaping the benefits of private ownership of their land; 2) Federal welfare programs that destroy initiative and independence; 3) The fiat power of tribal councils, which encourages widespread corruption; and 4) The suspension of constitutional protections for Indians on reservations. . . .

There are over 500 federally recognized tribes and about 300 federal Indian reservations in the United States. These range in size from the Navajo Reservation, the largest with nearly 16 million acres, to many smaller reservations of less than 1000 acres. Some are less than 100 acres in size. In all, some 53 million acres of Indian land—an area about the size of the New England states—are held in trust by the United States. Of this total, 77 percent is classified as "tribal trust" (owned collectively by tribes), 20 percent is "individual trust" (owned by individual Indians), and 2 percent is owned by agencies of the federal government. The remaining 1 percent is unclassified as to ownership status.

The trust lands, both tribal and individual, are administered and managed by the Bureau of Indian Affairs. Established in 1824 as part of the War Department, the BIA was transferred to the Department of the Interior when that department was created in 1849. The Bureau completely dominates reservation life. Besides controlling tribal resources on trust lands—including leasing of mineral, agricultural, grazing, timber, and water rights—the BIA oversees a myriad of welfare, education, social service, and development programs. It is also a major tribal employer. Eighty percent of its 14,000 employees are Indians.

Privatizing the Reservation

Besides the trust lands, there are on the Indian reservations many private property owners, both Indian and non-Indian, who hold fee title to their land with essentially the same rights as private property owners elsewhere. This fee simple ownership [without restrictions as to heirs or transfer of ownership], which amounts to between 16 and 20 percent of reservation land, is a legacy of the General Allotment Act (or Dawes Act) of 1887. The idea behind allotment was to establish individual Indian ownership of reservation land through a process similar to homesteading. This would, it was believed, promote Indian agricultural development and encourage assimilation of Indians into white society. The size of the allotments varied widely from one reservation to another, from as little as 10 acres to as much as 400 acres.

Owning vs. Controlling Indian Land

In a society where land ownership has traditionally been synonymous with wealth, the group which holds the largest blocks of privately owned land are the poorest, American Indians. Why?

From the beginning of the European invasion of this continent, the control of the development of the land and its natural resources quickly passed from the control of the Native Peoples to a series of outside governments. Even after the establishment of the United States government and the subsequent recognition of Indian nations as domestic sovereign dependent nations under a special trust relationship, Indian nations have been under the domination of outside control. Development has been permitted only at the discretion of—and often, the whims of—federal officials. The attitude most often reflected has been that of a dictator, sometimes benevolent, with a series of social welfare programs designed, first to isolate, and then, to assimilate Native Peoples.

Maggie Gover, *You Don't Have to Be Poor to Be Indian*, 1979.

Historians and academics almost universally have decried the allotment era as an abysmal failure and another rapacious assault on Indian lands by the white man. To support this view they cite the millions of acres that were privatized and are no longer under tribal or BIA control. To be sure, as in previous dealings with the Indians, there were some who acted unethically, even criminally, in defrauding allottees of their land. But that is not to say that all or even most of the results of the Dawes Act were harmful to Indians. Indeed, if you visit a reservation today you can readily see some of the benefits. The Indian homes, farms, ranches, and enterprises that are the best kept, most productive, and most prosperous are those properties to which the owners hold fee title. They stand in stark contrast to the dilapidated trust properties all around them.

These private property owners also are less likely to be dependent upon government assistance and less likely to fit the negative stereotype that non-Indian society often associates with Indians. This phenomenon should not surprise anyone. In spite of much propaganda to the contrary, the American Indian is a *homo economicus*, the same as the members of all other races and ethnic groups. As has been demonstrated over and over again with the privatization of government housing projects all over the world, individual private property owners invariably manage their property and their lives far better than government could ever hope to. . . .

In many cases, Indians sold their reservation parcels in order to acquire non-reservation land that was more compatible with their needs and desires. Thus there are today many Indian ranchers and farmers operating off the reservation on an even footing with non-Indians. Probably few of these would agree that they would be better off on the reservation. So, too, many other Indians moved to small towns and cities, where they may or may not have been better off than those who stayed on the reservation. It is also worth noting that there are scholars like Professor Fred McChesney of Emory University who have studied the Dawes Act era and feel that the criticism has been badly misplaced. McChesney points out that "it was not privatization but restrictions on fully defined property rights that made land ownership difficult for Indians."

Misunderstanding Indian Culture

Most of the policy failures concerning the Indian reservations stem from an enduring and tragic misunderstanding of the Native American tribal cultures. Most non-Indians have mistakenly viewed all Indian tribes as communistic in nature, and therefore incompatible with private ownership of land. Typical of this viewpoint is this excerpt from a minority report of the House Committee on Indian Affairs published in 1938:

> From the time of discovery of America, and for centuries probably before that, the North American Indian has been a communist. Not in the offensive sense of modern communism, but in the sense of holding property in common. . . . The very idea of property in the soil was unknown to the Indian mind.

This errant view has been repeated in the textbooks and literature so often that it goes largely unchallenged and has become the accepted dogma on Indian socio-politico-economic development.

"I know that is the prevailing notion today, as it has been for a long time, but it is completely wrong," says Indian scholar Fred Hatch, a member of the Sault Ste. Marie Chippewas, "and it continues to lead to wrongheaded approaches to federal policies with the Indians." Hatch, a practicing attorney in Sayner, Wisconsin, who has taught Indian treaty law and anthropology at the University of Wisconsin at Milwaukee, says it is understandable that many anthropologists, historians, and observers might misinterpret certain Indian customs as being collectivistic. "But to conclude that because Indians often hunted, gathered, planted, and harvested in groups that they were therefore communistic totally misses the mark. The reliable anthropological evidence shows that, to the contrary, nearly all of the North American Indians were fiercely individualistic."

Their group or communal activities were voluntary, born out of convenience and the need for common defense and social security in an often harsh environment. But individual private ownership of both personal property and even land was the established norm. . . .

Not only does the communal nature of the BIA's trust policy run contrary to Indian tradition; it is, arguably, the major factor contributing to the Indian's continuing condition of dependency and alienation. All of the talk about Indian "self-determination" is just so much wind-blown rhetoric as long as government bureaucrats control all Indian land. . . .

Federal Money, Moral Decay

Dan Cole was born a member of the Cherokee Nation in Oklahoma 75 years ago. The study of Indian history, tradition, and folklore has been a lifelong pursuit for him. Not just "book learning" mind you, but extensive, firsthand, live experience among the Indians of the United States and Canada and the Eskimos, Aleuts, and Indians of Alaska. During the late 1940s, '50s, and '60s, Cole spent considerable time in Alaska, much of it working as a civil engineer supervising the construction of installations for the U.S. Coast Guard. His hiring of Eskimo and Indian construction crews was unprecedented. Although he is an Indian, he was considered an outsider, and it took many months of working, hunting, and fishing alongside the natives before he was accepted as one of the tribe and allowed to learn the tribe's sacred stories, songs, and traditions.

"By our standards they were considered very poor," Dan Cole remembers. "Their annual income at that time was about $50-$80 per year. They lived in log or sod homes that were unheated. Their diet consisted mainly of fish, seal, and whale. But they were healthy and happy." Then came Alaska's statehood in 1959. "One of the first things that happened was federal money started pouring in. Free food, welfare checks. There was no incentive to go out and brave the elements to fish and hunt, or to hold a job. They started to stay in town to drink and gamble. Their family lives and tribal unity began to disintegrate. . . . Their diet shifted to potato chips and soda pop so that they were soon in bad health and their teeth were falling out." It was devastating, says Cole, and it happened so quickly. He has seen the same tragic results on reservations throughout the United States and on the Flathead Reservation in western Montana where he now lives and raises cattle.

"I grew up during the Depression in the Oklahoma dust bowl, so I'm familiar with poverty," Cole told the *New American,* "but I'm real troubled by what I see now, because it's a poverty of the soul, a moral decay, that's destroying us. Indians are wards of the government, with no responsibilities." On the Flathead Reservation, for instance, Indians are furnished with housing, with the heat, utilities, and telephone all paid for by the government. In addition, he says, Indians receive federal surplus foods, federal food stamps, federal welfare payments, income payments from the sale of tribal timber, and income from the Kerr Dam and Flathead Lake. Beyond that, they have year-round unrestricted hunting and fishing rights. It's a person with high principles and strong character who doesn't succumb to such blandishments.

And the BIA is continually dreaming up new ways to waste money. "Their newest fiasco here on the Flathead Reservation," says Cole, "is the new $3.5 million Two Eagle High School at Pablo. They're really pushing this 'Indian culture' thing now, so they decided to create this new tribal school that would draw Indian students out of the local public and private schools," he explains. But, in his words, it's been "a complete disaster. They have a fancy new building, new computers, free trips—but no discipline, no teaching, and no learning." Absenteeism, drinking alcohol on campus, sleeping or listening to stereos in class, and other behaviors not usually considered conducive to academic excellence are rife at Two Eagle.

What does Dan Cole see as the solution? "Abolish the BIA and the reservation system before they abolish the Indian. Allow Indians to have true self-determination, with responsibility for their own lives like everybody else." Cole asserts that most Flathead Indians supported just such a proposal by former tribal leader Bill Moriteau, now deceased. But the BIA and tribal leaders squashed it primarily because it would end their power, privileges, and personal access to millions of dollars in tribal funds. "The liberals all yell about how we should be ending apartheid in South Africa," says Cole, "but they want to see our version of it maintained here in America."

Dictatorship and Corruption

Verna Lawrence agrees with Dan Cole. Mrs. Lawrence is a Sault Ste. Marie Chippewa and a former member of the Chippewa tribal council. . . . "Federal Indian policies are destroying the Indians," says the outspoken Mrs. Lawrence. "They have already largely destroyed the initiative, independence, and self respect of the Indian people. They're turning them into irresponsible children who look to the federal government to pro-

vide their every need. I've never used any of my Indian benefits. I've earned everything I have, and I've taught my children
to do the same. I get fighting mad when I see these politicians,
bureaucrats, and tribal leaders with their hands out for more
tax dollars."

According to Verna Lawrence, if you want proof of the axiom
that "power tends to corrupt and absolute power corrupts absolutely," just go to virtually any Indian reservation. "Native
Americans have all the rights of American citizenship—they are
American citizens—until they set foot on the reservation. Then
they have no rights whatsoever. Tribal leaders exercise absolute
'sovereign' authority. They can lock you up and throw away the
key if they want to and you have no recourse, no right to due
process, no right to jury trial—nothing."

This has led to graft, corruption, nepotism, and other abuses
of tribal authority on a massive scale. It's a national scandal,"
says Lawrence. "Tribal officials act like third-world petty dicta-
tors, appointing their family members and cronies as the tribal
police, tribal judges, and other specially created posts, appropri-
ating tribal funds for their personal use. There's no accountability." Only a few of the most blatant examples—like Chief Peter
McDonald of the Navajo Nation—have ever been exposed in the
media, she says. . . .

Julie Cryderman, a Chippewa who lives off the reservation,
. . . [believes] that federal paternalism and control must end if
Indians are to survive in any viable capacity.

And what of tribal sovereignty? "Tribal sovereignty is rub-
bish," she snaps. "I'm an Indian, and proud of it, but I'm also an
American citizen. And I wouldn't give up my rights under the
Constitution for anything. You can still be an Indian off the
reservation, but you're not an American when you're on the
reservation: you're a ward of the government and at the mercy
of the tribal leaders." Charges of corruption and abuse by tribal
leaders came up repeatedly in interviews with Indians all across
the country.

"Let Them Grow Up!"

What about concerns that a new allotment program will expose Indians to exploitation by con artists and land grabbers?
"They're already being exploited on the reservation by some of
the worst con artists and land grabbers imaginable, for heaven's
sake," responds Verna Lawrence. "Yes, some of them will fritter
away their property and their opportunity, just as they are doing
now, but others will use it to build a decent life for themselves
and their families. And they have a right to that. It's their land,
not the government's, the BIA's, or the tribal council's. Let
them grow up! They should have the same right to succeed or

171

fail that every other American has. It's really time for this communal ownership and trusteeship to end.". . .

Dependency upon government for one's material welfare is always incompatible with personal liberty, progress, and prosperity. But, during times of increasing social polarization and budgetary constraints that force cuts in programs with numerically and politically weak constituencies, the danger of having one's property, life, and livelihood directly controlled by government bureaucrats and a fickle political process becomes obvious. As a minority of less than 1 percent of the population, Native Americans are especially vulnerable. Their present "privileged" status has been guaranteed primarily by the sympathies of the majority. But, as Indian militancy and the costs of judicially imposed "Indian rights" victories erode that sympathy base, individual Indians should realize that their interests would be better served by disentangling themselves from the tribal-federal relationship.

True self-determination for the Indians can only come about once the federal government relinquishes control over their property and their lives. This would also mean ending the federal policy of treating the Indians collectively as a communal-property society. An equitable allotment policy, allowing Indians to enjoy the benefits of private property and to choose their economic future, may offer the best (perhaps the only) solution to a difficult conundrum.

Under this approach, those Indians who are so inclined could pool their individual parcels to create their own communally owned tribal reservations. Some might choose to retain title to the surface rights on their land while deeding subsurface rights over to the tribe, or vice versa. Following the lead of environmental groups like the Nature Conservancy that buy land to be set aside and preserved in its natural condition, groups of Indians could add to their tribal holdings by purchasing the allotments of those Indians who are willing to sell. They might decide to incorporate as either a for-profit or non-profit entity. With revenues generated from development of their timber and mineral resources and other assets, they could continue to purchase additional land from non-Indians as well. Numerous options are available when freedom is brought into the equation and coercion is removed. Some voluntary market approach of this sort is most likely the only way for Native Americans to secure a real future for themselves, while preserving their Indian culture and heritage.

"Latinos entering the labor market . . . [have found] unstable employment, diminished job opportunities, and extreme impoverishment."

Economic Restructuring Has Caused Poverty Among Hispanics

Rebecca Morales and Frank Bonilla

The economic expansion of the 1980s presented a paradox, according to Rebecca Morales and Frank Bonilla, authors of the following viewpoint; the rich got richer, while the poor—especially Hispanics—fell farther behind. The authors examine the economic restructuring that has accelerated in the last three decades, and conclude it has combined with factors unique to the Hispanic population to make poverty a persistent and growing problem among this group. Morales and Bonilla are the authors of *Latinos in a Changing U.S. Economy: Comparative Perspectives on Growing Inequality*, from which this viewpoint is taken.

As you read, consider the following questions:

1. What caused the overall decline in real wages (wages measured by purchasing power) since the 1980s, according to the authors?
2. What distinct characteristics of the Hispanic-American population contribute to a high rate of poverty for this group, according to Morales and Bonilla?
3. What do the authors mean by the term "human capital"?

Excerpted from Rebecca Morales and Frank Bonilla, *Latinos in a Changing U.S. Economy: Comparative Perspectives on Growing Inequality*, pages 1-2, 4-7, 9, 11-12, 14-16, 21-22, 25-26, © 1993 by Sage Publications, Inc. Reprinted by permission of Sage Publications, Inc.

It is now widely understood that one of the economic consequences of the unprecedented expansion of the 1980s in the United States is that the rich got richer while the middle class stagnated and the poor fell farther behind. This growing economic division left a deep imprint on society. Aggregate measures document not only growing income inequality, but also a massive transference of wealth. White family incomes and net worth rose, even as these indicators fell among African Americans and Latinos. The resources available to individuals more narrowly defined their ability to improve and invest in communities, thereby reinforcing spatial demarcations in the spread of economic and social inequality.

The reality that opportunities for upward mobility in the United States were not part of the economic boom of the 1980s raises serious questions. This reversal of an historical trend toward equality is leading some to ask whether it is the product of a decade of excess. The absence of tangible improvements, despite efforts to stimulate the economy, leads others to question whether the polarization is instead a harbinger of other more enduring problems. These are troubling prospects. We pose these questions from the perspective of Latinos, a group that realized demographic growth at nearly 10 times the rate of non-Hispanic whites and more than 5 times that of African Americans between 1980 and 1990. Members of this large and expanding segment of society are having to come to terms with the possibility that they may never reach parity with the average American without concerted efforts to change their circumstances that must involve the nation as a whole.

What Causes Inequality Faced by Latinos?

The problem lies in how to interpret the dilemma confronting Latinos in light of recent trends. There are several competing views. One is that the disparity felt by Latinos is a function of their own attributes, such as English language and educational limitations, or what is widely referred to as their human capital. Another is that the situation is the product of institutional constraints, such as failures of the educational system or of protections for workers' compensation or benefits reflected in a weakened social safety net. Yet a third line of reasoning is that structural barriers such as occupational shifts place enormous obstacles in the path to economic advances. The geographical distribution of wealth and poverty arguably adds another dimension. Urban segmentation is seen by some as generating the growth of an urban underclass, a dynamic that is compounded by international trends. Within minority neighborhoods, environmental blight and social disorganization further erode the prospects for economic recovery. To come to terms with these views, we begin our examination of the reality confronting Latinos with a question: To what can we attribute the persistent and growing inequality facing Latinos today? . . .

Research indicates that since the 1970s, national low-wage employment rose and middle-strata jobs declined. The change in employment structure occurred in the wake of a sectoral shift. Manufacturing employment dropped 3% from 1969 to 1989 even as jobs in the service sector grew by 93%. The net result is that manufacturing declined in relative importance from 29% of all jobs to 19% while services increased from 42% to 54%. The structural changes adversely affected white men, minority men and women, youths, and full-time as well as part-time workers in all parts of the country. . . .

Reducing Inequality: An Economic Imperative

By any standard, Hispanics lost ground economically during the 1980s. Hispanics' median family income declined both in real dollars and in comparison with other groups. Poverty among Hispanic children remained substantial. Hispanic woman-maintained families were unable to improve their economic status. And, in addition to the prevalence of poverty, the degree of hardship facing poor Hispanics also deepened. . . .

In the 1990s, reducing inequality between Hispanics and the rest of society will not be a moral preference, but an economic imperative. Hispanics will constitute about one-third of overall labor force growth between now and the end of the century, and a growing proportion of taxpayers supporting Social Security, Medicare and other transfer payment systems needed to support an aging society. An untrained and underemployed labor force will not only retard direct economic output, but increase demand for public assistance and diminish the tax base necessary for the support of essential government services. Improving the Hispanic community's economic standing—and the human capital characteristics of individual Hispanics—clearly serves the economic interest of the nation. A modest investment in the Hispanic community will provide substantial returns to society.

Leticia Miranda and Julia Teresa Quiroz, *The Decade of the Hispanic: An Economic Retrospective*, 1990.

The nature of jobs coming out of the restructuring disadvantaged the newest groups to enter the work force. In part, this is because casual part-time jobs, or those defined as less than 35 hours per week, constituted nearly one quarter of net job creation. . . . Employment throughout the 1980s has also been characterized by a sharp decline in real wages. Lower wages resulted from the replacement of high-wage manufacturing by lower-paying service employment and increase of less stable jobs, but also from a stationary minimum wage. In 1981, the federal minimum wage was set at $3.35 per hour, and did not change until 1990. Because the minimum wage is set in nominal terms, inflation eroded its value over time. In 1991, a full-time minimum-wage worker earned $8,840 per year, which was 3% below the federal poverty level for a family of three and 26% below the poverty level for a family of four. From 1973 to 1990 the average weekly wage dropped from $315 to $258 (inflation-adjusted to 1982 dollars), thereby erasing half of the gains in real wages made since World War II.

Real wages fell more rapidly during recessions and never fully recovered during expansions. With each setback, wages became more unequally distributed. The growing inequality of wages is captured in statistics that show that from 1979 to 1987, real wages of male workers between the ages of 25 and 64 declined an average of 2% per year among the bottom one fifth of the wage distribution, but increased by 0.5% among those in the highest one fifth. For females the data are slightly less negative, but similar in outcome.

The nature of the new employment structure has hurt both whites and minorities, though the burden has been far greater for people of color. Nearly 60% of net new employment since 1979 held by all workers paid poverty level wages, yet at the other extreme, 17.6% of net new white employment was in jobs that pay three times the poverty level. . . .

The paradox of economic growth and income inequality is multidimensional. At one level it is an outcome of economic restructuring. When probed deeper, the situation appears to be tied to problems of greater job instability, lower wages, declining social services, the urban concentration of less educated minorities and immigrants, a spatial mismatch of jobs to workers, and a process of environmental deterioration. In the face of these trends, Latinos entering the labor market in the last decade have encountered difficult conditions. For many, the outcome has been unstable employment, diminished job opportunities, and extreme impoverishment.

The Latino Profile

Latinos in the United States display several distinct characteristics: high rates of immigration and reproduction, low levels of education, high rates of urbanization, concentration in low-paying jobs, and high levels of poverty. These traits are both cause and consequence of the restructuring.

The U.S. Bureau of the Census reports that during the 1980s the Hispanic population increased by 34%, as opposed to 7% for

176

the non-Hispanic population. Immigration is a major contributor, with approximately one half of the growth resulting from net migration. Reproduction is also high, as shown in an overall fertility rate among Hispanic women of 106 births per 1,000 women as opposed to 67 for non-Hispanic women. The high rates of immigration and reproduction are reflected in a population that is younger than that of the nation as a whole. Latinos maintain a median age of 25 years against a national median of 32 years.

Youth and immigrant status have contributed to a less educated population. In 1986, only half of adults 25 and older were high school graduates, as compared to more than three fourths of all whites and more than three fifths of African Americans. Only 1 in 10 Latinos was a college graduate. In the decade from 1980 to 1990, the white population realized an increase in college enrollment from 31.8% to 39.4%, and African Americans saw a gain from 27.6% to 33.0%, but Latinos suffered a decline from 29.8% to 29.0%. Therefore, this group has entered the labor force with fewer acquired skills than the average for the nation.

Low Wages and Losing Ground

Latinos are also an overwhelmingly urban population. Their rates of urbanization (90%) far exceed those for the nation as a whole (75%), and they are clustered in the most dynamic metropolitan areas of the United States, such as Los Angeles and New York, and those areas most exposed to international influences, such as Miami. As a consequence, their concerns are integrally tied to those of the nation's metropolises.

Within these labor markets, Latinos reveal low occupational attainment. In 1988, Latino men were more likely to be employed as production workers and less likely to be managers than the population as a whole, and Latinas were more likely to be operators or in service occupations and less likely to be employed in managerial or technical occupations than the general population. Low-wage occupational concentration is particularly evident among Mexicans and Puerto Ricans, though it exists among all subgroups. Latinos are not only low-wage workers, but after adjusting for inflation, they have lost ground with respect to wages in recent years. Latino men averaged $49 per year *less* in 1987 than in 1978. In part this was because 23.8% of these Latino men were minimum-wage workers.

These forces translate into low average incomes. The average family income among Latinos fell by 12.7% from 1978 to 1982 after adjusting for inflation (a drop of $1,585), compared to 9.5% among white families, and 15.5% among African Americans. In the period of economic recovery from 1982 to 1987, the average income of white families grew by 11.4%, and 13% among African Americans, but only 6.3% among Latinos. In 1987, 6 out of every 10 Latino families were among the poorest two fifths of the total population, but only 1 in 10 was among the wealthiest one fifth. Latinos are clearly overrepresented at the economic bottom.

Latinos Fall Further into Poverty

Poverty has thus become a pressing issue. From 1978 to 1987, Latino poverty rose nearly one third, from 21.6% to 28.2%. By contrast, the poverty rates for both whites and African Americans reflected a much smaller increase (from 8.7% to 10.5% for whites and from 30.6% to 33.1% for African Americans). With each recession, Latinos fell further into poverty.

Though poverty and inequality are concerns shared by all Latinos, they are of greatest immediacy for Puerto Ricans, Mexicans, and certain recent immigrant groups such as Dominicans. Puerto Ricans display the greatest distress with 40.3% classified as poor in 1987, the highest rate for any racial or ethnic group in the nation. This was followed by Mexicans at 28.3%, up from the 1978 level of 20.6%. Family poverty rates were 37.9% for Puerto Ricans, and 25.5% for Mexicans, followed by Other Hispanics (26.1%), Central and South Americans (18.9%), and Cubans (13.8%).

Against this profile, we can start to construct a logic for Latino impoverishment and low economic standing. According to prevailing views, impoverishment among many is the result of unemployment. In 1991 when the unemployment rate for the nation as a whole was 6.7%, it was 9.4% for Hispanics. Among the subgroups, these figures were 11.8% for Puerto Ricans, 9.6% for Mexicans, 8.5% for Cubans, and 8.2% for Other Hispanics. . . . In addition, poverty is increasingly linked with single-parent families. Approximately half of the Hispanic families living below the poverty level are headed by women. This problem is most apparent among Puerto Ricans, with the highest rate of families headed by females (43%).

Few Options for Improvement

For those still in the work force, persistent poverty appears to be directly linked to the erosion of wages, the nature of Latino employment, and cutbacks in government assistance—or structural and institutional causes—in concert with certain specific attributes of this population that shape their employability—or aspects of human capital. These factors interact to disadvantage Latinos as they enter the work force and provide few options for improving the situation.

Thus, because of Latino concentration in low-wage jobs, erosion of the minimum wage affected Latinos more severely than the general population. The proliferation of low-wage employment and loss of opportunities for upward mobility created structural barriers to advancement. These barriers were aggravated by unresolved problems of wage discrimination.

Further, layered upon the problematic transformation of an economy and society are the limitations of the people themselves. Low educational status has been repeatedly linked to poor economic performance among Latinos. The influx of new immigrants with low educational attainment, combined with the failure of schools to meet the needs of Latino students and inadequate on-the-job training, all contribute to wage and income polarization.

And because Latinos are largely urbanized, they disproportionately feel the effects of the suburbanization of better paying jobs, and loss of support from government programs and social expenditures upon urban areas. Sharp federal program cuts throughout the 1980s had their most detrimental effect on low-income households. As Latinos constitute 9%-17% of the beneficiaries of low-income programs (or twice their level of representation in the population) they were about twice as likely to feel the loss as the population as a whole. . . .

Latinos have historically constituted a perversely appropriated stock of low-cost, easily expendable labor. This function was not predicated on citizenship or language, as some of the most impoverished were citizens and English speakers. Rather it was an issue of redefining the workings of the labor market to make it more responsive to the competitive climate at the expense of Latino and other low-wage labor. Though this economic strategy was, in fact, fed by high rates of immigration, and by high numbers of new Latino entrants into the labor force, it was reinforced by national policies designed to encourage unfettered market competition through notions of labor market flexibility. This concept of flexibility, which could be applied selectively prior to the most recent restructuring, is universal today. . . .

Latinos Bear the Brunt of Restructuring

Latinos in the U.S. economy . . . have all too frequently absorbed the brunt of economic risks and provided flexibility in the labor market. . . . The recent surge in inequality has produced (a) a widening gap between minority male and white male incomes as minority male incomes fell more rapidly, (b) a widening between minority female and white female incomes despite trends toward a closing of the gender income gap, and (c) a more rapidly widening income gap within Latino and African-American populations than among whites. The principal dynamics driving increased wage inequality since the mid-1970s are (a) a widening gap between higher- and lower-income wage earners and a declining share of middle-income earners, (b) a

179

widening gap between a white concentration in upper-income groups and a disproportionate minority concentration in lower-income groups, (c) a widening gap between immigrant and non-immigrant incomes, (d) widening gaps between high and low educational achievement, and (e) renewed or increased ethnoracial wage discrimination. From this aggregate analysis, the significance of direct racism, or differences in earnings not accounted for by age, education, or experience, is shown to be less important in explaining why Latinos are doing poorly in the U.S. labor market than are structural and human capital variables.

"Hispanics are [wrongly] perceived to be a disadvantaged minority—poorly educated, concentrated in barrios, economically impoverished."

The Extent of Hispanic Poverty Is Exaggerated

Linda Chavez

Statistics on the achievements of Hispanic Americans are skewed by the continuing immigration of unskilled, uneducated, non-English-speaking Hispanics into this country, charges Linda Chavez in the following viewpoint. While Hispanic leaders complain of a lack of economic progress for Hispanic Americans, she asserts, they ignore the achievements of many, especially those who were born in the United States. Contrary to the prevailing picture, she says, most Hispanic Americans have moved into the economic mainstream. Chavez is the author of *Out of the Barrio: Toward a New Politics of Hispanic Assimilation*, from which this viewpoint is taken.

As you read, consider the following questions:

1. According to Chavez, who are the "most invisible Hispanics" today?
2. How did Cubans achieve economic success in the United States, according to the author?
3. According to Chavez, what evidence do Hispanic advocates use to prove Mexican Americans are permanently disadvantaged? How does she refute this argument?

"Each decade offered us hope, but our hopes evaporated into smoke. We became the poorest of the poor, the most segregated minority in schools, the lowest paid group in America and the least educated minority in this nation." This view of Hispanics' progress by the president of the National Council of La Raza [Raul Yzaguirre], one of the country's leading Hispanic civil rights groups, is the prevalent one among Hispanic leaders and is shared by many outside the Hispanic community as well. By and large, Hispanics are perceived to be a disadvantaged minority—poorly educated, concentrated in barrios, economically impoverished; with little hope of participating in the American Dream. This perception has not changed substantially in twenty-five years. And it is wrong.

Hispanics have been called the invisible minority, and indeed they were for many years, largely because most Hispanics lived in the Southwest and the Northeast, away from the most blatant discrimination of the Deep South. But the most invisible Hispanics today are those who have been absorbed into the mainstream. The success of middle-class Hispanics is an untold—and misunderstood—story perhaps least appreciated by Hispanic advocates whose interest is in promoting the view that Latinos cannot make it in this society. The Hispanic poor, who constitute only about one-fourth of the Hispanic population, are visible to all. These are the Hispanics most likely to be studied, analyzed, and reported on and certainly the ones most likely to be read about. A computer search of stories about Hispanics in major newspapers and magazines over a twelve-month period turned up more than eighteen hundred stories in which the word *Hispanic* or *Latino* occurred within a hundred words of the word *poverty*. In most people's minds, the expression *poor Hispanic* is almost redundant.

Has Hispanics' Progress Stalled?

Most Hispanics, rather than being poor, lead solidly lower-middle- or middle-class lives, but finding evidence to support this thesis is sometimes difficult. Of course, Hispanic groups vary one from another, as do individuals within any group. Most analysts acknowledge, for example, that Cubans are highly successful. Within one generation, they have virtually closed the earnings and education gap with other Americans. Although some analysts claim that the success of Cubans is due exclusively to their higher socioeconomic status when they arrived, many Cuban refugees—especially those who came after the first wave in the 1960s—were in fact skilled or semiskilled workers with relatively little education. Their accomplishments in the United States are attributable in large measure to diligence and hard work. They established enclave economies, in the traditional immigrant mode, opening restaurants, stores, and other émigré-oriented services. Some Cubans were able to get a foothold in industries not usually available to immigrants. They formed banks, specializing in international transactions attuned to Latin American as well as local customers, and made major investments in real estate development in south Florida. These ventures provided big profits for only a few Cubans but jobs for many more. By 1980 Miami boasted some two hundred Cuban millionaires and 18,000 Cuban-owned businesses, and about 70 percent of all Cubans there owned their own homes (a rate that exceeds that of whites generally). But Cubans are as a rule dismissed as the exception among Hispanics. What about other Hispanic groups? Why has there been no "progress" among them?

The Fight Is to Be Treated the Same

The history of American ethnic groups is one of overcoming disadvantage, of competing with those who were already here and proving themselves as competent as any who came before. Their fight was always to be treated the same as other Americans, never to be treated as special, certainly not to turn the temporary disadvantages they suffered into the basis for permanent entitlement. Anyone who thinks this fight was easier in the early part of this century when it was waged by other ethnic groups does not know history. Hispanics have not always had an easy time of it in the United States. Even though discrimination against Mexican Americans and Puerto Ricans was not as severe as it was against blacks, acceptance has come only with struggle, and some prejudices still exist. Discrimination against Hispanics, or any other group, should be fought, and there are laws and a massive administrative apparatus to do so. But the way to eliminate such discrimination is not to classify all Hispanics as victims and treat them as if they could not succeed by their own efforts. Hispanics can and will prosper in the United States by following the example of the millions before them.

Linda Chavez, *Out of the Barrio: Toward a New Politics of Hispanic Assimilation*, 1991.

The largest and most important group is the Mexican American population. Its leaders have driven much of the policy agenda affecting all Hispanics, but the importance of Mexican Americans also stems from their having a longer history in the United States than does any other Hispanic group. If Mexican Americans whose families have lived in the United States for generations are not yet making it in this society, they may have a legitimate claim to consider themselves a more or less permanently disadvantaged group, like blacks. That is precisely what Mexican American leaders suggest is happening. Their proof is that statistical measures of Mexican American achievement in education, earnings, poverty rates, and other social and economic indicators have remained largely unchanged for decades. In 1959 the median income of Mexican-origin males in the Southwest was 57 percent that of non-Hispanics. In 1989 it was still 57 percent of non-Hispanic income. If Mexican Americans had made progress, it would show up in improved education attainment and earnings and in lower poverty rates, so the argument goes. Since it doesn't, progress must be stalled.

In the post-civil rights era, the failure of a minority to close the social and economic gap with whites is assumed to be the result of persistent discrimination. Progress is perceived not in absolute but in relative terms. The poor may become less poor over time, but so long as those on the upper rungs of the economic ladder are climbing even faster, the poor are believed to have suffered some harm, even if they have made absolute gains and their lives are much improved. However, in order for Hispanics (or any group on the lower rungs) to close the gap, they must progress at an even greater rate than non-Hispanic whites; their apparent failure to do so in recent years causes Hispanic leaders and the public to conclude that Hispanics are falling behind. Is this a fair way to judge Hispanics' progress? In fact, it makes almost no sense to apply this test today (if it ever did), because the Hispanic population itself is changing so rapidly. This is most true of the Mexican-origin population.

New Immigrants Skew Statistics

In 1959 the overwhelming majority of persons of Mexican origin living in the United States were native-born, 85 percent. Today only about two-thirds of the people of Mexican origin were born in the United States, and among adults barely one in two was born here. Increasingly, the Hispanic population, including that of Mexican origin, is made up of new immigrants, who, like immigrants of every era, start off at the bottom of the economic ladder. This infusion of new immigrants is bound to distort our image of progress in the Hispanic population, if each time we measure the group we include people who have just arrived and have yet to make their way in this society.

A simple analogy illustrates the point. Suppose we compared the achievement of two classes of students in the same grade as measured by a standardized test administered at the beginning and the end of the school year, but the only information by which we could assess progress was the mean score for the class. Let's say that the mean score for Class A was 100 points on the initial test, a score right at the national average, and that

Class B scored 75. In the test given at the end of the school year, Class A scored 150 (again the national average) and Class B scored 110. Both classes made progress, but Class B still had not eliminated the gap between it and Class A and remained significantly below the national average. Having only this information, we would be justified in believing that students in Class B were continuing to lag in educational achievement.

But suppose we discovered that Class B had grown by one-half by the time the second test was given and that the other class had remained stable. In Class A thirty students took the test at the beginning of the school year, and the same thirty took it at the end. In Class B, however, fifteen new students were added to the class between the first and the second test. We would have no way of knowing what the average final test score meant in terms of the overall achievement of students in Class B until we knew more about the new students. Suppose we then found out that half of them were recent, non-English-speaking immigrants. We could reasonably assume that the addition of even five such students would skew the test results for the entire class, presumably lowering the class mean. Unless we had more information, though, we still wouldn't know what exact effect the scores of the new students had on the class mean or how much progress the original students had actually made over the year.

Hispanic Leaders Ignore the Obvious

Hispanics in the United States—and the Mexican-origin population in particular—are very much like Class B. In 1980 there were about 14.6 million Hispanics living in the United States; in 1990, nearly 21 million, an increase of about 44 percent in one decade. At least one-half of this increase was the result of immigration, legal and illegal. This influx consists mostly of poorly educated persons, with minimal skills, who cannot speak English. Not surprisingly, when these Hispanics are added to the pool being measured, the achievement levels of the whole group fall. It is almost inconceivable that the addition of two or three million new immigrants to the Hispanic pool would not seriously distort evidence of Hispanics' progress during the decade. Yet no major Hispanic organization will acknowledge the validity of this reasonable assumption. Instead, Hispanic leaders complain, "Hispanics are the population that has benefitted least from the economic recovery" [National Council of La Raza]. "The Myth of Hispanic Progress" is the title of a study by a Mexican American professor, Jorge Chapa, purporting to show that "it is simply wrong to assume that Hispanics are making gradual progress towards parity with Anglos." "Hispanic poverty is now comparable to that of blacks and is expected to exceed it by the end of this decade," warns the Hispanic Policy Development Project.

Hispanics wear disadvantage almost like a badge of distinction, as if groups were competing with each other for the title "most disadvantaged." Sadly, the most frequently heard complaint among Hispanic leaders is not that the public ignores evidence of Hispanics' achievement but that it underestimates their disadvantage. "More than any group in American political history, Hispanic Americans have turned to the national statistical system as an instrument for advancing their political and economic interests, by making visible the magnitude of social and economic problems they face," says a Rockefeller Foundation official, Kenneth Prewitt. But gathering all Hispanics together under one umbrella obscures as much information as it illuminates, and may make Hispanics—especially the native born—appear to suffer greater social and economic problems than they actually do.

In fact, a careful examination of the voluminous data on the Hispanic population gathered by the Census Bureau and other federal agencies shows that, as a group, Hispanics have made progress in this society and that most of them have moved into the social and economic mainstream. In most respects, Hispanics—particularly those born here—are very much like other Americans: they work hard, support their own families without outside assistance, have more education and higher earnings than their parents, and own their own home. In short, they are pursuing the American Dream—with increasing success.

Periodical Bibliography

The following articles have been selected to supplement the diverse views presented in this chapter.

Douglas J. Besharov — "The Moral Voice of Welfare Reform," *Responsive Community*, Spring 1993. Available from 714 Gelman Library, George Washington University, Washington, DC 20052.

John Sibley Butler — "Self-Help and Adjustment to American Society," *Agenda*, Fall 1990. Available from NCNE, 1367 Connecticut Ave. NW, Washington, DC 20036.

Ron Daniels — "Confronting the 'State of Emergency,'" *Z Magazine*, June 1993.

Ruth Denny — "Indian Casinos Hit the Jackpot," *Utne Reader*, November/December 1992.

John Hood — "Children's Crusade," *Reason*, June 1992.

Paul Klebnikov — "Showing Big Daddy the Door," *Forbes*, November 9, 1992.

Sylvester Monroe — "The Gospel of Equity," *Time*, May 10, 1993.

Victor Perlo — "Racism and Poverty," *Political Affairs*, February 1993.

Sue Anne Pressley — "Poverty by Government Decree," *The Washington Post National Weekly Edition*, July 19-25, 1993.

Barbara Ransby — "The Undeclared War on Black Women," *Crossroads*, February 1993.

David Segal — "Dances with Sharks," *The Washington Monthly*, March 1992.

Andrew E. Serwer — "American Indians Discover Money Is Power," *Fortune*, April 19, 1993.

Richard Vedder and Lowell Gallaway — "Declining Black Employment," *Society*, July/August 1993.

Roger Wilkins — "Don't Blame the Great Society," *The Progressive*, July 1992.

Alan Wolfe — "The New American Dilemma," *The New Republic*, April 13, 1992.

Elizabeth Wright — "Opportunities Unlimited: A Black Success Story," *Issues and Views*, Summer 1992. Available from PO Box 467, New York, NY 10025.

Why Does an American Underclass Exist?

POVERTY

Chapter Preface

Nearly as much rhetoric has been expended on what to call that segment of society that is mired in urban poverty as on examining the causes of and possible cures for their enduring destitution. Jason DeParle credits William Julius Wilson with legitimizing the term *underclass* in his 1987 book, *The Truly Disadvantaged*. But by 1990, Wilson said, the word had become "hopelessly polluted in meaning." While he intended the term to refer to inner-city dwellers restricted by cultural factors, he complained that some used it pejoratively in arguments that the poor created their own situation, and it had picked up a racist connotation. Wilson suggested a substitute: *ghetto poor.*

Why such agonizing over a word? The answer lies in the attempts to assign blame for the circumstances of the nation's most hopelessly impoverished. Consider the impact of *homeless* versus *bum*, or *hobo* versus *tramp* or *vagrant*. Similarly, *ghetto poor* implies an external cause of poverty—the situation into which one is born, perhaps—that is not acknowledged by such terms as Victorian England's *undeserving poor.*

The undeserving poor of the last century were those able-bodied people who did not work hard enough to support themselves: sots and lazybones, the sluggish and the shiftless. The deserving poor, on the other hand, were generally widows and their children, orphans, the extremely elderly, and the ill or disabled. Society accepted an obligation to provide some support for the deserving poor, many of whom felt ashamed of having to accept charity, but the undeserving poor were on their own.

By contrast, today's qualifications for deserving help have been stretched beyond the Victorian's ability to comprehend. Extensive welfare programs are buttressed by a rhetoric of "entitlement to benefits" that seeks to nullify the stigma of charity. Some see such welfare programs as morally right and necessary, society's obligation to a deserving poor who are incapacitated not by age or illness, but by society's structures and failures. Others believe such programs sap the will or desire of recipients to better themselves. They feel that welfare for the undeserving poor has created the underclass.

The authors of the following viewpoints take strong stands on the ever-shifting concept of deserving and undeserving poor as they debate why an American underclass has developed—why the inner-city ghettoes are now filled not with hard workers just passing through on their way to a better life, but with generations of people who see no way out of poverty.

"The underclass . . . makes urban life at the comfortable levels of well-being not only pleasant but possible."

Capitalism Relies on a Permanent Underclass

John Kenneth Galbraith

The underclass serves a crucial role in preserving the comfort of the wealthy, argues well-known economist John Kenneth Galbraith in the following viewpoint. Galbraith notes that in the past, the underclass—those who worked for low pay in unpleasant jobs—was a temporary stop on the way up for those who were escaping even worse conditions. But economic growth in the United States has slowed and many companies have found cheaper unskilled labor in other countries. Thus, the author finds, not only is the underclass a permanent part of the economic system but succeeding generations now find themselves locked in poverty. Galbraith is the Paul M. Warburg Professor of Economics Emeritus at Harvard University.

As you read, consider the following questions:

1. What two kinds of work does Galbraith discuss?
2. According to the author, what was the major reason for the immigration legislation of 1990?
3. Galbraith notes that in the past, members of the underclass were not necessarily discontented with their lot. What does he believe has changed to increase their unrest?

On no matter is American social thought in its accepted and popular manifestation more insistent than on social class or, more specifically, the absence thereof in the United States. We have a classless society; to this we point with considerable pride. The social mythology of the Republic is built on the concept of classlessness—the belief, as President George Bush once put it, that class is "for European democracies or something else—it isn't for the United States of America. We are not going to be divided by class."

Yet truth, if sufficiently obvious and inescapable, does obtrude. Presidential oratory, however well-intended and even eloquent, does not serve entirely to suppress it. Determinedly and irrevocably into the American language has come the modern reference to "the underclass." There are individuals and families that, it is conceded, do not share the comfortable well-being of the prototypical American. These people, this class, are concentrated in the centers of the great cities or, less visibly, on deprived farms, as rural migrant labor or in erstwhile mining communities. Or they are the more diffused poor of the Old South and of the region of the Rio Grande in Texas. The greater part of the underclass consists of members of minority groups, blacks or people of Hispanic origin. While the most common reference is to the underclass of the great cities, this is at least partly because its presence there is the most inescapably apparent.

So much is accepted. What is not accepted, and indeed is little mentioned, is that the underclass is integrally a part of a larger economic process and, more importantly, that it serves the living standard and the comfort of the more favored community. Economic progress would be far more uncertain and certainly far less rapid without it. The economically fortunate, not excluding those who speak with greatest regret of the existence of this class, are heavily dependent on its presence.

The underclass is deeply functional; all industrial countries have one in greater or lesser measure and in one form or another. As some of its members escape from deprivation and its associated compulsions, a resupply becomes essential. But on few matters, it must be added, is even the most sophisticated economic and social comment more reticent. The picture of an economic and political system in which social exclusion, however unforgiving, is somehow a remediable affliction is all but required. Here, in highly compelling fashion, the social convenience of the contented replaces the clearly visible reality.

The Definition of *Work*

Appreciation of this reality begins with the popular, indeed obligatory, definition of work. Work, in the conventional view, is pleasant and rewarding; it is something in which all favored by occupation rejoice to a varying degree. A normal person is proud of his or her work.

In practical fact, much work is repetitive, tedious, painfully fatiguing, mentally boring or socially demeaning. This is true of diverse consumer and household services and the harvesting of farm crops, and is equally true in those industries that deploy workers on assembly lines, where labor cost is a major factor in the price of what is finally produced. Only, or in any case primarily, when this nexus between labor cost and price is broken or partly disassociated, invariably at higher income levels, does work become pleasant and, in fact, enjoyed. It is a basic but rarely articulated feature of the modern economic system that the highest pay is given for the work that is most prestigious and most agreeable. This is at the opposite extreme from those occupations that are inherently invidious, those that place the individual directly under the command of another, as in the case of the doorman or the household servant, and those involving a vast range of tasks—street cleaning, garbage collection, janitorial services, elevator operation—that have an obtrusive connotation of social inferiority.

There is no greater modern illusion, even fraud, than the use of the single term *work* to cover what for some is, as noted, dreary, painful or socially demeaning and what for others is enjoyable, socially reputable and economically rewarding. Those who spend pleasant, well-compensated days say with emphasis that they have been "hard at work," thereby suppressing the notion that they are a favored class. They are, of course, allowed to say that they enjoy their work, but it is presumed that such enjoyment is shared by any *good* worker. In a brief moment of truth, we speak, when sentencing criminals, of years at "hard labor." Otherwise we place a common gloss over what is agreeable and what, to a greater or lesser extent, is endured or suffered.

A Continuing Need for Workers Who Are Poor

From the foregoing comes one of the basic facts of modern economic society: the poor in our economy are needed to do the work that the more fortunate do not do and would find manifestly distasteful, even distressing. And a continuing supply and resupply of such workers is always needed. That is because later generations do not wish to follow their parents into physically demanding, socially unacceptable or otherwise disagreeable occupations; they escape or seek to escape the heavy lifting to a more comfortable and rewarding life. This we fully understand and greatly approve; it is what education is generally meant to accomplish. But from this comes the need for the resupply or, less agreeably, for keeping some part of the underclass in continued and deferential subjection. . . .

In the latter years of the last century and until World War I, American mass-employment industry and the less agreeable urban occupations drew their work force extensively from Eastern Europe as well as from the labor surplus of American farms. As this supply diminished, poor whites from the Appalachian plateau and, in greatly increasing numbers, blacks from the South moved to take their place. The assembly plants and body shops of Detroit were once staffed by workers from the adjacent farms and small towns of Michigan and Ontario, as well as by immigrants from Poland and elsewhere in Europe. As that generation went on to personally more attractive or socially more distinguished occupations, the assembly lines there reached out to more distant refugees from poor farming and mining areas and to the erstwhile sharecroppers and other deprived rural workers of the Deep South. With the latter recruitment Detroit became a city of largely black population; the automobile industry would not have survived had it had to rely on the sons and daughters of its original workers. Nor would many other public and private services have been available in tolerable form.

Stahler. © *Cincinnati Post*. Reprinted with permission.

In more recent times, migration from Mexico, Latin America and the West Indies has become a general source of such labor. For many years now, legal provision has been made for the importation of workers for the harvesting of fruit and vegetables, there being very specific acknowledgment that this is something native-born Americans cannot be persuaded in the necessary numbers to do. There is here, somewhat exceptionally, a clear legal perception of the role of the underclass.

In the immigration legislation of 1990, there was at last some official recognition of the more general and continuing need for immigrant labor. Although much of the discussion of this measure turned on the opening of the door to needed skilled workers (and compassionately to relatives of earlier migrants), the larger purpose was not in doubt. There would be a new and necessary recruitment of men and women to do the tasks of the underclass. Avoided only was mention of such seemingly brutal truth. It is not thought appropriate to say that the modern economy—the market system—requires such an underclass, and certainly not that it must reach out to other countries to sustain and refresh it.

The Darker Side

It is important to note and emphasize that the contribution of the underclass is not confined to disagreeable industrial and agricultural employment. In the modern urban community, as noted, there is a vast range of tedious or socially demeaning jobs that require unskilled, willing and adequately inexpensive labor. To this need the underclass responds, and it makes urban life at the comfortable levels of well-being not only pleasant but possible. There is, however, the darker side.

In the inner cities of the United States . . . there is a continuing threat of underclass social disorder, crime and conflict. Drug dealing, indiscriminate gunfire, other crime and family disorientation and disintegration are now all aspects of everyday existence.

In substantial part, this is because a less vigorously expanding economy and the movement of industry to economically more favored locations have denied to the underclass those relatively stable and orderly industrial employments once available in the large cities. But also, and more importantly, the normal upward movement that was for long the solvent for discontent has been arrested. The underclass has become a semipermanent rather than a generational phenomenon. There has been surprisingly little comment as to why minority communities in New York, Chicago, Los Angeles and elsewhere, once poor but benign and culturally engaging, are now centers of terror and despair. The reason is that what was a favoring upward step in economic life has now become a hopeless enthrallment.

Yet, considering the sordid life to which the modern underclass is committed, and especially when their life is compared with that of the contented majority, it is an occasion for wonder that the discontent and its more violent and aggressive manifestations are not greater than they are. One reason . . . is that for some of the underclass life in the cities, although insecure, ill-rewarded and otherwise primitive, still remains, if tenuously, better than that from which they escaped. The great black migration to the North after World War II was from a rural existence, classically that of the sharecropper, with rudimentary shelter and clothing; no health care; hard farm labor; exploitative living costs; little in the way of schooling; no voting rights; forthright, accepted and enforced racial discrimination; and, withal, extreme invisibility. Urban life, however unsatisfactory, was an improvement. So also for those moving from Puerto Rico and in the recent past from Latin America. For many the comparison is not with those who are more fortunate but with their own past position. This latter comparison and its continuing memory in the culture unquestionably has had [a] tranquilizing effect on the American underclass. . . . It is one unnoted reason, along with ineligibility because of recent arrival or illegal presence, that underclass voter turnout in elections is relatively low.

Lack of Mobility Will Cause Resentment

While the urban areas inhabited by the underclass have seen outbreaks of violence in the past, notably the widespread riots in the second half of the 1960s, the more surprising thing, nonetheless, is their relative tranquillity. This, however, is something on which no one should count in the future. It has existed in the past because, as noted, the underclass has been in the process of transition—that from a lesser life, and with the prospect of generational escape. As this process comes to an end—as membership in the underclass becomes stable and enduring—greater resentment and social unrest should be expected. A blockage in the movement upward and out of the underclass will not be accepted. However, although it will not be accepted, it will not in the ordinary course of events be anticipated.

It is not in the nature of the politics of contentment to expect or plan countering action for misfortune, even disaster, that, however predictable and predicted, is in the yet undisclosed future. Such planning, invoking as it always does public action—provision of good educational opportunity, good public housing and health care, competent attention to drug addiction, family counseling, adequate welfare payments—is systemically resisted by the contented electoral majority. In what is the accepted and, indeed, only acceptable view, the underclass is deemed the source of its own succor and well-being; in the extreme view, it requires the spur of its own poverty, and it will be damaged by any social assistance and support. None of this is, of course, quite believed; it serves, nonetheless, to justify the comfortable position and policy.

195

"It's time to . . . extend the capitalist economy across our whole society, and put it to work for all of our nation's people."

Socialist Policies Created America's Underclass

Jack Kemp

As the rest of the world looks to America for advice on democracy and capitalism, it is time to apply our knowledge right here at home, says Jack Kemp, former secretary of the U.S. Department of Housing and Urban Development in the following viewpoint. The democratic capitalist economy works for those who are in it, but welfare has led to a second, socialist economy in America, which creates rather than alleviates poverty. A return to capitalist principles for the entire population, Kemp asserts, will help the poor reenter the mainstream economy.

As you read, consider the following questions:

1. How did the desire to help the poor lead to increased poverty, according to Kemp?
2. According to the author, what do the poor want?
3. Why does the author believe that cutting the capital gains tax (the tax on the profit made when an asset is sold for more than it cost) would benefit the poor?

From Jack Kemp's speech "An Inquiry into the Nature and Causes of Poverty in America and How to Combat It," delivered at the Heritage Foundation, June 6, 1990.

All around the world, despite the resistance of the old guard, freedom and free markets, democracy and capitalism are increasingly on the march. From Eastern Europe and Latin America to Africa and Asia and even the Soviet Union, people are dreaming of freedom and democracy after decades and even centuries of oppression, poverty, despair, and debt. . . .

Yet, in such revolutionary times, Charles Dickens's observation on the French Revolution may well still apply: it can be the best of times and the worst of times simultaneously. Here in the U.S., we're enjoying unprecedented economic growth and opportunity, yet . . . there are some parts of our nation and all too many of our people left out and left behind, suffering from the tragedy of homelessness, poverty that stretches over generations, and a sense of hopelessness and despair about the future.

As [Heritage Foundation president] Ed Feulner said, the world is looking to us for advice on the free market ideas of Adam Smith: "They don't want lectures on income redistribution and capitalist exploitation, they want income and capitalism."

Ed is right; but . . . I know that not only is Eastern Europe looking to us for market-oriented answers, but so is East Harlem, East St. Louis, and East L.A.

If we are to present the example of democratic capitalism and the rule of law to the rest of the world, we've got to make it work for the low-income people and distressed neighborhoods and communities right here in our own country. . . .

Poor People Want Opportunity

Traveling across the country, I've seen thousands upon thousands of low-income people and families in public housing communities eagerly seeking change and responding positively to our ideas. They don't want more government promises and egalitarian welfare schemes, they want to live in neighborhoods free from crime and drug abuse, with good jobs and opportunities to own property and homes; they want quality education so that they and their children can live better lives. They want what we all want—a chance to develop their talent, potential, and possibilities.

Our friend Kimi Gray of Kenilworth-Parkside said that her residents and public housing tenants throughout the country may be registered Democrats, but they work with Republicans because Republicans are "the ones that seem to understand that we do not want to stay a poor and permanent underclass."

Well, of course that's true. And that's how Mr. Lincoln built the Republican Party. As he said, "When one starts poor, as most do in the race of life, free society is such that he knows he can better his condition: he knows that there is no fixed condition for his whole life."

A debate over how to increase the wealth and opportunities of the poor plays to the strengths of our Party's Lincoln wing—our most authentic roots.The Democrats will win any debate over redistribution. After all, that's what they are on this earth for. But that's the debate of yesterday. Today's debate is how to tap and unleash the wealth, talent, and potential in low-income communities and cities all over America.

A Tale of Two Economies

In 1984, Governor Mario Cuomo of New York electrified the Democratic Convention with his tale of America as two cities, one rich and one poor, permanently divided into two classes. He talked about the rich growing richer and the poor becoming poorer, with the conclusion that class conflict, if not warfare, was the only result, and redistribution of wealth was the solution.

But with all due respect to Governor Cuomo, he got it wrong. America is not divided immutably into two static classes. But it is separated or divided into two economies. One economy—our mainstream economy—is democratic capitalist, market-oriented, entrepreneurial, and incentivized for working families whether in labor or management. This mainstream rewards work, investment, saving, and productivity. Incentives abound for productive human, economic, and social behavior.

It was this economy led by President Ronald Reagan's supply-side revolution of tax rate cuts in 1981 that generated 21.5 million new jobs, more than 4 million new business enterprises, relatively low inflation, and higher standards of living for most of our people. This economy has created more jobs in the 1980s than all Europe, Canada, and Japan combined. And according to the U.S. Treasury, federal income taxes paid by the top 1 percent of taxpayers surged by over 80 percent—up from $51 billion in 1981 to $92 billion in 1987. Harvard and White House economist Lawrence Lindsey estimates that by 1985, economic output was between 2 and 3 percent higher than it would have been without the tax cut.

But the best news of the eighties was that good policies lead to good results, confirming what deep down we always understood, that the real wealth of America comes not from our physical resources, but our human resources; not from things, but from ideas.

But there is another economy—a second economy that is similar in respects to the Eastern European or Third World "socialist" economy if you will—and it is almost totally opposite to the way people are treated in our mainstream capitalist economy, and it predominates in the pockets of poverty throughout urban and rural America. This economy has barriers to productive human and social activity and a virtual absence of economic incentive and rewards that deny entry to Black, Hispanic and other minority men and women into the mainstream, almost as effectively as hiring notices 50 years ago that read "no Blacks (or Hispanics or Irish or whatever) need apply."

Noble Intentions Gone Awry

The irony is that the second economy was set up not out of malevolence, but out of a desire to help the poor, alleviate suffering, and provide a basic social safety net. But while the intentions were noble, the results led to a counterproductive economy. Instead of independence, it led to dependency. In an effort to minimize economic pain, it maximized welfare bureaucracy and social costs that are near pathological.

Now, let's pause, and step away from our orthodox notions and examine this from afar. What if you wanted to create poverty. What policies and principles would you use to destroy the economy of cities and make people dependent on government? How would you do it? Let me offer some suggestions:

1. Impose steeply graduated and progressive tax rates and then inflate the currency to push people into ever higher tax brackets.
2. Reward welfare and unemployment at a higher level than working and productivity.
3. Tax the entrepreneur who succeeds in the legal capitalistic system much higher than in the illicit underground economy.
4. Reward people who stay in public housing more than those who want to move up and out into private housing and homeownership.
5. Reward the family that breaks up rather than the family that stays together.
6. Encourage debt, borrowing, and spending rather than saving, investing, and risk-taking.
7. But most of all, if you really wanted to create poverty and dependency, weaken and in some cases destroy the link between effort and reward.

Examples abound of how Third World disincentives have created poverty in inner cities. I read a *Wall Street Journal* article about a woman on welfare in Milwaukee, Wisconsin, who tried to put away a few pennies, nickels, dimes, and dollars so that one day she could do what every other mother wants to do, send her daughter to college. She managed to build a savings account of just over $3,000, but there was a catch. The social welfare agency said she was violating welfare rules. She was taken into court, prosecuted for fraud, and fined $15,000. But since she didn't have $15,000, they just took her $3,000, gave her a year's sentence in jail, but suspended it.

Guess what? According to the same *Wall Street Journal* article, she now spends every cent she gets, and she must rely on government subsidies to pay for just about everything. . . .

The good news is that government policies can change and that good policy can lead to good results. Productive human effort can be promoted, behavior can be modified or altered. Work effort can be unleashed. The forces that cause poverty can be reversed. President Bush said that for these seeds of productive behavior to grow, we must "give people—working people, poor people, all our citizens—control over their own lives. And it means a commitment to civil rights and economic opportunity for every American."

Welfare Promotes Self-Destructive Behavior

The problem with the welfare state is not the level of spending, it is that nearly all of this expenditure actively promotes self-destructive behavior among the poor. Current welfare may best be conceptualized as a system that offers each single mother a "paycheck" worth an average of between $8,500 and $15,000 a year, depending on the state. The mother has a contract with the government: She will continue to receive her "paycheck" as long as she fulfills two conditions: 1) she does not work; and 2) she does not marry an employed male. I call this the incentive system made in hell.

Robert Rector, *Policy Review*, Summer 1992.

Along with planting a billion new trees in the decade of the nineties, we ought to plant the seeds of millions of new minority enterprises. In other words, expanding the base of capitalism and access to capital can alter the conditions of poverty. . . .

As columnist William Raspberry wrote ". . . when assets are present, people begin to think in terms of the asset. If a young mother owns her own home, she begins to pay attention to real estate values, property taxes, the cost of maintenance and so forth. . . . Note," he says, "that it is the assets themselves that create this effect, as opposed to just educational programs or exhortations toward better values."

Stuart Butler and Bob Woodson point out that to the liberals, empowerment means giving power to government to control our lives. But empowerment really means not control over others, but freedom to control one's own affairs. The poor don't want paternalism, they want opportunity—they don't want the servitude of welfare, they want to get jobs and private property. They don't want dependency, they want a new declaration of independence.

In that spirit, let me outline some ideas for a national agenda to help low-income people and our nation find the keys that will unlock the shackles and cycles of poverty and despair.

A National Agenda

First, cut the capital gains tax to 15 percent for the nation and eliminate it altogether in distressed inner cities and rural communities we would designate as Enterprise Zones. President Bush correctly implored the Democratic majority in Congress to cut the capital gains tax rate and finally—after ten years—to establish what 37 states have already implemented, Enterprise Zones, as a national policy.

The capital gains tax reduction isn't to help the rich or secure old wealth, but to free up or unlock old capital and old wealth to help new business, new risk-takers, job-creation, and economic growth. Virtually every survey shows that the major problem for inner city entrepreneurs is the absence of seed capital. The capital gains tax reduction, coupled with Enterprise Zones, will help "unlock" existing, status-quo capital to fund and support a whole new generation of budding entrepreneurs in America's inner cities where economic opportunity is needed most.

When the top capital gains tax rate was reduced from 49 percent to 20 percent, the number of small company start-ups more than doubled, rising to 640,000 and creating 15 million new jobs. By dramatically reducing the capital gains tax rates again, and greenlining inner city neighborhoods, we can expand the economy and put that enormous job-creating potential to work where it is needed most.

Not only would a lower capital gains tax rate help the poor, but it would also increase tax revenues. Lower capital gains rates would greatly increase the number of capital gains transactions passing through federal, state, and local tax gates, raise the total value of assets throughout the economy, and make the economy bigger, more efficient, and more productive.

Second, an expansion of resident management and urban homesteading in public housing can empower residents to acquire private ownership and control of their homes and receive pride and dignity of ownership.

Third, housing vouchers and certificates should be significantly increased and expanded so as to give low-income families greater choice and more freedom where to live, while expanding access to affordable housing for those most in need.

Fourth, a new version of tax reform is needed to remove low-income families from the tax rolls and dramatically increase the after-tax income of welfare mothers and unemployed fathers who go to work.

In 1948, at the median income, a family of four paid virtually no income taxes, and only $30 a year in direct Social Security taxes (1 percent). In 1990, the same family's tax burden would be over $6,000. To be comparable to 1948, the personal exemption—the tax allowance for the costs of nurturing children—would have to be well over $6,000. Instead, it is only $2,000.

Fifth, a dramatic expansion of the earned income tax credit, the creation of up to a $6,000 exemption for children under 16, and a Child Care tax credit to roll back this tax burden on low-income families and unemployed parents.

Sixth, helping homeless people who now wander aimlessly in streets or are warehoused in shelters. The Congress should pass a Shelter Plus Care program to expand community-based mental health facilities, drug abuse treatment, job training, and day care. This program will help homeless Americans get shelter, transitional housing, and support services to help them reenter the mainstream economy.

Seventh, in order to enhance education and opportunity, we've got to expand true choice and competition through magnet schools, education vouchers, tuition tax credits, and the type of choice-enhancing policies that Wisconsin state Representative Polly Williams and Detroit Councilmember Reverend Keith Butler recommend.

Eighth, Congress should pass legislation including IRAs for first-time homebuyers, the low-income housing tax credit, and Operation Bootstrap linking housing vouchers to strategies for gaining self-sufficiency.

Winning the War

My friends, over 200 years ago Adam Smith wrote the recipe for creating wealth. It was titled *An Inquiry into the Nature and Causes of the Wealth of Nations.* Today, I'm asking for an inquiry into the nature and causes of the wealth of *cities.* It's a variation on Adam Smith's theme of "natural liberty.". . . Our greatest assets are not in the wealth we see around us but the potential which is unseen . . . in the minds yet to be educated, in the businesses not yet opened, the technologies not yet discovered, the jobs waiting to be created. Wealth is not what we've done, but what we have yet to do.

This is a country of dreams. America has long dreamed of a better future for people everywhere. America's permanent revolution has brought a fresh air of freedom that's blowing around the world. Yes, it's a struggle. Yes, we need to stay strong. Yes, we need to maintain our alliances. Yes, we must maintain peace through strength. But also it's time to bring the revolution back home to America to extend the capitalist economy across our whole society, and put it to work for all of our nation's people.

"What produced the good life for individuals did not produce it for cities."

American Values Created the Underclass

James Q. Wilson

The rising tide of prosperity enabled productive people to desert the cities, leaving only the poor and criminals, according to James Q. Wilson, author of the following viewpoint. Wilson, a well-known political scientist and professor of management at UCLA who has advised presidents on urban policy, charts an expansion of personal freedom in the United States and examines the seeming contradictions of democracy. While most people thought that prosperity would produce widespread decency, the author believes a triumvirate of cherished American values—prosperity, freedom, and democracy—has contributed to the creation and entrenchment of the underclass in America's cities.

As you read, consider the following questions:

1. How, according to the author, has prosperity contributed to the creation and perpetuation of the urban underclass?
2. What examples does Wilson give of the two ways freedom has expanded in the United States in the past thirty years?
3. Why has democracy failed to solve the problems of the urban underclass, in the author's view?

From James Q. Wilson, "The Contradictions of an Advanced Capitalist State," *Forbes*, September 14, 1992. Reprinted by permission of *Forbes* magazine, © Forbes Inc., 1992.

Karl Marx thought that the contradictions of capitalism were the inevitability of declining profits and exhausted markets. He got it only slightly wrong: Those turned out to be the problems of *communist* states. The problems of advanced capitalist, democratic societies are not economic at all, they are political and cultural.

The U.S. has pursued happiness with greater determination and more abundant success than any other nation in history. For 45 years it waged, with steady resolve and remarkable forbearance, a Cold War that preserved the security of the Western world without sacrificing its liberty in the process. So remarkable has been our achievement that millions of people from every corner of the globe have come here to be part of America. And what have they found? A nation of grumpy citizens, convinced that their country, or at least its government, has gone to hell in a hand basket.

More Americans today than at any time since the late 1950s say that they distrust the people who manage their affairs: Around 75% believe that they have little or no confidence in the government.

Part of this grumpiness reflects the recent recession. As we recover from those bad times, we will recover a bit from our bad mood. But only a bit. The decline in popular confidence did not begin with the recession, or the Bush Administration, or Watergate or Vietnam; it began in the early 1960s and has been going, with only occasional and modest upticks, ever since. Whatever irritates us, it has been irritating us for a long time. . . .

Why Were We Euphoric?

Before trying to explain why the public is so grumpy now, I think it worth asking why they were so euphoric before. Maybe low public confidence in government is the norm and the high confidence that existed in the 1950s was the aberration. It's not hard to imagine why we felt so good then. We had just waged, with great success, an immensely popular war for a manifestly good cause; at the end of the war we were indisputably Top Nation, with a currency that was the world's standard, a productive capacity that was unrivaled, export markets that took everything we produced and begged for more and a monopoly on the atom bomb.

My guess is that Americans have usually been suspicious of their politicians and that the Eisenhower-era euphoria was unusual, perhaps unprecedented. . . .

But even if we discount the slide on the grounds that we were overdue for a return to normalcy, there are features of the current anger that strike me as more troublesome than anything we can attribute to the post-Ike hangover.

One is the condition of our inner cities. It is not just that they are centers of unemployment, high crime rates, school dropouts and drug abuse; that has, alas, always been the case. Today, however, the problems seem more pervasive, more widespread and more threatening than in the past. Once there were bad neighborhoods to be avoided; elsewhere, life was, if not prosperous, at least orderly. Today the signs of decay seem omnipresent—panhandlers and graffiti are everywhere, senseless shootings can occur anywhere and drug use has penetrated even the best schools.

To cope with these problems in the past we have relied on the schools and the police. But today that reliance seems misplaced; the schools don't teach students, the police can't maintain order.

Indeed, the government as a whole seems to be out of control. . . .

Why do these problems exist?

There are three reasons: prosperity, freedom and democracy.

© 1989 by Ace Backwords.

For a century or more, dangerous drugs have been consumed. Middle-class people used opium, jazz musicians used heroin, stockbrokers sniffed cocaine. But starting in the 1960s, these drugs moved out of the elite markets and entered the mass market. The reason was that the nation had become prosperous enough so that ordinary people could afford them. The discovery of crack cocaine in the early 1980s brought that drug within the reach of almost everyone. Everybody knows that drug addicts often steal to support their habits. What most people don't know is that today many addicts do not have to steal to do this; they can get by on the strength of part-time jobs, family support and public aid.

The inner city has always been a haven for criminals who could take advantage of its anonymity, disorder and low-cost housing. So long as they had to search out their victims on foot, the victims were neighbors. The availability of cheap automobiles put everyone within reach of burglars and robbers. As these offenders began to share in the general prosperity, they were able to replace fists with guns and cheap Saturday-night specials with modern semiautomatic weapons.

We have always had youth gangs in our cities, but even as late as the 1950s they were armed, if at all, with knives. When I was growing up in southern California, a dangerous gang was one whose members had made zip guns out of lengths of tubing taped to crude wooden stocks and loaded, one round per gun, with .22-caliber bullets. Today many gangs can afford Uzis, MAC-10s and 9mm pistols.

All of these changes should have been anticipated because there is no way to confine prosperity to law-abiding people only. The extraordinary standard of living that makes Americans the envy of much of the world extends to the criminal as well as the noncriminal; the rising tide has, indeed, lifted all boats, including those carrying pirates.

Prosperity Does Not Always Produce Decency

What frustrates many Americans, I think, is that their hard-earned prosperity was supposed to produce widespread decency. They had been taught to believe that if you went to school, worked hard, saved your money, bought a home and raised a family, you would enjoy the good life. About this they were right. But they also thought that if most people acted this way their communities would improve. About this they were not right. What produced the good life for individuals did not produce it for cities.

The reason is that prosperity enabled people to move to the kinds of towns Americans have always wanted to live in—small, quiet and nice. As the middle class moved out to the suburbs they took with them the system of informal social controls that had once helped maintain order in the central cities. As employers noticed that their best workers were now living outside these cities, they began moving their offices, stores and factories to the periphery.

Prosperity not only enhanced the purchasing power of urban criminals, it deprived them of the legitimate jobs that had once existed as alternatives to crime and it emancipated them from the network of block clubs, PTAs and watchful neighbors that are the crucial partners of the police.

As we Americans got better off individually, our cities got worse off collectively. This was probably inevitable. But it left us feeling angry and cheated.

Freedom in the last 30 years has undergone an extraordinary expansion in at least two ways. The powers exercised by the institutions of social control have been constrained, and people, especially young people, have embraced an ethos that values self-expression over self-control. The constraints can be found in laws, court rulings and interest-group pressure; the ethos is expressed in the unprecedented grip that the youth culture has on popular music and entertainment.

One should not exaggerate these constraints. The police, for example, must now follow much more elaborate procedures in stopping, arresting and questioning suspects. This is burdensome, but it is not clear that it has materially reduced their ability to solve crimes or arrest criminals. Most homicides, robberies and burglaries are solved because there is eyewitness testimony or physical evidence; confessions are not typically the critical determinant of a successful prosecution. An important exception involves consensual crimes, such as drug dealing. Lacking a victim or a witness, many prosecutions depend on undercover drug purchases or overheard conversations, and what can be purchased or overheard is now far more tightly regulated.

The Difficulty of Maintaining Order

These constraints have become particularly restrictive with respect to the police's ability to maintain order. Gangs, vagrants, panhandlers, rowdy teenagers and graffiti painters were once held in check by curbside justice: threats, rousts and occasional beatings. Today the threats are emptier, the rousts rarer, the beatings forbidden. In many places vagrancy and public drunkenness have been decriminalized. In cities where the police kicked or arrested graffiti painters they now must organize graffiti paint-out campaigns.

Many of the same restraints have reduced the authority of the schools. Disorderly pupils can still be expelled, but now with much greater difficulty than once was the case. The pressure to pass students without demanding much of them has intensified. As the freedom of students has grown, that of teachers has shrunk. The immense bureaucratic burdens on classroom teachers have deprived them of both time and power, with the result that they have both less time in which to teach and less authority with which to make teaching possible.

The expansion in personal freedom has been accompanied by a deep distrust of custodial institutions. The mentally ill were deinstitutionalized in the belief that they would fare better in community mental health clinics than in remote asylums, but there weren't enough clinics to treat the patients, the patients were not compelled to enter the clinics and their families were unequipped to deal with them. The mentally ill and the drug dependent now constitute a majority, it is estimated, of homeless adults on the streets.

Americans have two chief complaints about our government.

One is that it seems unable or unwilling to cope adequately with the costs of prosperity and the darker side of freedom. The other is that it has not managed to extend that prosperity and freedom to everyone. These two views are not in principle incompatible, but many Americans suspect that in practice they are. That is one reason, I think, that race relations are, at least rhetorically, so bad. Whites think the government is too tolerant of crime, gangs, drug abuse and disorderly behavior; blacks think it is too preoccupied with law and order and not concerned enough with ending racism and widening opportunities. Public reaction to the Los Angeles riots expressed that tension.

Democracy vs. Popular Expectations

But even if that tension did not exist, it is not clear that democracy, American style, could effectively meet popular expectations. Those expectations are that government should be nonintrusive and have a balanced budget; spend more money on education, health care, crime control and environmental protection; strike the right balance between liberty and order; and solve the problems of racism, drug abuse, school failures and senseless violence. . . .

But democracy, American style, does not lend itself to making tough choices. The reason is simple: the Constitution of the United States.

That Constitution was written not to make governing easy but to make it hard; not to facilitate choices but to impede them; not to empower leaders but to frustrate them. The constitutions, written and unwritten, of European democracies are very different: They were designed to allow the government to govern, subject only to the periodic checks of a popular election. Here, popular participation is encouraged; there, it is discouraged. Here, the courts can overturn presidential and congressional actions; there, they cannot. Here, many officials have the power to say "no" and none has the power to say "yes" and make it stick; there, a prime minister can say "yes" and make it stick. . . .

Once in office, politicians know that it is their personal visibility and not their party's slogans that affect their chances of staying in office. Accordingly, they organize the Congress so that all members will have large staffs, all members will be able to introduce high-profile bills (even if many are doomed to defeat) and as many members as possible will have a chance to chair a committee or subcommittee. When a bill is passed, it is in everyone's interest to insure that it contains something for every important constituency; if the result is confusion or contradiction, the bureaucracy can be left with the task of sorting things out. When the bureaucracy can't sort it out—when it can't both build highways and make it easy for people to go to court to block highway construction—Congress and the White House can blame the mess on "the bureaucrats" and promise that heads will be knocked and names taken.

In making policy in a highly participatory system, officials will have no incentive to say that the government shouldn't tackle a problem or doesn't know how to solve it and every incentive to claim that government must "do something" and that they know just what to do. As a result, we have crime bills that don't reduce crime, drug abuse bills that don't curb drug abuse, education bills that don't improve learning and disability insurance that can't define "disability." The more such things are done, the more interest groups will have an incentive to organize lobbying efforts and open offices in Washington. The more such offices are opened, the more pressure there will be for more bills and the smaller the chances that any given bill will make much sense.

What Americans don't see is a constitutional system at work in an era of big government and mass participation; what they do see are the things that they don't like about politics. . . .

They see a government that cannot solve the critical problems of our time. They don't see that no other free government has solved those critical problems, either. European democracies run big deficits (often they are, relative to GNP [gross national product], bigger than ours), are equally baffled by youth disorders and drug abuse and have made even less progress in combatting racism.

What, a citizen may ask, do we get out of all of this confusion, pettiness, incompetence and gridlock?

Prosperity, freedom and democracy.

"The poorest poor don't work [because] their poverty is less an economic matter than a cultural one."

A Lack of Moral Values Created the Underclass

Myron Magnet

In the following viewpoint, Myron Magnet argues that the underclass consists of people who are unwilling to work their way out of poverty. Magnet contends that the sexual revolution and the counterculture of the sixties challenged the values that made Americans prosperous, and eventually led the poor into a new, intractable poverty. Magnet, a member of the board of editors of *Fortune* magazine and a fellow of the Manhattan Institute for Policy Research, is the author of *The Dream and the Nightmare: The Sixties' Legacy to the Underclass,* from which this viewpoint is excerpted.

As you read, consider the following questions:

1. How are the prosperous implicated in the poverty of the underclass, according to Magnet?
2. What did the Haves seek for themselves, as well as for the poor, in the author's view?
3. Why does the author believe the behaviors celebrated by the Haves will imprison poor people in poverty? Why would this not also be true for the wealthy?

Excerpted from *The Dream and the Nightmare: The Sixties' Legacy to the Underclass* by Myron Magnet. Copyright © 1993 by Myron Magnet. Reprinted with permission of William Morrow and Company.

Weren't dizzying contrasts of wealth and poverty supposed to have gone out with Dickensian London? What are they doing flagrantly alive again, deeply ingrained in the basic texture of today's American cities?

The daily juxtapositions are so bizarre that they strain belief, however numbingly familiar they grow. In New York City, directly under the windows of the treasure-crammed five-million-dollar apartments that loom over glittering Fifth Avenue, for instance, sleep the homeless, one and sometimes two to a park bench, haggard, usually ill, huddled in rags turned dead gray with dirt and wear. In a gentrified neighborhood across town, bustling with upper-middle-class professionals, only a thickness of brick separates a building where staid burghers have paid upwards of three quarters of a million dollars for an apartment from the squalid crack house next door.

Not far away, for the last few Christmas seasons, the line of fur-coated holidaymakers jovially filing into a luxury food store to buy caviar advertised at "only" $260 a pound has adjoined the sullen line of ravaged paupers waiting for the soup kitchen to open at the church around the corner. Downtown, in the suave, postmodern towers that house health clubs, power lunches, and automated teller machines, grimy derelicts looking like leftovers from the Depression haunt the gleaming atriums for warmth and safety, while above sit dapper investment bankers, some of whom made seven-figure incomes rearranging the industrial order before they were forty. As for the urban parks and pillared train stations that speak of a once-confident civic pride and prosperity, how often are they now—graffitied, vandalized, reeking of human waste—but dreary gauntlets of beggary?

Or worse: think of the savage 1989 rape of a twenty-eight-year-old jogger by a "wilding" pack of Harlem teenagers in New York's Central Park. What starker contrast of Haves and Have-Nots could be found than between the victim, a Wall Street investment banker ambitious to excel in every pursuit, and her brutal attackers, unregenerate beneficiaries of a wide array of social programs designed to uplift the "disadvantaged"?

What Is Wrong with the Country?

Like Death interrupting the dumbstruck banquet, the poverty and vice that pervade America's cities appall the prosperous. What's wrong with the country, they worry, that such problems are everywhere? Does the same system that enriches the Haves simultaneously degrade the Have-Nots? Does the comfort of the prosperous somehow rest upon the debasement of their poorest fellow citizens, the homeless and the underclass? Are the prosperous *responsible* for the condition of the poor?

When the Haves think about their relation to the poor, the im-

211

ages that come to mind feed their anxiety and sense of guilt: their brother's keeper . . . the biblical grandee Dives with the beggar Lazarus at his mansion gates . . . the religious duty to aid the poor. They think of Dickens's *Christmas Carol* or of "Good King Wenceslas," embodiments of that Victorian paternalist ethic that holds masters responsible for the condition of their dependents. . . .

But happily, modern society isn't hierarchical, in Victorian fashion. Today's Haves aren't the "betters" or the "masters" of the Have-Nots, and today's worst-off poor are nobody's mistreated dependents or exploited employees: they are radically disconnected from the larger society, and they don't work. Victorian philanthropy isn't equal to their plight.

Impersonal and economic, rather than intimate and moral like the Victorian notions, modern theories hold the prosperous, as a class, responsible for the condition of the poor, as a class. Take Jesse Jackson's much-trumpeted theory of "economic violence," holding that the Reagan administration mindset that unfettered the rich simultaneously immiserated the poor by unraveling the social safety net. The rich got a tax break, leaving less revenue to go to the poor. A more sophisticated formulation holds that in the eighties the Haves created a world economy that handsomely rewards themselves while constricting opportunity for the Have-Nots.

The eloquent fact that means-tested federal welfare spending rose 44 percent between 1980 and 1987, however, explodes a theory like Jackson's. And further refuting this whole line of thought, the eighties boom that enriched the tycoons created an astonishing 18.4 million new jobs, both skilled and unskilled, offering a way out of poverty to almost any poor person with the willingness and discipline to work.

So even if the economic developments of the eighties did increase the disparity in income between the rich and the poor, those developments don't explain why we have an underclass or why the homeless haunt the streets. Since low-skill jobs exist in profusion, since work today will normally lift people above the poverty line, and since opportunity for further advancement is open to those with the ambition and energy to seize it, for the able-bodied, poverty in America is no longer an utterly ineluctable fate: one can choose to try to escape, by legitimate rather than criminal paths, with a good chance of success.

Why Do the Poor Stay Poor?

But in that case, America's deepest-rooted poverty starts to look more than a little mysterious. If jobs do exist, as they did throughout the eighties, why do large numbers of very poor people remain in poverty? The emblem of this mystery, ubiqui-

212

tous in big cities, is the panhandler begging outside McDonald's, right under the *Help Wanted* sign.

The key to the mystery of why, despite opportunity, the poorest poor don't work is that their poverty is less an economic matter than a cultural one. In many cases, the Have-Nots lack the inner resources to seize their chance, and they pass on to their children a self-defeating set of values and attitudes, along with an impoverished intellectual and emotional development, that generally imprisons them in failure as well. Three, sometimes four generations have made the pathology that locks them in—school-leaving, nonwork, welfare dependency, crime, drug abuse, and the like—drearily familiar.

But the underclass culture they live in is far from being wholly of their own invention. Underclass culture has its own very distinct inflection, to be sure; but for all its idiosyncratic peculiarity it is a dialect, so to speak, shaped more by the culture as a whole, and by the singular history of underclass communities within that culture, than by any independent, internal dynamic.

Ramirez/Copley News Service. Reprinted with permission.

That's why the prosperous are indeed implicated in the poverty of the poor, even though they don't extract their BMWs from the hides of the underclass the way mine owners squeezed profits out of abused children in the early days of the Industrial Revolution, when "economic violence" was more than rhetoric.

The Haves are implicated because over the last thirty years they radically remade American culture, turning it inside out and upside down to accomplish a cultural revolution whose most mangled victims turned out to be the Have-Nots.

An Honorable Aim

This was the precise opposite of what was supposed to happen. For when the Haves began their cultural revolution a generation ago, they acted in the name of two related liberations. Above all, impelled by the fervor of the civil rights movement, they sought the political and economic liberation of the Have-Nots, the poor and the black. The ideal that guided them was a vision of democracy; their honorable aim was to complete democracy's work, to realize democratic values fully by making American society more open and inclusive. Out of this democratic impulse sprang the War on Poverty, welfare benefit increases, court-ordered school busing, more public housing projects, affirmative action, job-training programs, drug treatment programs, special education, *The Other America*, Archie Bunker, *Roots*, countless editorials and magazine articles and TV specials, black studies programs, multicultural curricula, new textbooks, all-black college dorms, sensitivity courses, minority set-asides, Martin Luther King Day, and the political correctness movement at colleges, to name only some of the almost endless manifestations.

The deep changes in the majority culture's beliefs about the nature of democratic society and the poor's place within it had momentous consequences for the worst-off. But in addition to trying to liberate the poor and excluded from their marginality, the cultural revolution sought a second, even more spectacular liberation, which also shaped the fate of the poor, indirectly but far-reachingly.

This was the personal liberation that the Haves sought for themselves. Chafing against what the avant-garde writers and "sick" comedians of the fifties lambasted, only sometimes correctly, as that era's life-denying repression and conventionality, the Haves yearned to free themselves from a sense of anxious, stifling conformity, to claim a larger, more fulfilling life than that of an Organization Man or Man in the Gray Flannel Suit, or as a faceless atom in a Lonely Crowd, as titles of some of the era's influential texts had it.

That longing found two epochal expressions. The first was the sexual revolution, whose attitudes, diffused throughout the culture by advertising, movies, popular music, and television, so transformed values and behavior that they ultimately reshaped family life, increasing divorce, illegitimacy, and female-headed families on all levels of society.

The second manifestation was the sixties counterculture. As its name announced, the counterculture rejected traditional bourgeois culture as sick, repressive, and destructive. Bourgeois culture's sexual mores, based on guilt, marriage, and the perverse belief that present gratification should be deferred to achieve future goals, were symptoms of its pathology. Its sobriety and decorum were mere slavish, hypocritical conformism; its industriousness betokened an upside-down, materialistic value system; its family life was yet another arena of coercion and guilt. This culture went hand in hand with an inherently unjust capitalist economic order, and a political order whose murderousness was plainly revealed by "Amerika's" war in Vietnam.

By contrast, "letting it all hang out," expressing yourself, acting upon what you really feel, "doing it"—all this constituted authentic, liberated selfhood, healthy and life-affirming. Such free expressiveness would get you closer to the counterculture's cherished ideal of a guilt-free, undivided selfhood, described in the therapeutic language of psychoanalysis as filtered through counterculture gurus like Norman O. Brown and Herbert Marcuse.

Do Your Own Thing

Consistent with that ideal, you didn't have to live by the disciplines of work and family and citizenship but could drop out from one or all, forging your own "alternative life-style," as the phrase went, more valid and authentic, and certainly more communitarian, than the conventional one. . . .

The cultural revolution's yoking together of personal and political liberations had a curious effect. It dignified the purely personal, making self-cherishing seem unselfish, almost civic-minded. Conversely, the irresponsibility that could mark the quest for personal liberation sometimes got carried over into social policy, too. . . .

Partly because of this confusion of the selfish and the civic, the cultural revolution failed in devastating ways in both of its two large intentions. Instead of ending poverty for the Have-Nots—despite the civil rights movement, despite the War on Poverty—the new cultural order fostered, in the underclass and the homeless, a new, intractable poverty that shocked and dismayed, that seemed to belong more to the era of ragged chimney sweeps than to modern America, that went beyond the economic realm into the realm of pathology. Poverty turned pathological because the new culture that the Haves invented— their remade system of beliefs, norms, and institutions—permitted, even celebrated, behavior that, when poor people practice it, will imprison them inextricably in poverty. It's hard to persuade ghetto fifteen-year-olds not to get pregnant, for instance, when the entire culture, from rock music to upscale perfume

215

commercials to highbrow books, is intoxicated with the joy of what before AIDS was called "recreational" sex.

Worse, during the sixties and seventies, the new culture of the Haves, in its quest for personal liberation, withdrew respect from the behavior and attitudes that have traditionally boosted people up the economic ladder—deferral of gratification, sobriety, thrift, dogged industry, and so on through the whole catalogue of antique-sounding bourgeois virtues. As social thinker Irving Kristol puts it, "It's hard to rise above poverty if society keeps deriding the human qualities that allow you to escape from it."

Moreover, the new culture held the poor back from advancement by robbing them of responsibility for their fate and thus further squelching their initiative and energy. Instead of telling them to take wholehearted advantage of opportunities that were rapidly opening, the new culture told the Have-Nots that they were victims of an unjust society and, if they were black, that they were entitled to restitution, including advancement on the basis of racial preference rather than mere personal striving and merit. It told them that the traditional standards of the larger community, already under attack by the counterculture, often didn't apply to them, that their wrongdoing might well be justified rebellion or the expression of yet another legitimate "alternative life-style." It told them that, if they were mentally ill, they were really just marching to a different drummer and should be free to do their marching in the streets—which is where many of them ended up, homeless. . . .

A Crisis of Values

No wonder that so many complain that America is undergoing a crisis of values. That crisis—real enough—is not caused by greed, contrary to what is often alleged. It is the unsurprising result of three decades of holding basic beliefs in abeyance and using questionable means to try to achieve a worthy social end. It is the result of making a democratic cultural revolution that ended—tragically—by making a travesty of the democratic values it had set out to uphold. . . .

The bitter paradox that is so hard to face is that most of what the Haves have already done to help the poor—out of decent and generous motives—is part of the problem. Like gas pumped into a flooded engine, the more help they bestow, the less able do the poor become to help themselves. The problem isn't that the Haves haven't done enough but that they've done the diametrically wrong thing. "If people could just stop making things worse," concludes economist Thomas Sowell ruefully, "it would be an enormously greater contribution than they're likely to make any other way."

"It isn't dependency . . . that keeps people trapped; it's the fear . . . that they can't do anything about their condition."

Lack of Hope Perpetuates the Underclass

William Raspberry

Everyone is born financially dependent. Thus it cannot be the fact of dependency itself that traps people in poverty, reasons William Raspberry in the following viewpoint. When people feel that they do not matter to society, Raspberry believes, or when they feel that their efforts to change their lives will have no effect, their despair becomes a self-fulfilling prophecy. Raspberry is a nationally syndicated columnist.

As you read, consider the following questions:

1. What similarities and differences does Raspberry find between high school students and people on welfare?
2. Why does the author feel that merely earning an income would not be a solution to the self-esteem problems of the poor?
3. What single change does Raspberry feel would help poor people most? Why does he think the welfare system cannot effect this change?

William Raspberry, "The Myth of Financial Dependency," *Liberal Opinion Week*, June 15, 1992, © 1992, Washington Post Writers Group. Reprinted with permission.

Robert Woodson had finished his lecture at the prestigious prep school and was into the question-and-answer period when the subject turned to the crippling effects of welfare.

Isn't it true, someone wondered, that dependency robs people of their initiative—even their morality—and thwarts the natural striving toward self-sufficiency?

It was a slow, fat pitch to a black conservative who has been critical of government programs that get in the way of private self-help efforts. But instead of swinging for the fence, Woodson barehanded the ball and tossed it back.

"How many of you work for what you have?" he asked his mostly white, mostly well-off audience. "How did you pay for your clothes, your tuition, your summer camp?"

"My parents. . . ."

"No, I'm asking what did *you* pay for? And if you haven't paid for any of the things you enjoy, does that compromise *your* integrity, *your* initiative, *your* striving toward self-sufficiency?"

Helplessness Creates Despair

The point is on target. It isn't financial dependency that creates the frustration and despair that sometimes overwhelm poor people. It is helplessness—the belief, daily reinforced, that they cannot make any significant difference in their world, in their immediate neighborhoods or in their own lives.

College-bound prep school students, as Woodson understands, believe they matter. Everything conspires to make them believe it: the spoken and unspoken expectations regarding their future contributions, their parents' investment in their education, their own well-honed sense of entitlement. And that's why their financial dependency doesn't bother them.

"My point wasn't to embarrass anyone," the president of the Washington-based National Center for Neighborhood Enterprise explained later. "It's just that I get so used to hearing the well-off come down on poor people, arguing that being dependent robs them of their morale and their morality, that I wanted to find a way to shake up the students' thought patterns.

"Not just affluent youngsters but also a lot of ordinary middle-class people have that same view of things. They look at welfare recipients—particularly those who have been on welfare for a time, or whose parents were recipients—and they assume that the reason they stay on it is because it becomes comfortable to them to the point that they actually desire it.

"I tell them, 'If you don't desire dependency, given the level of comfort your parents can afford to give you, why would you imagine that poor people desire to live at the subsistence level?'"

It isn't dependency or a lack of desire to do better that keeps people trapped; it's the fear-bordering-on-certainty that they can't do anything about their condition. The cure is not to eliminate the dependency but to instill the confidence that their efforts matter, that they have gifts to share.

"Hopeless" Message Skews Debate on Underclass

Words like "permanent," "irreducible" and "unending" pop up routinely in stories about the underclass, constantly reemphasizing the powerful message that the "underclass," alas, is hopeless, a message that skews public debate from constructive questions such as "How can we best help the poor?" to insidious questions such as "Why should we help the poor at all?"

Clarence Page, *Liberal Opinion Week,* January 14, 1991.

Sure, but wouldn't it boost their confidence to know they were earning their own way? Most assuredly. But not necessarily in terms of income. Different people earn their way by different means. The Kennedy children, to take perhaps America's best known example, have never worried that their financial dependency would somehow cripple them. Rather they have accepted as a matter of family-inculcated course that their wealth, however unearned, carries with it the freedom—and the duty—to serve.

It's not about financial independence but about a belief in one's own efficacy. And that has less to do with who pays the bills than with a sense of having at least the potential to carry one's weight. There is, for instance, no reason to suppose that those who work their way through college (as I did) see themselves as having more *potential* than those who (like my children) have their education paid for. The critical thing is to inculcate the attitude that a college education, however financed, carries with it a set of social obligations.

A Self-Fulfilling Prophecy

The sense of helplessness—of inefficacy—that so many poor people have is more a matter of attitude than of objective fact. People do better, for themselves and for others, when they believe they can; and every failure is viewed as only a temporary setback. They lapse into despair when they believe that nothing they can do will really make any difference; and every setback becomes "proof" of their helplessness.

We need to find ways to persuade those who see themselves as helpless that they aren't really helpless at all—that their efforts matter.

We need to teach people—all people, but especially our children—not to define themselves in terms of their income or its sources but in their potential for being useful.

And we need to teach ourselves that we can't do these things solely by transforming the welfare system. The feeling of efficacy and the sense of social obligation cannot be delivered along with a welfare check. Or, for that matter, with a seven-figure bequest.

"Individual actions . . . are required to escape the poverty trap."

Lack of Commitment Perpetuates the Underclass

Murray Weidenbaum

The central questions about poverty, notes Murray Weidenbaum in the following viewpoint, are these: How do people fall into poverty, and how can they be moved out of poverty? The author finds the answers to these questions in three interrelated goals that can make the difference between poverty and prosperity for most people: completing high school, marrying (and staying married), and staying employed, even at the minimum wage. Weidenbaum, director of the Center for the Study of American Business at Washington University in St. Louis, is author of a book on America's economy, *Rendezvous with Reality*.

As you read, consider the following questions:

1. What evidence does the author offer to support his contention that government spending does not cure poverty?
2. What institution does Weidenbaum believe is powerfully connected to the problem of poverty?
3. How are the three goals the author outlines interconnected, in his view?

Murray Weidenbaum, "It's Up to Individuals to Fight the War on Poverty," *Los Angeles Times*, September 23, 1990. Reprinted with the author's permission.

The most recent debates on income distribution in the United States have degenerated into a clash among statisticians and those who use those statistics. Some experienced analysts conclude, from their inspection of the data, that the distribution of income is becoming more unequal, and especially that the upper income classes are gaining at the expense of people with lower incomes.

Simultaneously, other professionals conclude that the degree of income equality did not change significantly in the 1980s and that, when fringe benefits and income-in-kind payments are properly taken into account, the poverty problem is far less severe than it has been portrayed.

I take a "plague on both your houses" view. Whether the total tally of the poor has been rising or falling, the hard fact is that there are a great many poor people in the United States. The basic thrust of the debate should be shifted to a far more useful set of questions: How do people fall into poverty? How can they be helped to move out of poverty?

Americans Are Not Heartless

First of all, it is inaccurate for Americans to castigate themselves as a heartless society. Over the past 25 years, federal spending for income support to individuals multiplied over five times in constant dollars. Any way it is measured, the per capita outlay of public funds to fight poverty has been expanding faster than inflation and real outlays also have grown faster than the number of poor people.

The continuing problem is that while these expensive efforts now represent a far larger share of the nation's resources than was devoted when Franklin D. Roosevelt and Lyndon B. Johnson sat in the Oval Office, the large outlays have not produced the promised results.

There is virtually universal agreement in the United States that those who are physically or mentally unable to support themselves should be helped by society. Such assistance should be provided in adequate amounts and with a minimum of hassle. Over the years, however, a profound broadening has occurred in the qualification for such aid. Low or no income has become the only basis necessary to qualify for the receipt of welfare. The earlier terms, "handouts" and "charity," have been transformed into "transfer payments" and "entitlements."

Many long-term welfare recipients are beset by deep-rooted personal and social problems not quickly cured by money. There is a powerful connection between the health of the family as an institution and the depths of the poverty problem.

A few examples will help. Nine out of 10 families on welfare are headed by women. Men living alone have twice the unem-

222

ployment rates of family men. Nearly three-fourths of the children on welfare are on the rolls because neither of their parents is willing to support them. Frequently, the father has left the home or never took responsibility for the child in the first place.

To Escape Poverty, Just Follow the Rules

- Go to high school, work modestly hard, and graduate.
- If you father or bear children, be married. If you're married, try to stay that way, unless conditions are abusive.
- Hold a job, unless extenuating circumstances are legitimate.
- Don't abuse drugs or alcohol.
- Don't break the law. . . .

The most deadening and persistent poverty in this society would be much less if these rules were followed.

More than a few people, needless to say, don't like talking this way. It smacks of blaming victims, they say. It's simplistic and not a little racist, they contend. But, the fact of the matter is, many adults who are poor are not victims in the sense the "system" has done them in, as is claimed by a quarter-century of liberal reflex. They have done in themselves and, too frequently, their children.

Mitchell B. Pearlstein, *St. Paul Dispatch*, May 20, 1990.

Without judging the moral basis of these alternative lifestyles, it is apparent that much of the cost of such actions is not borne by the individuals making those decisions, but by the children and by society as a whole.

Focusing on a positive approach, a distinguished panel of both liberal and conservative analysts issued a report, "The New Consensus on Family and Welfare." The panel stated, "An indispensable resource in the war against poverty is a sense of personal responsibility." The panel also noted that climbing out of poverty is something the *individual* must do, albeit with some help from society.

How to Escape Poverty

More often than not, all it takes for a person to leave the ranks of the poor is three things: 1) completing high school, 2) getting and staying married (even if not on the first try), and 3) staying employed, even if at modest pay such as the statutory minimum wage. The three factors are closely interrelated. The high school diploma helps in getting a job. The wages received enable the person to get married and to begin raising a family. The obligation to support a family encourages the person to stick with the

223

job or to quickly find another.

An examination of the available data is useful in destroying some widely held myths. Poverty is primarily a children's, not a senior citizens', problem. Three and a half million of the elderly are poor, while 13 million children are. About three-fourths of the elderly own their homes. The average family headed by someone 65 to 74 years of age holds more than twice the dollar assets than the typical family headed by a person 35 to 44 years old. The older the head of the family, the wealthier the family is likely to be—through age 74.

Also, very few men, black or white, who are heads of households are even near poverty—if they just have a high school education. In 1986, less than 5% of black males and less than 10% of black females who met these simple requirements were in poverty. Of adult black males who were high school graduates in 1986, 86% had family incomes more than twice the poverty level.

When a woman on welfare takes on a full-time job, the odds are overwhelming that she is lifting herself out of poverty. Few women working steadily earn only the minimum wage. The median annual earnings of full-time female workers without a high school diploma are higher than the minimum wage. Raising a child is often cited as a reason for unmarried women staying on welfare. The fact is that most mothers are now working, including a slight majority of those with children under six.

Government Can Help

There is much that government can and should do to reduce poverty. That includes conducting a sensible macroeconomic policy that yields a growing economy, which in turn generates a rising supply of jobs. Strengthening the educational system—perhaps by opening up more competition—would surely help. And continuing to provide large sums of money to alleviate distress will be necessary for the foreseeable future.

Nevertheless, the most important actions generating poverty are personal—producing children out of wedlock, getting divorced, dropping out of school and waiting for the dream job to come along before starting to work.

All in all, however, the message that arises from any detailed examination of poverty in the United States is upbeat. The solution is within reach of most people. Marriage and family prevent poverty. Schooling prevents poverty. Working at almost any job prevents poverty. Individual actions—rather than more generous government expenditures—are required to escape the poverty trap.

Periodical Bibliography

The following articles have been selected to supplement the diverse views presented in this chapter.

Andre Carothers	"When Enough Is Too Much," *E Magazine*, January/February 1993.
Jason DeParle	"What to Call the Poorest Poor?" *The New York Times*, August 26, 1990.
Alan Ehrenhalt	"The Underclass and the Suburban Solution," *Governing*, June 1993.
Richard I. Kirkland Jr.	"What We Can Do Now," *Fortune*, June 1, 1992.
Joe Klein	"How About a Swift Kick?" *Newsweek*, July 26, 1993.
Marvin H. Kosters	"The Rise in Income Inequality," *The American Enterprise*, November/December 1992.
Neil McLaughlin	"Beyond 'Race vs. Class': The Politics of William Julius Wilson," *Dissent*, Summer 1993.
Charles Murray	"The Legacy of the 60's," *Commentary*, July 1992.
Dee Myles	"The Crisis of Capitalism and the African American Family," *Political Affairs*, April 1993.
Thomas Sowell	"Serving Is Not Servitude," *Forbes*, March 1, 1993.
Paul Starr	"Civil Reconstruction," *The American Prospect*, Winter 1992. Available from New Prospect, Inc., PO Box 383080, Cambridge, MA 02238.
William Tucker	"Chronicler Without a Clue," *The American Spectator*, June 1991.
Camilo José Vergara	"A Guide to the Ghettos," *The Nation*, March 15, 1993.
William Voegeli	"Poverty and the Victim Ploy," *First Things*, November 1991. Available from First Things Readers Service, 129 Phelps Ave., Suite 312, Rockford, IL 61108.
David Whitman	"The Surprising News About the Underclass," *U.S. News & World Report*, December 25, 1989/January 1, 1990.
James Q. Wilson	"Crime, Race, and Values," *Society*, November/December 1992.

225

Can Government Efforts
Alleviate Poverty?

POVERTY

Chapter Preface

One of the most vexing questions facing those who wish to reform America's massive welfare system is what to do about the mothers of very young children. When the welfare program Aid to Families with Dependent Children (AFDC) was originally established in 1935 as Aid to Dependent Children, it recognized, writes Gilbert Steiner in *The State of Welfare*, a "national commitment to the idea that a mother's place is in the home." But by the mid-1980s, over half of all married women with children under six were in the work force, at least part time. Many began to feel that "welfare mothers" should take their place in the labor force, too.

Current welfare policies make working a poor choice for many single mothers: AFDC benefits, combined with Medicaid, food stamps, and sometimes housing aid, often "pay" better than a job at minimum wage, especially when child care costs, transportation, and other job-related expenses are factored in. Thus reformers seek to reduce benefits in order to make welfare a less attractive lifestyle. Cutting off benefits seems to some critics the only way to get people "off the welfare rolls and into the work force."

"Two years and out" has become a rallying cry for those who urge that benefits be cut off, even for single mothers, after two years. Proponents of this plan say providing benefits for two years would give someone a chance to regroup after a loss, get job training, perhaps establish a home. After that, benefits would end, so the person would supposedly be forced to get a job.

But applying this strategy to single mothers on welfare raises a host of questions, as former secretary of health, education, and welfare Joseph A. Califano Jr. points out:

> Is it fair? Suppose the mother gets sick? Suppose she really tries and can't find a job? Will the government guarantee her a job? How much will care for her children cost when she works, and is the taxpayer going to pick up the tab? Will welfare recipients be the only people guaranteed taxpayer-bankrolled child care when they go to work? Is such a guarantee politically feasible?

While many reformers have no problem with refusing benefits to able-bodied adults, the fact that ending help for mothers can endanger their children illustrates the complexity of the issues involved when the government attempts to alleviate poverty.

The authors of the following viewpoints argue whether various government policies have aggravated or alleviated poverty. Many believe that the most effective aid must be given on the local level; they realize that the farther from the problem, the easier it is to forget that poverty has a human face.

"There are perverse incentives to maintain poverty because we have a whole industry built on the backs of poor people. "

The Welfare Industry Perpetuates Poverty

Robert L. Woodson, interviewed by Lloyd Eby and Lawrence Criner

Seventy cents of every dollar spent on welfare goes to the welfare bureaucracy, charges Robert L. Woodson in the following viewpoint. Woodson asserts that this "poverty service industry" is irrationally set up so the success or failure of a project has no relationship to the amount of money spent on it. He proposes programs that bypass bureaucracy and funnel funds directly to jobs for the poor because they would cost less and be more effective. Woodson is founder and president of the National Center for Neighborhood Enterprise, which provides support to grass-roots organizations working to revitalize urban communities. He was interviewed by Lloyd Eby and Lawrence Criner, assistant senior editor and associate senior editor, respectively, for the *World & I.*

As you read, consider the following questions:

1. How are normal economic and social policies of U.S. society inverted for the poor, according to Woodson?
2. Does the author believe the current welfare system causes or cures poverty? Explain.
3. What specific changes in the welfare system does the author propose to make it more effective?

From an interview of Robert L. Woodson by Lloyd Eby and Lawrence Criner titled "The Key to Success Is the Neighborhood." This article appeared in the September 1992 issue and is reprinted with the permission of *The World & I,* a publication of The Washington Times Corporation, © 1992.

THE WORLD & I: What is your overall assessment of this country's social-welfare program?

Robert L. Woodson: It's been a colossal failure. The overall thrust toward poor people has been successful in some limited areas, but it's been like feeding the birds by feeding the elephants.

W&I: Where did we go wrong?

Woodson: Things worked best when, in the thirty years from the thirties to the sixties, we transferred cash directly to individuals, without a lot of overhead and without providing a lot of services to people. Then Lyndon Johnson started the Great Society, and there was a twenty-five-fold increase in the amount of money that we spent on social services from the sixties to the present day, but what we did was take cash and translate it into services. Thus, a whole service industry was born, with a proliferation of schools of social work, all kinds of abstract master's degrees, all of this foolishness.

As a result, the United Way and the government and corporations and foundations began to invest in the service industry as a principal means to help the poor, so that now seventy cents of every dollar goes to the industry; only thirty cents goes to the poor people themselves.

There are perverse incentives to maintain poverty because we have a whole industry built on the backs of poor people; they ask not which problems are solvable but what's fundable.

Spending More Does Not Work

W&I: Some critics claim that we've never really been serious about these persistent problems and never spent enough money on them, and that a just society is one that takes care of those who are in need. What about that?

Woodson: The question is, what have we gotten for what we spent? What is the relationship between expenditures and outcomes?

If we keep spending money on a football team and they keep losing games, would we say it's because we're not spending enough? Suppose we double the expenditure and they continue to lose? Would we then say, well, we're not spending enough?

That argument has been used to continue to proliferate and expand the welfare bureaucracy without any reference to outcomes at all.

The policies that normally influence behavior outside of poor communities are exactly inverted for the poor. The rest of us are encouraged to save money. But if you are on welfare and you accumulate assets in excess of $1,000, you can be sent to jail. The rest of us prosper because we choose our doctors, our lawyers, where we send our kids to school, everything. That's what democracy is all about. For poor people, those things are all dictated by government policy: Public schools, where their children will go to school; food stamps, what they can buy; public housing, where they live. Medicaid determines who their doctors will be. Legal services, who their attorneys will be.

In our market economy, if a store or business fails to deliver quality goods and services to their customers in a courteous way, the business will go under, no matter how much the management spends on it. But in our poverty industry it doesn't matter whether or not social services are effective or schools teach. There is no relationship between satisfaction of the customer and expenditures on the project. It defies common sense how anybody could conceive of a system in which the amount of money being spent is not related at all to whether or not the customers feel or believe that they are benefited. You don't hear poor people say, "We're not spending enough."

The issue is this: An awful lot is being spent on poverty, but not enough is being spent on poor people themselves.

The welfare shaft.

Reprinted by permission: Tribune Media Services.

W&I: Do you agree with Charles Murray's claim that welfare inevitably or indirectly is a cause of poverty?

Woodson: No. I think that Charles goes a little too far. I do think it's a contributing factor. I think that not just welfare but the whole thrust of the new society undermined existing community institutions. There was a tremendous supplanting of the functioning of those traditional institutions that really represented the moral infrastructure of those communities.

For instance, on Indian reservations, old people used to tell stories to kids, and they had a role and the kids had a sense of continuity. In the sixties they were replaced with poverty workers, who read to the kids. The function of churches, where a janitor could come and be an executive on Sunday morning, was supplanted by poverty agencies.

During the sixties we were moving toward specialization and training for several reasons, including the challenge of *Sputnik*. In engineering and mathematics, you became a specialist, and the same phenomenon occurred within our social environment. We began to specialize more, and the more we specialized and the more we professionalized, the more the institutions that were intended to help the poor became detached from the realities of the poor. We just came in and administered massive transplants into the body of low-income communities. If you were to administer massive transplants into the human body, regardless of the intention, the body would reject it. . . .

Strengthen Support Structures

W&I: You emphasize support structures, the family, informal social organizations. The view you espouse is antithetical to the present driving mainstream social policy.

Woodson: I know it. That's exactly why we're in this mess we're in. I look at the present situation and reflect on the black community and remember that up until 1959, 78 percent of all black families were whole, and women were raising their own children.

W&I: People are worried now about the breakdown of the black family and the rise of illegitimacy. Has welfare contributed to that?

Woodson: Not as Charles Murray seems to think. The data just does not support the claim that kids are having babies so they can move out and live on their own, because about 96 percent of them live in the homes of the baby's grandparents; so they're not going out and establishing their own separate households. I think a lot of these kids have no sense of belonging to anything so they consciously go out and get pregnant. I've had them tell me so. They get pregnant in order to have something to own.

By contrast, the woman who taught me a lot of what I know about the power of the informal sector is a hairdresser who's now around eighty years old, Mercedes Grier. Around thirty years ago she used to have about nineteen young girls between thirteen and fifteen in her living room every Friday night. They would just visit and talk with one another, and every other weekend she'd take them on an excursion somewhere in a public bus. In two years only one of those girls became pregnant. Yet she didn't have a pregnancy prevention program.

Because the girls felt their own sense of belonging, they didn't have to realize that in the form of a baby. They could derive this sense the way most kids do, from a family. Take the Kenilworth-Parkside housing complex here in D.C.; there is strong leadership and community involvement, so teen pregnancy has virtually been eliminated there. You don't see girls walking around pregnant.

So there are examples of what happens when people are called to themselves. It can have a tremendous impact. It's the only thing that works that I know of.

Transforming Welfare

W&I: If you had the power to do by fiat whatever you want on this set of issues, what would you do?

Woodson: First I would call a moratorium on all these social-welfare policies. I would have an immediate review of them.

I would move to elevate the cap on accumulated assets, so that people receiving welfare could accumulate up to $10,000 in assets.

I would have an aggressive program of transitions from welfare to work, any kind of work. I would promote job creation and enterprise formation. There are examples where people have established small businesses in low-income communities.

I would look at what we're spending on government programs. Consider Meals on Wheels; it spends billions of dollars delivering meals to the elderly and other people in those communities. Why can't we set up catering companies among low-income people and let them generate jobs and businesses by delivering services, like Meals on Wheels, to one another? This has been pioneered in St. Louis, where residents purchased a company and it went from providing 240 meals a day to 2,000 meals.

I would then mobilize those in the business community to roll up their sleeves and act as mentors to these groups to make it possible for them to deliver meals to day-care centers and to the public schools. Much money is spent to provide meals to schools, prisons, and other institutions. There's no reason why we cannot make it possible for low-income people—who cook very well!—to develop sufficient business acumen and skill to deliver these meals and feed all those people.

I would reduce Medicaid costs by examining the overuse of emergency rooms by poor people who don't have access to their own physicians, and I would take some Medicaid funds and invest them in community-based nonprofits that would be empowered to examine the factors that contribute to the overuse of emergency rooms. By investing in these you would, again, create jobs, create skills, but you would be driving down the cost of Medicaid because fewer people would use the emergency services. And you would then see a decline in the need for those funds, funds that then can be used for other health purposes.

Then I would move into preventive health: health screening in poor communities, and nutrition and antismoking efforts. In other words, I would redirect the resources of our social-welfare industry and instead sponsor and support locally based efforts that will create jobs and expand skills, while actually driving down public expenditures.

I'd have residents take over public housing. Where they have been empowered to take on management responsibilities, the operating costs have dramatically declined by an average of 60 percent and income from rent collection has increased. So it is quite possible to support a whole array of grass-roots efforts using public funds that can actually create jobs while driving down the amount of needed funds.

I'm impressed by one program in Denver, called Women's Employment Network. They propose that we should contract out the intake function of the welfare office to a private, non-profit agency. Anyone coming on welfare would have to sign a self-sufficiency agreement and then sign a contract, which would include a profile of what that person's capacities and skills were, what his or her needs were.

Most people need day-care services while they receive job training. So in this program the recipients live in a facility for six to eight months, where kids are cared for while the participants receive training. They have moved people into the work force. About 80 percent of the people coming through would be able to move out into some form of work, possibly to one of these catering companies I described. But there will also be some people who will need long-term assistance.

Reducing the Welfare Bureaucracy

With that arrangement you don't have to fire any existing social workers, but you would cease hiring. Because you are reducing the number of people coming in and staying in that system, the welfare bureaucracy would shrink by attrition as people retire. . . .

W&I: You talk a lot about local themes, local initiatives, local control, and so on. The past thirty years we've tended to look to government for these things. So let me ask, then, what do you think the proper role of government is, and what are its limitations in this set of issues?

Woodson: I think government should be on tap but not on top. Government should create an environment to support private action. Government should be what it was intended to be. I think when it does intervene, it should be in cases of emergency. What was intended to be an ambulance system has been institutionalized into a transportation system.

If there's a disaster, government should move in, clean up, do what it has to do, then pull out. Its role is to ensure that private entities function properly. Aside from the fundamental functions, government should always seek to be least intrusive.

W&I: It's unusual to hear a black man say these things because the majority of so-called black leaders have been highly statist, highly in favor of government.

Woodson: Well, you find that the higher their income, the angrier they are, the more elitist, and the more removed they are from the rank and file. . . .

"I'm Very Optimistic"

W&I: Let me conclude by asking you—I don't mean this as a psychological question—are you optimistic or pessimistic?

Woodson: I'm very optimistic because in my work I see so many signs of health. I go into these low-income communities, and I see twenty-five kids in a little rundown public-housing home who are taking Bible studies from this lady who is helping them finish high school. I see the two thousand kids who are now declaring themselves as parents, and I see people who were on drugs for ten years saying that they've gone through conversion and they're rehabilitated.

You can't be around people who have been through all they've been through and not feel optimistic and know that if they have been among society's dregs and if they can change, and if neighborhoods that were overrun by drug addicts are suddenly safe and sound and on their way to recovery, then something different is very possible.

I'm probably one of the few people in Washington who are simply delighted with our deficits because they're compelling us to embrace innovations that we would not otherwise be sitting here talking about. As Ben Franklin said, nothing concentrates the mind more than the prospect of hanging in the morning. So when we're under that imperative, we are motivated to come up with something fast.

"As the American welfare state has grown . . . , the rate of poverty has declined by nearly 40 percent."

The Welfare Industry Has Greatly Reduced Poverty

Theodore R. Marmor, Jerry L. Mashaw, and Philip L. Harvey

When judging the effectiveness of welfare programs, the public often ignores social insurance programs such as Social Security, a part of the welfare state that has been immensely successful in reducing poverty, charge Theodore R. Marmor, Jerry L. Mashaw, and Philip L. Harvey in the following viewpoint. On the other hand, the authors point out that those who believe poverty would decrease if welfare funds went directly to the poor instead of through the welfare system are ignoring the fact that means-tested cash-transfer programs (aimed specifically at those in need) have been inefficient at reducing poverty. Marmor is a professor of politics and public policy at the Yale School of Organization and Management. Mashaw is Tweedie Professor of Law and Management at Yale Law School. Harvey is an associate at the law firm of Debevoise & Plimpton in New York City.

As you read, consider the following questions:

1. What is the poverty gap? What kind of program, according to the authors, would be explicitly aimed at closing the poverty gap?
2. Describe the difference between social insurance programs and means-tested cash transfers. Why do the authors believe the former are more effective in reducing poverty?
3. What do the authors see as the primary functions of the welfare state in America?

Excerpts from *America's Misunderstood Welfare State: Persistent Myths, Enduring Realities* by Theodore R. Marmor, Jerry L. Mashaw, and Philip L. Harvey. Copyright © 1990 by Basic Books. Reprinted by permission of Basic Books, Inc., a division of HarperCollins Publishers, Inc.

Over the past several years we have repeatedly quizzed our colleagues, students, and other nonspecialist acquaintances about their understanding of American social welfare policy. We have been particularly interested in their conception of the place "welfare" occupies in the "welfare state" and in their view of the relationship between American welfare efforts and the incidence of poverty. We have heard expressed repeatedly the same ideas—a collection of beliefs that reflect, in distilled form, the reporting of both the daily press and standard journals of news and commentary concerning welfare in America. On our view, there exists something like a set of standard beliefs among well-educated adults concerning welfare, poverty, and the welfare state. . . .

The Conventional Wisdom

What about the relationship between welfare, the welfare state, and poverty? The conventional wisdom is that welfare and the welfare state have failed to solve the problem of poverty. But the stories about the dynamics of this failure are radically different. In one version failure is attributable to lack of effort. We never fought the cash War on Poverty that might have been ushered in by the family-assistance plans of either the Nixon or Carter administrations. And the great growth of the welfare state, in social insurance payments, has not been targeted at the poor. A competitive version views our antipoverty expenditures as sufficient to cure income poverty if giving money to the poor could actually cure poverty. On this view, the persistence of poverty is powerful evidence of the pernicious tendency of welfare to produce, rather than alleviate, dependency. Once again, however, the conventional wisdom is badly mistaken.

What has happened to poverty? Changes in the incidence of poverty in the United States are sensitive to what is measured, how, and over what time period. The most basic measure that we will use is the "official" poverty estimate reported by the Census Bureau's Current Population Survey (CPS). That estimate focuses on absolute levels of self-reported, annual cash income. There are many reasons to view this poverty estimate skeptically. Nevertheless, the census numbers are the most widely used by the press, commentators, and policymakers, and they have been compiled systematically over a considerable period of time. The CPS figures thus provide a reasonable picture of trends even if the absolute levels of poverty reported are contestable and contested.

First, the numbers for the past three decades simply belie the claim of failure. The CPS reports that the incidence of poverty fell from 22.2 percent in 1960 to 13.5 percent in 1988, a decline of 39 percent. We *have* made progress in reducing poverty over the past 30 years. This reduction might even be described as substantial. To be sure, this progress is attributable to rising average income levels as well as to government transfer programs, but the latter have had an important effect. In 1987, the nation's overall poverty rate would have been 20.6 percent instead of 13.5 percent were it not for these transfers. Moreover, the decline has been greater than these figures suggest, because the CPS data do not take into consideration the increasing importance of in-kind benefits in boosting the real income of poor households. If the value of food and housing benefits were counted, contemporary poverty rates would be 1.5 percentage points below the reported figures. . . .

Social Security Works

Social Security is one of America's biggest successes. It has dramatically improved the quality of life for older Americans. Fifty years ago most elderly people were dependent on relatives or public charity. A large proportion were destitute. Thanks to Social Security, most older people now live decently and independently.

Alice M. Rivlin, *Los Angeles Times*, May 12, 1991.

It is possible that the public is unimpressed with our longer-term progress against poverty because it has heard something about how much we have paid to achieve it. After all, the poverty gap, the difference between the incomes of the poor before taxes or transfer payments and the amount necessary to raise all families to the poverty floor in any given year, is far less than the amounts spent each year on social welfare programs. In 1987, for example, the poverty gap was about $124 billion, while welfare state expenditures totaled more than four and a half times that amount. Spending for means-tested programs alone, those presumably targeted at the poor, totaled close to $159 billion. Is this not evidence of, if not a failed, at least a spectacularly inefficient welfare state? We will approach these issues in reverse order.

Antipoverty efficiency. Two things need to be understood under this heading. One is straightforward, if occasionally rather technical: Poverty reduction is a very imprecise measure of the efficiency of even our means-tested, cash-assistance programs. The other is an apparent paradox: Poverty reduction has been accomplished largely through programs that do not target the poor.

The efficiency of a program is, broadly speaking, a measure of its capacity to conserve resources while accomplishing its purposes. An antipoverty program that closes 10 percent of the poverty gap at a cost of $15 billion is more efficient than a program that has the same effect at a cost of $20 billion. It is also more efficient than a program that spends $15 billion but closes only 5 percent of the poverty gap. So far so good.

Now, which programs of the American welfare state are explicitly designed to close the poverty gap? Answer: None. Such a program is, of course, imaginable. It would be a negative income tax that used the poverty line as its standard of need. To the extent that the income of a family or an individual fell below the poverty line, a payment would be made sufficient to bring them up to the poverty floor, but no higher. No one already above the poverty line would receive anything. Unless such a program had extremely high administrative expenses it should be very efficient at achieving its clear, and apparently single, objective—closing the poverty gap.

The American Welfare State

But Congress has consistently refused to adopt such a forthright program of poverty reduction. The programs that make up the American welfare state are quite different. Social insurance payments are based, not on demonstrated lack of income, but on prior contributions and the occurrence of a defined risk—death, disability, retirement, or medical expense. Means-tested programs providing cash assistance are largely directed toward groups that have experienced similar risks but are either not covered or not adequately covered by contributory social insurance programs (the aged, blind, and disabled poor, and children who have either lost or never had the support of one or both of their parents). Means-tested programs providing in-kind assistance (Food Stamps, medical care, shelter, job training, and the like) are primarily intended to contribute to the recipients' capacity for independent living and eventual self-support. Viewed as an assault on poverty defined in terms of a lack of current cash income, these programs are quite inefficient—they are over- and undergenerous, as well as over- and underinclusive. But direct poverty reduction is but one purpose of the American welfare state and not the sole purpose of any of its programs. Any program will appear inefficient if its efficiency is judged in relation to purposes different from those it is actually designed to serve.

To worry about the efficiency of the American welfare state from the perspective of an interest in eliminating poverty is thus really to worry about the *purposes* of our current welfare state and its programmatic expression. If there is a failure here, it is a failure of aims, not of execution. There is no evidence that a significant portion of welfare state expenditures is going to the wrong people or for the wrong purposes or at excessive administrative expense. Perhaps we should have a welfare state directed primarily at the elimination of the current income poverty of all Americans. That we do not now have one signals, not that our welfare state is inefficiently administered, but that it is pursuing different goals.

The idea that a more efficient antipoverty welfare state requires an alteration in our current programs and their goals is, of course, not a new one. It was one of the guiding principles of prior unsuccessful efforts to enact something like a negative income tax. And it animates some current suggestions for redirecting social insurance payments to the truly needy. In both cases, however, reformers talk primarily about better targeting of payments to achieve more efficient antipoverty effects. What is missing from their talk is an appreciation for the diverse goals that actually animate the American welfare state—a failure that inevitably leads to frustration and ineffective policy prescription.

A Paradox of Efficiency

To see this more clearly, let us recast our inquiry into antipoverty "efficiency" in terms of antipoverty "effectiveness." The revised question is not, "Which programs have the greatest percentage of their dollars targeted on the poor?" but, "Which programs eliminate the largest percentage of poverty?" The answer is the paradoxical one that we mentioned earlier: cash social insurance payments, the programs that most clearly are *not* directed at the poor, are the most effective at reducing poverty.

The difference between the effectiveness of social insurance and means-tested cash transfers in lifting people out of poverty is quite staggering—700 percent in 1985. In that same year, social insurance payments were nearly three times as effective as means-tested cash and in-kind programs combined. Nor is this differential effectiveness limited to the aged poor. Although social insurance, particularly Social Security retirement pensions, clearly has its greatest antipoverty impact on the aged, social insurance payments to the disabled and to the survivors of deceased workers eliminate nearly four times as much poverty among the non-aged poor as do means-tested cash benefits. The conclusion is thus inescapable: In the United States, social insurance has been a dramatically more effective antipoverty strategy than has welfare. Or, to put it in terms of our paradox, efficiency is ineffective.

The reasons for this paradox are not hard to find. Although their poverty is not the occasion for a social insurance transfer, many who receive social insurance payments would otherwise be poor. Because Social Security now covers over 90 percent of the population and pays substantial benefits, it has large effects.

Perhaps more important, because social insurance has overwhelming popular support, it is much more resilient politically in times of fiscal strain. The last dozen years have seen considerable retrenchment in means-tested programs, while social insurance cutbacks during that time have been extremely modest. Whereas means-tested cash benefits lost a third of their overall antipoverty effectiveness in the period 1979-85, social insurance lost only 9 percent of its antipoverty effectiveness. And while the power of social insurance to lift the non-aged poor out of poverty declined by 15 percent in that period, cash welfare payments lost 54 percent of their antipoverty efficacy.

The most resilient and most effective programs have been those for the aged. This is true even of the means-tested programs. The most significant antipoverty success story is Social Security pensions, which now prevent destitution among 71 percent of the aged. The growth of welfare state transfers between 1967 and 1985 reduced the poverty rate for elderly individuals by almost 12 percentage points, and most of this progress was attributable to the growth of social insurance benefits rather than means-tested programs. The elderly have thus been transformed from the age group most likely to suffer from poverty into the age group least likely to be poor. . . .

A Brief Recapitulation

Cash assistance to the poor has never been a large part of our welfare state and is literally dwarfed by social insurance expenditures. This pattern of expenditure fits our preferences for pooling common risks and the creation of opportunity as the primary functions of the welfare state. The American public may care about the elimination of poverty, but it is not keen on addressing income poverty through the simple expedient of cash transfers to the poor. Fortunately, however, our large and growing welfare state, particularly its social insurance component, does prevent much poverty. As the American welfare state has grown over the last three decades, the rate of poverty has declined by nearly 40 percent.

"Public jobs would . . . offer both mothers and non-mothers a way out of poverty."

Public Jobs Programs Should Replace Welfare

Mickey Kaus

Society cannot control some of the factors that create and perpetuate an underclass of ghetto poor, but it can control welfare, points out Mickey Kaus in the following viewpoint. To break the cycle of welfare dependency, he believes, welfare should be abolished in favor of public jobs, similar to those provided by the government's Works Progress Administration (WPA) in the 1930s to help the nation recover from the Great Depression. According to the author, WPA-type jobs that pay just under the minimum wage will help restore self-respect, provide job references, and create discipline and structure that will eventually transform ghetto welfare culture into part of the larger working society. Kaus is the author of *The End of Equality,* from which this viewpoint is taken.

As you read, consider the following questions:

1. Why does Kaus suggest that public jobs should pay slightly less than the minimum wage?
2. How does the author justify forcing mothers of young children off welfare?
3. Why does Kaus believe a public-jobs program would make two-parent families more common?

Welfare may not have been a sufficient condition for the growth of the underclass, but it's hard to see how contemporary liberals can deny that it was a necessary condition. . . . AFDC's [Aid to Families with Dependent Children] "give them cash" solution enabled an underclass to form, just as FDR [President Franklin D. Roosevelt] might have predicted. Which raises the obvious question: could altering this necessary ingredient somehow "de-enable" the underclass?

Certainly, if we're looking for a political handle on underclass culture, there is none bigger than the benefit programs that constitute the economic basis—the "mode of production," a Marxist might say—of the ghetto. In the average "extreme social problem" neighborhood, 34 percent of the households are on welfare. According to the Congressional Budget Office, cash welfare (mainly AFDC) is some 65 percent of the above-ground income of single mothers in the bottom fifth of the income distribution—up from 45 percent in 1970. A second, hidden chunk of ghetto GNP is illegal income, including income from the sale of drugs. But after interviewing urban welfare mothers in confidence about where they really get their money, Christopher Jencks and Kathryn Edin report that AFDC and food stamps account for 57 percent of their incomes. Work accounts for 12 percent, crime only 9 percent. Even assuming crime is a bigger factor than that (especially for young ghetto men), it's not a factor the larger society has been able to control. Welfare is something society *can* control. . . .

Changing Welfare

Changing welfare offers a chance to transform the economic role of the ghetto poor without tying them to their dying neighborhoods. Instead of attempting to somehow teach mainstream culture to people who spend most of their day immersed in ghetto culture, we could make ghetto culture economically unsustainable. . . .

That means something like this: replacing AFDC and all other cash-like welfare programs that assist the able-bodied poor (including "general relief" and food stamps) with a single, simple offer from the government—an offer of employment for every American citizen over eighteen who wants it, in a useful public job at a wage slightly below the minimum wage for private sector work. The government would supplement the wages of all low-wage jobs, both public and private, to ensure that every American who works full-time has enough money to raise a normal-sized family with dignity, out of poverty.

In this system, if you could work and needed money, the government would not give you a check (welfare). It wouldn't give you a check and then try to cajole, instruct, and threaten you into working it off ("workfare") or "training it off." It would give you the location of several government job sites. If you showed up and worked, you would be paid for your work. If you don't show up, you don't get paid. Simple.

Unlike welfare, these public, WPA-style [Works Progress Administration; public works] jobs would be available to everybody, men as well as women, single or married, mothers and fathers alike. No perverse "anti-family" incentives. It wouldn't even be necessary to limit the public jobs to the poor. If Donald Trump showed up, he could work too. But he wouldn't. Most Americans wouldn't. There'd be no need to "target" the program to the needy. The low wage itself would guarantee that those who took the jobs would be those who needed them, while preserving the incentive to look for better work in the private sector.

© Don Meredith. Reprinted with permission.

Perhaps most important for Civic Liberals (as for FDR), such work-relief wouldn't carry the stigma of a cash dole. Those who worked in the neo-WPA jobs would be earning their money. They could hold their heads up. They would also have something most unemployed underclass members desperately need: a supervisor they could give as a job reference to other employers. Although some WPA workers could be promoted to higher-paying public service positions, for most of them movement into the private sector would take care of itself. If you have to work anyway, why do it for $4 an hour? The whole problem of "work incentives" that obsesses current welfare policy dwindles into insignificance when what you're offering is work itself, rather than a dole that people have to then be "incentivized" (that is, bribed) into leaving.

Those who didn't take advantage of the neo-WPA jobs, however, would be on their own as far as income assistance went. No cash doles. Mothers included. The key welfare question left unresolved by the New Deal—do we expect single mothers with children to work?—would be resolved cleanly and clearly in favor of work. The government would announce that after a certain date able-bodied single women who bear children would no longer qualify for cash payments. Young women contemplating single motherhood couldn't count on AFDC to sustain them. As mothers, they would have to work like everyone else. The prospect of juggling motherhood and a not-very-lucrative public job would make them think twice. . . . But the public jobs would also offer both mothers and non-mothers a way out of poverty.

Most Mothers Work

Most American mothers, 67 percent, now work. Most single mothers work. Today's liberals are eager to acknowledge these facts of modern life when it suits their purposes—when arguing for parental leave, or deriding Phyllis Schlafly's "Ozzie and Harriet" vision of the ideal family. But they can't have it both ways. If mothers are expected to work, they're expected to work.

If poor mothers are to work, of course, day care must be provided for their children whenever it's needed, funded by the government if necessary. To avoid creating a day-care ghetto for low-income kids, this service will have to be integrated into the larger system of child care for other American families. That will be expensive. But it won't necessarily be as expensive as you might think. When free day care has been offered to welfare mothers who work, demand has fallen below predictions. "It is never utilized to the extent people thought it would be," says Barbara Goldman of the Manpower Demonstration Research Corporation (MDRC). Most welfare mothers, it seems, prefer to make their own arrangements. (Whether those arrangements are any good is another question. The government might want to take steps to actually encourage day care, as part of an "acculturation" campaign to get underclass kids out of the home and into classrooms at an early age.)

What happens if a poor single mother is offered decent day care, and a WPA-style job, and she refuses them? The short answer is that nothing happens. There's no penalty. Also no check. Perhaps she will discover some other, better way of feeding herself and her family. If, on the other hand, her children are subsequently discovered living in squalor and filth, then she has neglected a basic task of parenthood. She is subject to the laws that already provide for removal of a child from an unfit home. The long answer, then, is that society will also have to construct new institutions, such as orphanages, to care for the children whose parents so fail them. . . .

What if women take the jobs but still don't form two-parent families? Suppose the work-for-welfare swap goes well. A life on welfare becomes impossible. Young women who would previously have had children and gone on welfare now go to work, have children, and put them in day care. But has the underclass culture really been transformed if these women don't form stable two-parent families? After all, as Nicholas Lemann reminds us, many of the black family patterns we lament today were in evidence before AFDC, when black women and men had little economic alternative to working.

Transforming Ghetto Culture

There are three answers to this question. The first is that, yes, the ghetto-poor culture would be transformed. A working matriarchy is very different from a non-working matriarchy. If poor women who work to feed themselves and their children prefer to stay unmarried—supporting their children without help from a stable working partner—that's their choice. At least they are out of the welfare culture; they will be able to participate in the larger working society with dignity.

The second answer, which naturally follows from the first, is that many working mothers will not want to make that choice. Certainly it's doubtful that they'll be willing to share their hard-earned paychecks with non-working men the way they might have been willing to share their welfare checks. Once work is the norm, and the subsidy of AFDC has been removed, the natural incentives toward the formation of two-parent families will reassert themselves. Why go crazy trying to raise a kid on $10,000 a year when you can marry another worker and live on $20,000 a year? It makes no sense. Soon enough ghetto women will be demanding and expecting that the men in their lives offer them stable economic support.

Finally, the next generation off welfare—men as well as women, even men growing up in single-mother homes—will be better prepared not only to find jobs but to get the skills that will let them find "good jobs." That's because they will have grown up in a home where work, not welfare, is the norm, where the rhythms and discipline of obligation pervade daily life. A growing body of evidence shows that one of the most important factors in determining success at school is whether a child comes from a working home. Simply put, if a mother has to set her alarm clock, she's likely to teach her children to set their alarm clocks as well.

Replacing Welfare Will Work

Eventually, replacing welfare with work *can* be expected to transform the entire culture of poverty. It won't happen in one generation, necessarily, or even two. But it will happen. Underclass culture can't survive the end of welfare any more than feudal culture could survive the advent of capitalism.

"There is no reason to think that A.F.D.C. mothers can become 'self-sufficient' when growing millions of currently employed workers cannot."

Proposals for Public Jobs Programs Are a Charade

Richard A. Cloward and Frances Fox Piven

Millions of qualified, experienced workers are looking for work, while many jobs for unskilled workers are being transferred to the cheaper labor markets of the Third World. In this situation, argue Richard A. Cloward and Frances Fox Piven in the following viewpoint, the call to force poor, unskilled welfare recipients off welfare and into the work force is a symbolic charade, an unworkable response to public fears and dissatisfactions about the troubled economy. There are too few jobs available now, they point out, and there is little money in government budgets to create public jobs for this population. Cloward and Piven are the authors of *Regulating the Poor: The Functions of Public Welfare*, a 1971 book updated and reissued in 1993.

As you read, consider the following questions:

1. Summarize the findings of the reports on "workfare" programs (which require welfare recipients to work) cited by Cloward and Piven.
2. Why do the authors feel that the savings realized from eliminating welfare benefits will not offset the costs of government jobs programs?
3. What effect do the authors believe work programs would have on the community life in poor neighborhoods?

From Richard A. Cloward and Frances Fox Piven, "The Fraud of Workfare." This article is reprinted, with permission, from the May 24, 1993, issue of *The Nation* magazine, © The Nation Company, Inc.

During the 1992 presidential campaign, Bill Clinton repeatedly promised to "reform" the welfare system. Polls showed it was his most popular issue, and it continues to be a sure-fire applause-getter in speeches. . . . The general direction Clinton intends to take is well known: Some job training, more workfare, new sanctions and an effort to cut women off the rolls after two years.

Such proposals reflect a rising tide of antiwelfare rhetoric, whose basic argument is that people receiving public assistance become trapped in a "cycle of dependency." Thus, Senator Daniel Patrick Moynihan grandiosely proclaims in the press that "just as unemployment was the defining issue of industrialism, dependency is becoming the defining issue of postindustrial society." Conservative political scientist Lawrence Mead warns that "dependency" signals "the end of the Western tradition." The national press announces that dependency has reached epidemic proportions. According to these accounts, rising unemployment, declining wage levels and disappearing fringe benefits need not concern anyone. "The old issues were economic and structural," Mead says, and "the new ones are social and personal."

To cope with these new issues, the critics urge that women on welfare be put to work. Near-miraculous social and cultural transformations are predicted once welfare mothers are shifted into the labor market. Cohesion will be restored to family and community, crime and other aberrant behaviors will disappear and poverty will decline. Mickey Kaus, who advocates replacing welfare with a W.P.A. [Works Progress Administration]-style jobs program, invokes a grand historical parallel: "Underclass culture can't survive the end of welfare any more than feudal culture could survive the advent of capitalism."

The Labor Market Is Already Saturated

But there is no economically and politically practical way to replace welfare with work at a time when the labor market is saturated with people looking for jobs. Unemployment averaged 4.5 percent in the 1950s, 4.7 percent in the 1960s, 6.1 percent in the 1970s and 7.2 percent in the 1980s, and job prospects look no better in the 1990s. The labor market is flooded with immigrants from Asia and Latin America, and growing numbers of women have taken jobs to shore up family income as wages decline. Confronted with an increasingly globalized economy, corporations are shedding workers or closing domestic plants and opening new ones in Third World countries with cheap labor. Meanwhile, defense industries are making huge work-force cuts.

Moreover, employers are increasingly offering "contingent work"—part-time, temporary and poorly paid. Some 30 million people—over a quarter of the U.S. labor force—are employed in such jobs. A substantial proportion of them would prefer perma-

248

nent, full-time jobs but cannot find them. Contingent workers are six times more likely than full-time workers to receive the minimum wage, and they are much less likely to receive health and pension benefits.

Because most mothers who receive Aid to Families with Dependent Children are unskilled, they can command only the lowest wages and thus cannot adequately support their families, a problem that will grow worse as wages continue to decline. According to the Census Bureau, 14.4 million year-round, full-time workers 16 years of age or older (18 percent of the total) had annual earnings below the poverty level in 1990, up from 10.3 million (14.6 percent) in 1984 and 6.6 million (12.3 percent) in 1974. There is no reason to think that A.F.D.C. mothers can become "self-sufficient" when growing millions of currently employed workers cannot. In a study of the finances of welfare families, sociologists Christopher Jencks and Kathryn Edin found that "single mothers do not turn to welfare because they are pathologically dependent on handouts or unusually reluctant to work—they do so because they cannot get jobs that pay better than welfare."

Research on workfare programs bears this out. Sociologists Fred Block and John Noakes concluded that participants typically cannot find jobs that pay more than welfare. Reviewing the research in the field, the Center on Budget and Policy Priorities found that—highly publicized stories of individual successes notwithstanding—only a handful of people in workfare programs achieved "a stable source of employment that provides enough income for a decent standard of living (at least above the poverty line) and job-related benefits that adequately cover medical needs." Still another general survey, this one sponsored by the Brookings Institution, reports that none of the programs succeed in raising earnings of welfare mothers more than $2,000 above grant levels. Political scientists John E. Schwarz and Thomas J. Volgy write in their book *The Forgotten Americans*, "No matter how much we may wish it otherwise, workfare cannot be an effective solution" because "low-wage employment riddles the economy." They note that in 1989 one in seven year-round full-time jobs, or 11 million, paid less than $11,500, which was roughly $2,000 below the official poverty line for a family of four. . . .

"Economy" Measures Would Be Too Expensive

Another reason to be skeptical about welfare-to-work programs is that, although they are promoted as economy measures, they would in fact be very expensive if implemented widely. Federal and state expenditures for A.F.D.C. now run about $20 billion, supplemented by another $10 billion in food stamp costs for welfare families. But workfare programs would cost tens of billions more. Administrative costs alone would overshadow any savings from successful job placements. And to this must be added the much larger costs of government-subsidized child care and health care—essential to mothers going off welfare, since the private market is curtailing such benefits for newly hired workers. Economist James Medoff estimates that the proportion of new hires who receive health benefits dropped from 23 percent to 15 percent during the past decade. Christopher Jencks estimates that A.F.D.C. mothers working at the minimum wage would have to be given "free medical care and at least $5,000 worth of other resources every year to supplement their wages," at a cost of up to $50 billion, a quixotic sum that Congress is unlikely to appropriate. Mickey Kaus offers a similar estimate of the cost of his recommendation for a mandatory jobs program for the poor. Congress is certainly not unmindful of these costs, as it shows by its endless squabbling over whether health and day care benefits should be given to working recipients at all.

Given these constraints, the results of existing workfare programs are predictable enough. Studies show that a substantial proportion of welfare recipients who find jobs end up reapplying for welfare because they cannot survive on their earnings, even with welfare supplements, and because temporary child care and Medicaid supports run out, or because of periodic crises such as layoffs or illness in the family. Nevertheless, the charade goes on, as experts and politicians promise to put an end to welfare "dependency." None of it makes pragmatic sense.

Irrational Assertions

Other professed goals of these work programs are equally irrational, such as the unsubstantiated assertions that putting welfare recipients to work would transform family structure, community life and the so-called "culture of poverty." Kaus insists that "replacing welfare with work can be expected to transform the entire culture of poverty," including family patterns, because "it's doubtful" that working women would "be willing to share their hard-earned paychecks with non-working men the way they might have been willing to share their welfare checks." Therefore, "the natural incentives toward the formation of two-parent families will reassert themselves." But Kaus presents no data to support the assumption that the source of a woman's income influences marriage or living arrangements. In our judgment, marriage rates might indeed increase if jobs paying adequate wages and benefits were available to men, as well as to women on welfare who choose to work, but that outcome seems entirely unlikely in view of current economic trends.

It is also doubtful that putting poor women to work would improve the care and socialization of children, as Kaus claims. "If a mother has to set her alarm clock, she's likely to teach her children to set their alarm clocks as well," he says, thus trivializing the real activities of most of these women. Many A.F.D.C. mothers get their children up every morning and, because of the dangers of the streets, escort them to school, walk them home and keep them in their apartments until the next morning. Forcing these overburdened women to work would add a market job to the already exhausting job of maintaining a home without sufficient funds or services while living in dangerous and disorganized neighborhoods.

Reprinted by permission of Mike Luckovich and Creators Syndicate.

Putting welfare recipients to work is advertised as the way to reverse the deterioration of community life. This is hardly a new idea. The minutes of a meeting of academics, intellectuals and administrators in New York City after Richard Nixon's 1968 presidential election reported a consensus that the rising welfare rolls accompanied by spreading urban riots and other manifestations of civil disorder proved that "the social fabric . . . is coming to pieces. It isn't just 'strained' and it isn't just 'frayed'; but like a sheet of rotten canvas, it is beginning to rip. . . ." Converting A.F.D.C. to a workfare system was the remedy; work would restore the social fabric.

More likely, removing women from their homes and communities would shred the social fabric even more. Putting mothers to work would deprive the poor community of its most stable element—the women who, for example, have mounted campaigns to drive drug dealers from their housing projects and neighborhoods. Sally Hernandez-Piñero, chairwoman of the New York City Housing Authority, emphasized the important social role played by the approximately 65,000 women raising children alone in the New York City projects: "Anyone with even a nodding acquaintance with these women knows them for what they are, the sanity of the poor community, resourceful survivors of abandonment, slander and brutality. . . . In many poor communities, they are the only signatures on the social contract, the glue that keeps our communities from spinning out of control."

None of the critics convincingly explain why these women would contribute more to their communities by taking jobs flipping hamburgers. Nor do they explain why it would not be better public policy to shore up income supports (the real value of A.F.D.C. benefits has fallen by 43 percent since the early 1970s, and by 27 percent if food stamps are figured in) and social supports for women who are struggling to care for children under the junglelike conditions of urban poverty. Instead, the family and community work performed by these women—like the family and community work of women in general—is consistently ignored or devalued. . . .

Many welfare mothers do want to work, and they should have the chance, together with training and supportive benefits, such as day care and health care, as well as adequate wages and supplemental welfare payments. Under such conditions, many would take jobs, and coercion would be unnecessary. Realistically, however, such opportunities are not on the reform agenda. It is the charade of work that is on the agenda. . . .

Welfare Mothers: Convenient Political Scapegoats

Politicians understand the value of . . . symbolism, however, and rush to divert voter discontent over rising unemployment and falling wage levels by focusing on "welfare reform," knowing that welfare mothers, a majority of whom are black and Hispanic, make convenient scapegoats. Welfare is thus defined as a major national domestic problem—bad for the country and bad for the poor. It drains public budgets and reduces work effort. Allowing poor mothers to opt out of paid work saps their initiative and induces disabling psychological and cultural patterns that entrench their incapacity for work all the more. Deepening poverty ostensibly follows. As Lawrence Mead puts it, the new inequality in the

252

United States can be traced to the "nonworking poor."

Not only are better-off people encouraged to blame the poor for their own troubles but the rituals that degrade welfare recipients reaffirm the imperative of work at a time when wages are down, working conditions worse and jobs less secure. Kaus writes that while we cannot promise the poor who work that "they'll be rich, or even comfortably well-off" (and, he might have added, we cannot even promise them a living wage), "we can promise them *respect*" because they "would have the tangible honor society reserves for workers." The charade of work enforcement reform should thus be understood as a symbolic crusade directed at the working poor rather than at those on relief, and the moral conveyed is the shame of the dole and the virtue of labor, no matter the job and no matter the pay.

One thing seems clear: If Clinton and Congress actually adopt the proposed two-year cutoff of benefits in the current labor market, they will soon find themselves debating whether women unable to make it in the marketplace should be readmitted to the rolls. . . . If they are not, the streets would soon fill with homeless women and children, and the venerable body of theory and historical research that attributes riots and political disorder to economic insecurity would once against be put to the test. It is hard to believe that national politicians will take that risk.

"The government has decided that it is better for people to have no roof over their head than to live in places that do not have hot water."

Government Regulation Created a Housing Crisis for the Poor

Ernest van den Haag

Government regulations that define the minimal requirements for housing are too demanding, according to Ernest van den Haag, author of the following viewpoint. While any shelter from the elements would seem better than homelessness, he points out, landlords are no longer allowed to offer facilities without such amenities as heat, water, and electricity—amenities that would cost more than many poor people are able to pay. Thus regulations intended to protect people from substandard housing prevent them from finding any housing at all. Van den Haag, former John M. Olin Professor of Jurisprudence and Public Policy at Fordham University in New York, is a Distinguished Scholar at the Heritage Foundation, a conservative think tank in Washington, D.C.

As you read, consider the following questions:

1. What difference does van den Haag see between the used-car market and the housing market?
2. What four kinds of inexpensive housing does the author say have disappeared because of government regulation?

Ernest van den Haag, "Who Goes Homeless?" *National Review*, March 1, 1993. Copyright © 1993 by National Review, Inc., 150 E. 35th St., New York, NY 10016. Reprinted by permission.

How come there are so many homeless people in American cities? By now the literature has established that at least a third of them are drug-addicted or mentally disturbed and would not stay in a dwelling even if it were available to them. Still, many other homeless people simply cannot afford the rent at which apartments are available.

This seems strange. If you need a new jacket you usually can buy it. If you can't spend five hundred dollars, you can find one for fifty. If that is too much, you can go to a thrift shop and get a used one for ten dollars or less. How come? The market for old and new jackets is not regulated by the government.

Or consider cars. If you cannot afford a new one, used ones are available in many price ranges. A very cheap used car may not have air conditioning, a radio, or power windows; the upholstery may be torn, the roof may leak, the windows may be broken and the paint peeling. But if it runs and carries you where you want to go, it is better than no transportation.

Used Cars vs. Used Housing

Here is the difference. While the government lets you buy an old jalopy, provided it's not dangerous, government regulators will prevent you from moving into an apartment unless it has heating, hot and cold water, electricity, etc. Landlords are not allowed to rent old apartments without such facilities, let alone build new ones. Sure, life without these conveniences is hard. But wouldn't you prefer an apartment without hot water to sleeping on the street? You would; but the government would not. Unless the apartment has the minimal conveniences the regulations require, you are not allowed to move in and the landlord is not allowed to rent it to you.

In the past, people who were down on their luck could spend the night in a flophouse, so called because it consisted simply of a big enclosure. No bedding; heat and water in some cases, but not in all. You just flopped down, protected from the elements. The price was very low. Not a comfortable overnight stay. Yet, wasn't it better than sleeping on the street, which not only lacks the same amenities but also may be wet, cold, windswept, dangerous, and without even a communal bathroom? A locker was usually provided in these flophouses, as were some other facilities, however minimal. They were privately owned and profit-making. The owners competed with one another to offer the most for the money, attract customers, and increase profits. Not least, private owners could get rid of disruptive customers. Public shelters cannot, or at least do not. They are very expensive for taxpayers, yet yield so little benefit to users that many homeless people prefer the street even in winter.

More amenities, above all privacy, were provided by cage ho-

255

tels. These consisted of large rooms divided into cubicles by means of partial walls, and offered common washing facilities. Those who could afford a little more still relied on rooming houses, which were comparatively luxurious, or on boarding houses, which offered room and board cheaply. The latter two kinds of facilities often made use of old buildings, subdividing what had been spacious apartments.

All or Nothing

All of these places have disappeared, not because they were no longer needed or had become unprofitable, but because the government made them unprofitable, when it did not actually demolish them, or prohibit them from offering shelter. Politicians, bureaucrats, and bleeding hearts waxed indignant about the deprivations people suffered in cheap lodgings which lacked minimal amenities. Their solution? Get rid of these cheap lodgings. The former customers, unable to afford more expensive lodging, now have to sleep on the street. In effect the government has decided that it is better for people to have no roof over their head than to live in places that do not have hot water. Yes indeed, the best can be the enemy of the better.

© Mike Keefe/*The Denver Post*. Reprinted with permission.

Common sense suggests that it is better to have transportation in a rundown jalopy, when that is all you can afford, than to have no transportation. Better to buy a second-hand jacket than to have none. And better to have some shelter, however bare, than to sleep on the street. But common sense ends where the government begins.

Nobody would be permitted to build a flophouse or an SRO [single-room occupancy hotel], or even to modify an existing building for such use—unless the facilities required by the government were installed. Which would drive the costs beyond the means of the prospective customers. In many cases the buildings are there, but cannot be utilized because they do not come up to government standards. Sure, the street doesn't either, but the government adamantly refuses to recognize that the street is the actual alternative. So do the many advocates for the homeless.

Whether automobiles or clothing, whatever in the normal course of events no longer satisfies the rich is utilized by the poor. They are and feel better off with second-hand things than they would without. Although there is increasingly a tendency for the government to get in the way, most second-hand markets are comparatively free and therefore efficient.

Suing the Landlord

Not so with housing. As Peter D. Salins and Jerard C. S. Mildner make clear in *Scarcity by Design* (Harvard, 1992), a landlord who tries to rent "substandard" apartments, at however low a price, will be haled into court. The looming fines, rent strikes, prosecutions, and civil suits make any such attempts unrewarding. On the other hand, a landlord who tries to charge what it actually costs him to maintain apartments in conformity with various ordinances will be prosecuted for exceeding rent ceilings. One need not be an economist to figure out that landlords will not rent, let alone build, apartments for which they cannot charge enough to cover the costs of the required amenities. Which means that apartments cheap enough for the poor to afford will not be built. So the homeless will have to continue sleeping on the street. Politicians and bleeding hearts will continue to deplore their fate. Money will be collected for them. The Civil Liberties Union will try to secure their right to sleep in subways and terminals. But no politician will lift a finger to get rid of the regulations that make the homeless homeless.

[Author's note:] I acknowledge with gratitude my debt to Professor Randall K. Filer's "Opening the Door to Low Cost Housing" (*The City Journal*, Summer 1992, Manhattan Institute, New York). My historical data are entirely due to his diligence.

"Rent control's toll on the housing stock has been devastating."

Rent Control Created the Housing Crisis

William Tucker

Rent control was a temporary wartime measure that has become entrenched in many cities, today covering about a fifth of America's rental housing. In the following viewpoint, William Tucker, author of *The Excluded Americans: Homelessness and Housing Policies*, charges that a policy intended to help the poor is instead exploited by the well-to-do or the well-connected. The result has been a deterioration or loss of affordable housing as landlords are unable to maintain their buildings, according to the author. Tucker is a reporter for a financial publication, *The Bond Buyer*.

As you read, consider the following questions:

1. Compare New York City's rental market before and after rent control, as depicted by Tucker.
2. In the study by Rolf Goetze cited by Tucker, how do the rent-controlled tenants compare as a group to those whose homes are not rent-controlled? Which group does Tucker feel would be more able to afford decontrolled rents?
3. How did rent control backfire on college students in Berkeley, California, and Cambridge, Massachusetts, according to the author?

March 1993 marked the 50th anniversary of the passage of the Emergency Wartime Residential Rent Control Act. Designed to prevent transient, well-paid wartime workers from outbidding local residents for apartments in industrial cities, the law was eventually extended to New York City—which had few wartime industries and reasonably high vacancy rates.

After the war, rent controls were abandoned everywhere except New York, where they have been extended by state law ever since. During the inflationary 1970s, a second wave of rent control ordinances captured Boston, Cambridge, and Brookline, Mass.; Newark; much of suburban Long Island and New Jersey; Washington; and more than half the population of California. Today more than 200 cities, containing about a fifth of the rental units in the country, are under rent control. The results have been disastrous.

Hardly a man is now alive who remembers what New York City was like before rent control. Who can recall the traditional "moving days" of April 1 and Oct. 1, when old leases expired and New Yorkers went hop-skipping across the city in pursuit of better apartments? Who remembers the "fall renting season," when landlords spent the month of August redecorating in order to attract prospective tenants returning from summer vacation? Housing was so cheap and plentiful that people routinely put their furniture in summer storage and rented a new apartment when they returned in the fall. New York was often called the "City of Nomads."

Dilapidated Housing

Today, most New Yorkers have become accustomed to the idea that finding an apartment requires Eastern European-style guile and duplicity. A few years ago, *New York* magazine recommended "joining a church or synagogue" as a good way of meeting people who might provide leads on a new apartment.

After 50 years of rent control, New York, which once had arguably the most beautiful housing stock in the world, now has the most dilapidated housing in America. Beautiful brownstones from the turn of the century now stand shuttered with window decals that feature drawings of curtains and flowerpots, designed to make it *appear* that someone is living in them. Over 70% of central Harlem has been taken for back taxes. The middle-class bureaucracy that manages this confiscated housing now swallows more money than the New York Public Library. Meanwhile, a whole generation of struggling, blue-collar landlords has been wiped out.

All this has done wonders for the city's perpetual fiscal crisis. Although few realize it, New York City borrows more money than any entity except the federal government. Despite its massive debt, New York remains a museum of decaying infrastructure. Where does the money go? Into housing construction. Over the past five years, the city government has spent $5.1 billion rehabilitating housing confiscated from private landlords.

Still, New Yorkers accept all this sheepishly, going to the shearing every year for taxes that are 170% of the national average with barely a whimper. At least the government is protecting them from their landlords.

What has happened is fairly predictable from economic theory, which forecasts supply shortages, disinvestment and deterioration of the product when price controls go into effect. What has been less explored is the "nomenklatura" phenomenon—the emergence of an elite capable of turning the regulations to its advantage.

Helping the Rich

Although rent control is always advertised as "helping the poor," the rich and well-connected have been the clear winners. In New York, rents in Harlem and the outer boroughs are at market levels, while all the "great deals" are on the Upper East Side, the Upper West Side and Greenwich Village—home of the cultural and financial elite.

Such luminaries as Deputy Mayor Barbara Fife, City Council President Ruth Messinger, former Mayor Ed Koch, James Levine, music director of the Metropolitan Opera, Alistair Cooke and ballerina Suzanne Farrell have all spent years benefiting from rent control.

The same pattern is beginning to emerge in other cities that adopted rent control during the "second wave" of the 1970s. Independent studies in Cambridge, Mass., and Berkeley, Calif., have found that the major benefits of rent control have gone to upper-income professionals who use their mastery of the bureaucracy and their superior networks of friends and connections to exploit the system.

In Cambridge, Rolf Goetze, a highly respected housing consultant, compiled statistics on residents' age and occupation from the city's 71,000-person voter registration records. He then compared the characteristics of tenants in rent-controlled housing with those of tenants and homeowners in the uncontrolled sector.

Profiling Rent-Controlled Tenants

Despite the tendency of high-income people to own their own homes, Mr. Goetze found rent-controlled apartments to be more densely populated with professional people in their prime earning years. Over 52% of rent-controlled tenants are age 30 to 49, compared with 34.4% in the noncontrolled sector. Senior citizens make up only 7.7% of the rent-controlled sector but 16.6%

in unregulated housing. Also under-represented in rent-controlled apartments are young people, age 18 to 29, who are 32.3% of the unregulated population but only 24.5% of those in controlled housing.

Mr. Goetze found the rent-controlled tenantry to be dominated by people classified as professional, managerial-administrative, technical-semiprofessional, clerical and skilled. The unregulated sector was populated by unskilled and semiskilled blue-collar workers, students, retired people, housewives, and the unemployed.

"The largest concentration of people in rent-controlled apartments seems to be white-collar professionals in their 30s and 40s," says Mr. Goetze. "Rent-controlled units are not concentrated in any particular neighborhood. It's just that, wherever they are, professional people seem to be more skillful at ferreting them out."

Creating Housing Shortages

Rent control policies ensure a shortage of affordable housing in the six states and nearly 200 urban areas where such regulations are in force. Economists long have taught that all price controls lead to shortages by discouraging production while stimulating increased demand. Rent controls are no exception. By eliminating incentives for construction of new housing and for proper maintenance of existing housing, rent control creates rental housing shortages. This makes it almost impossible for Americans with limited means to find the few units that occasionally do become available, since high demand ensures those units will usually go only to those who can afford broker's fees, exorbitant "key money" commissions, and bribes to landlords.

John Scanlon, "Homelessness: Describing the Symptoms, Prescribing a Cure," Heritage Foundation *State Backgrounder*, April 30, 1990.

Typical is Kenneth Reeves, a 1970 Harvard graduate and now mayor of Cambridge. Mr. Reeves still lives in the rent-controlled apartment he first rented in 1976. In an apparent gesture of populism, he even advertises his rent-controlled status in his campaign literature.

In Berkeley, Michael St. John, a Ph.D. in economics who has consulted for landlords for many years, is just completing a study for the Pacific Legal Foundation that reaches almost identical conclusions. "We've compared the population of Berkeley in 1980, just after rent control was instituted [1979], with the population of Berkeley today," says Mr. St. John. "It's already obvious that there has been an enormous shift toward the professional and white-collar classes. Welfare mothers form a much smaller portion of the population today, as do several other categories of older and poorer people. Berkeley probably would have gentrified anyway—the same thing has happened in neighboring towns —but rent control seems to have accelerated the process."

Revenge Backfires

Ironically, even though rent control was adopted in both Berkeley and Cambridge with the help of vast student-voter populations taking revenge on their "townie" landlords, today's college students do not seem to be getting any of the benefits.

Eva Floystrup, who with her carpenter husband has owned a building in Berkeley for 20 years, still rents to the six thirty-something professionals who came to her as Berkeley students 15 years ago. "I can't get rid of them," she says. "I have students coming up to me all the time saying, 'Why can't I find anyplace to live in Berkeley?' I tell them, 'We're still taking care of the Class of '79. If they ever leave, I'll have room for you.'"

Rent control's toll on the housing stock has been devastating, the inequities enormous. But remember, it's only temporary. As soon as Berkeley and Cambridge's "temporary housing shortages" are over—as soon as World War II winds down in New York—things will be getting back to normal.

"A major reason for this housing crisis is the shortage of low-rent and subsidized housing."

Cutbacks in Government Funds Created the Housing Crisis

Carl Rowan

The urban working poor often live in inadequate housing—if they are lucky, according to Carl Rowan, author of the following viewpoint. Many spend so much of their income on rent, he says, that they cannot afford other necessities. Even a minor financial crisis can result in their becoming homeless. Rowan blames cutbacks in federal funds for affordable housing, along with drops in welfare spending, for much of this housing crisis. Rowan is a nationally syndicated newspaper columnist.

As you read, consider the following questions:

1. What percentage of its income should a poor family spend on housing, according to the figures cited by Rowan?
2. Does the author explain why a failure to build new housing resulted in a drop in the number of existing housing units?
3. What change in the housing supply between 1970 and 1989 does the author describe? What effects does he believe this change has had on the poor?

Carl Rowan, "No Home Sweet Home for America's Poor," *Liberal Opinion Week*, December 28, 1992. Reprinted with special permission of North American Syndicate.

Just when Americans are feeling good and warm-hearted about our mission of mercy into Somalia, I hope I don't appear churlish in bringing up a special kind of suffering in our country.

I am talking about the millions of people who are at risk for disease and malnutrition because they cannot find affordable housing. Our urban working poor who can find shelter are paying so much for it that they can't buy proper food, clothing and other necessities of life.

A Severe Housing Crisis

Take the case of Audrey Wabash, who for four years tried futilely to get into public housing in this city. The *Washington Post* reported that she lived for a time on the streets and in a shelter for women—but could not get public housing.

After finding a job cleaning an office building, the 38-year-old single mother moved into a private apartment. It's just a small place in a neighborhood she considers so dangerous that she won't let her 14-year-old son live with her.

And it has brought new dilemmas. Well over half of Wabash's minimum-wage salary goes to pay the $425 monthly rent. Moreover, since she has a job and a place to live, she is now low on the priority list for subsidized housing, which has an average rent of $165 a month.

The plight of Audrey Wabash is shared by millions of poor Americans in cities across this country. A severe housing crisis has put affordable housing beyond their reach, reports the Center on Budget and Policy Priorities.

According to standards established by the [Ronald] Reagan administration, poor households should spend no more than 30 percent of their income on housing. (If Wabash were able to live by those guidelines, she would be paying a maximum of about $225 a month.) But according to the Center's report, three-fourths of the households earning less than $10,000 a year in all 44 metropolitan areas for which data are available paid more than 30 percent of their income for housing in the late 1980s.

In fact, says the report, affordable housing was so scarce that in 43 of the 44 cities, at least half of the poor spent more than 30 percent of their incomes on housing. (The figures are based on data collected between 1986 and 1989, but the situation has not improved since then, the Center says.)

Living in Fear

Think of the emotional burden those housing costs put on needy families. They live in constant fear that an unexpected medical expense, a tardy welfare check, or a job loss will lead to utility shut-offs or even eviction.

A major reason for this housing crisis is the shortage of low-rent and subsidized housing. During the 1980s the Reagan administration cut back federal efforts to build new affordable housing in favor of relying on the private market. The result was a drop of about one million low-rent units in the decade; by 1989 the supply reached its lowest level in 20 years.

At the same time, rents rose and the real value of cash assistance like Aid to Families with Dependent Children (AFDC) fell. In 39 of the 44 metro areas surveyed, the cost of a modest two-bedroom apartment was greater than the entire AFDC grant for a family of three.

IF IT WERE ONLY THAT SIMPLE

The upshot, according to the study, is that instead of the 400,000 surplus low-rent units America had in 1970, there were 4.1 million more renters than available units by 1989. Only one-third of poor urban renters received help with housing costs from any level of government in the late 1980s.

Impact of the Housing Squeeze

The impact of this housing squeeze is spelled out in other findings of the report:

• Applicants for housing assistance often languish on waiting lists for years. Along with overextended renters, they are prime candidates for the ranks of the homeless.

• Large numbers of the poor (over 50 percent in some cities) live in substandard or overcrowded housing.

• Whites as well as minorities are affected; nearly 90 percent of poor white households spent at least 30 percent of their incomes on housing in the late 1980s. However, blacks and Hispanics face more serious problems because they are more likely to be poor and they must battle various forms of discrimination in the housing field.

It's a somber note . . . but we must remember that housing woes are so widespread that suffering is just around the corner in our big cities.

*"There's no reason anyone has to sleep on the
street in St. Louis anymore."*

Local Governments Can Coordinate Private Efforts to End Homelessness

Katherine Barrett and Richard Greene

In 1993, Katherine Barrett and Richard Greene surveyed leaders of America's cities to find innovative problem solvers. In St. Louis, Missouri, they discovered that the city government shelters the homeless not by providing services to them directly, but by coordinating the efforts of private agencies that receive city dollars, charitable individuals and institutions, and private businesses. This coordination has led to better services, more efficient use of resources, and often lower costs. Barrett and Greene are contributing editors to *FW* (*Financial World*), a biweekly financial newsmagazine.

As you read, consider the following questions:

1. Barrett and Greene believe that large urban problems, such as crime, cannot be solved by just one city agency, such as the police. What is their reasoning? How is this idea put into practice in dealing with the homeless in St. Louis?
2. Why do the authors believe there will continue to be some homeless people in St. Louis? Does this reflect a breakdown in providing services to the homeless?
3. What do Barrett and Greene see as the key to St. Louis's success in dealing with the homeless?

The litany of evils that beset America's large cities is familiar stuff for viewers of the 11 o'clock news. Examples of violent crime, homelessness and the devastation of AIDS roll across the screen like evil floats in a parade from hell. The deterioration of downtowns and neighborhoods is a favorite topic of pundits of all political stripes.

"Whenever they do a story about Cleveland, they're sure to show a clip of the Cuyahoga River when it caught on fire in 1969," says one of that city's leaders. "That was a long time ago, and that river is now one of the cleaner ones in the U.S. But you can just count on it. When the story mentions Cleveland, there's our burning river again."

The nearly universal bad press accorded the nation's cities has led to the perpetuation of three great urban myths:

• Nothing ever gets better.
• The only way to make things better is to spend more.
• When you *do* spend more money, things only get worse.

Wrong. Wrong. And wrong.

From coast to coast there are cities making valiant efforts—often without huge expenditures—to better their lot. . . .

Each of the cities we have singled out has accomplished something in a way that other cities can replicate. "Somebody, somewhere has found the best way to do the job," says Frank Fairbanks, city manager of Phoenix. "The point is to focus on the best."

Comparing Notes

Benchmarking is clearly the most sensible route for cities interested in progress. Officials in Dallas have made a religion out of comparing notes with other municipalities. "I make a dozen calls a week to other cities," says Ryan Evans, Dallas's director of budget and research. "If you find out another city of similar size has a parks and recreation department that's operating $10 million less expensively, you're going to ask why. Why re-create the wheel all the time? That's a waste of resources."

Different conditions among cities, of course, are obstacles to the cross-pollination of ideas. Washington, D.C., is uniquely hamstrung by federal regulations. New York City's budget dwarfs the 10 next-largest cities combined. El Paso's future is deeply intertwined with that of Juarez, Mexico. But the biggest difference among cities is their ability to bring cash to the table. El Paso, which has one of the smallest per capita budgets of any large city, can hardly be expected to innovate on the scale of Portland, Ore., a city with relatively high per capita resources.

Limited resources shouldn't be an excuse for stifled progress, however. Oklahoma City, for example, is hardly rolling in dough. Yet it has repeatedly come up with helpful innovations such as its "Cellular Pothole Hotline," which permits drivers to punch a four-key code into their car phones and reach a 24-hour answering machine equipped to take complaints about potholes. Expensive? No. Useful? Very.

In truth, ideas that blossom in one place often fail to take root in another simply because they are not properly cultivated. Paul Epstein, a consultant and former manager of citywide productivity for New York City's mayor's office, calls the syndrome "pilot programmitis." The money is there to start innovative new services—mayors love ribbon cuttings and dramatic announcements. But when it's time for expansion or evaluation of services, the TV cameras disappear—and all too often, so does public support.

"It's terrific to get credit for being the initiator," says Kim Hopper, a research scientist at the Nathan Kline Institute who has extensively studied homeless programs. What's tough is getting the funding, the staff and the local support to keep something alive and vital after it's brought into existence.". . .

Creative Leadership and Cooperation

Homelessness has too many forms for unitary, centralized solutions. . . . Some solutions will cost money, but many important problems primarily need creative leadership. Homelessness offers important opportunities to politicians and other leaders who can achieve much by merely reassigning roles and responsibilities within a program and restructuring the way the money flows. . . .

In consideration of the homelessness issue . . . in Portland, Oregon, the mayor's office has become the focal point for persons with power and influence in the community to carry on a reasoned discussion about community problems and arrive at practical courses of action. . . . The business community sits at the table with the social service agencies and others, bringing both its economic interests and a commitment to help to the situation. The Chamber of Commerce, which set up a task force of its own on social concerns, has committed time and money. When everyone with influence over a problem participates, solutions seem to be more complete, with fewer unanticipated consequences.

Richard W. White Jr., *Rude Awakenings*, 1992.

Another significant enemy of good ideas is a lack of partnerships within the cities: between city hall and the city council; between the business community and the government; between city agencies. Most urban problems aren't simple enough for one agency to solve. Crime, for instance, is more than a police problem. Cities such as Dallas and Seattle are making a dent in high crime rates by combining the efforts of police, social service agencies and the business community. . . .

As important as the need for partnerships is a solid management base if innovative programs are to grow. Good accounting and financial reporting systems, honest budgeting and regular evaluation and measurement of agencies' accomplishments are vital. Cities need to be able to judge the quality of services delivered with their cost in mind; otherwise services are doomed to the inefficiency of the unaccountable. A motivated and well-managed work force also underlies any successful efforts. . . .

In 1985 it was difficult to take a casual stroll through sections of St. Louis without getting the unsettling feeling that you were tramping through someone's living room. The homeless slept on park benches or, when they got lucky, in broken-down cars. Shelter was in such short supply that Legal Services of Eastern Missouri sued the city on behalf of homeless individuals.

When the city aggressively accelerated its efforts to deal with the situation, it was met with suspicion, doubt and even outright contempt. "There were people from [social] agencies who refused to meet with me because I represented the city," says Rosemary Terranova, who was then director of the City of St. Louis Department of Human Services. "They wouldn't return my phone calls."

St. Louis Today

Today, in 1993, St. Louis has made enormous progress. "There's no reason anyone has to sleep on the street in St. Louis anymore," Terranova says. In fact, some 10,000 men, women and children use its shelters over the course of a year. Inevitably, some people—many of whom are mentally ill and substance abusers—will decline services. But by keeping facilities safe and clean, St. Louis has managed to reduce that number to a bare minimum.

Of course, simply getting people off the streets doesn't mean St. Louis has solved the problem of homelessness—a complex social ailment with a variety of deep-rooted causes. But the strides the city has made are remarkable. What's been done in St. Louis is very innovative and deserves to be replicated," says Michael Mayer, director of programs for the National Alliance to End Homelessness.

One of the most crucial elements in the St. Louis model was developed early on: The city defined itself not as a provider of services, but as a coordinator of various not-for-profit agencies that fed, clothed, transported and provided health care to the homeless. Careful review of those agencies assured that duplication was avoided, that agencies worked together efficiently and

270

that the quality of their services was kept high.

In awarding city funds, each private agency was chosen to handle a single aspect of the problem. One organization ran the hotline, another the transportation system. One provided life-skills classes—teaching budgeting, parenting, consumerism, the appropriate use of utilities, home repair and how to be a good tenant. Several agencies were in charge of individual shelters and others handled transitional housing—such as Hope House, a 50-unit furnished apartment building owned by the city of St. Louis.

The contracts themselves, which are bid for annually, require each recipient of city dollars to work closely with the others. "We created an overlay mechanism that not only induced but mandated that agencies collaborate in order to receive city funding," says Terranova, who is now executive director of the St. Louis Housing Resource Center, which provides the city's major homelessness prevention service. "The human services community is competitive and protective of turf. What's unique here is the high level of cooperation and collaboration."

Coordinating Efforts Is Key

Kim Hopper, a research scientist with the Nathan Kline Institute in Orangeburg, N.Y., has studied homelessness extensively. "The biggest dropped ball nationally," he says, "has been the lack of coordination in the deployment of resources by housing and development agencies and those that provide clinical and support services in psychiatry, health and substance abuse. If you get housing or services in the community without the other pieces, the investment turns out to be worthless."

Since 1986 a formal meeting of the St. Louis Homeless Services Network, which now has 135 member agencies, has been held monthly to share information. Smaller groups also meet frequently to discuss individual cases.

Moreover, St. Louis effectively drew charitable individuals and the private sector into the effort. Retailers and other corporate citizens often see the homeless as an enemy of profit. Who wants to eat in a restaurant when a grimy family is camped out front, begging? Given the opportunity to pitch in effectively, though, private companies often will.

In 1993 the city expects to contribute $2.5 million of its own funds and to receive twice that much from private sources to attack the problem. In July 1992, St. Louis began funding the Homeless Resource Bank, which acts as a warehouse for in-kind donations including food, furniture and baby equipment. By the end of 1992 it had received about $155,000 worth of household goods.

Efficiency is key. Until the late 1980s St. Louis was like many cities in its use of the "mission model" for its shelters. Two sets

271

of shelters were maintained. At 6 a.m., when nighttime shelters closed, the homeless were transported to daytime shelters, where children were picked up for school and later dropped off, before everyone was shifted back to the night shelter. "It was musical chairs," says Dorothy Dailey, director of the Homeless Services Program, part of the city's Department of Human Services. "We've now gone to 24-hour shelters with satellite centers for classes and day care within the shelters themselves. We've cut down substantially on our need for transportation."

Addressing the Causes of Homelessness

With the street problem under control, St. Louis has turned its attention to the causes of homelessness. Such preventive work is clearly sensible, but is still "a relatively rare programmatic effort," Mayer says.

Its major thrust, thus far, has been through the Housing Resource Center, which is now the first stop people make when they are having problems that may ultimately lead to homelessness. The agency, which is run by Catholic charities, performs such tasks as mediating with landlords when evictions are threatened or code violations are found. It also helps people get jobs and job training, and provides financial assistance and counseling to the potentially homeless.

The high price of shelters—including the cost of food, round-the-clock staff and the obvious need for security—makes preventive work exceedingly cost-effective. Consider: A $350 one-time payment can often help a marginally solvent family keep its apartment. Compare that with the $900 a month it costs to keep a family of four in a shelter.

"The common mistake has been to treat homelessness like a transient emergency," says researcher Hopper. "The sense of urgency may have been transient, but the crisis persists."

Periodical Bibliography

The following articles have been selected to supplement the diverse views presented in this chapter.

Teresa Amott — "Ending Poverty: Unconventional Wisdom," *Christianity & Crisis*, June 8, 1992. Available from 537 W. 121st St., New York, NY 10027.

Gordon Berlin and William McAllister — "Homelessness: Why Nothing Has Worked," *The Brookings Review*, Fall 1992. Available from 1775 Massachusetts Ave. NW, Washington, DC 20036.

Tom Bethell — "They Had a Dream," *National Review*, August 23, 1993.

Ruth Conniff — "Cutting the Lifeline," *The Progressive*, February 1992.

Richard L. Cravatts — "Loosen Codes and House the Homeless," *The Wall Street Journal*, February 6, 1992.

Robin Epstein — "Workfair," *In These Times*, March 8, 1993.

Sarah Griffen — "Poor Relations," *Dollars & Sense*, May 1992.

Joe Klein — "Cities, Heal Thyselves," *Newsweek*, July 5, 1993.

Joe Klein — "'Make the Daddies Pay,'" *Newsweek*, June 21, 1993.

Christopher Meade — "The Myth of Welfare," *Z Magazine*, September 1992.

John Mueller — "The Cost of Social Spending—Joblessness," *The Wall Street Journal*, July 13, 1993.

The New York Times — "Rethinking Welfare" series, July 5-10, 1992.

Michael Novak — "The Crisis of the Welfare State," *Crisis*, vol. 11, no. 7, July/August 1993.

Robert Rector — "Increase Well-Being, Not Just Welfare," *The Washington Times*, May 25, 1992.

Robin Toner — "Politics of Welfare: Focusing on the Problems," *The New York Times*, July 5, 1992.

William Tucker — "The Front Lines of Welfare Reform," *Insight*, August 16, 1993. Available from 3600 New York Ave. NE, Washington, DC 20002.

David Whitman — "Exodus of the 'Couch People,'" *U.S. News & World Report*, December 23, 1991.

The World & I — "Welfare in America," September 1992.

Yale Law & Policy Review — "Welfare Reform and Poverty," vol. 11, no. 1, 1993. Available from Yale Law School, 127 Wall St., New Haven, CT 06520.

For Further Discussion

Chapter 1

1. Robert Rector agrees with John E. Schwarz and Thomas J. Volgy that the official poverty figures do not accurately reflect the extent of poverty in the United States, but these authors draw very different conclusions. Create your own definition of poverty, then compare it with the ideas in these two viewpoints. Which viewpoint seems closer to your definition?

2. James W. Michaels believes that the condition of America's poor is improving, but Bettye Caldwell believes that escaping poverty today is more difficult than it used to be. What different measures of poverty do Michaels and Caldwell use to draw their conclusions? What implications would their differing conclusions have in formulating policies to alleviate poverty?

3. Shawn Miller and Rush H. Limbaugh III suggest that the problems of hunger and homelessness have been exaggerated for political reasons; Kevin Clarke and Ann Braden Johnson believe the problems have been minimized for political reasons. Which set of arguments do you find more compelling? Why? Do the authors' experiences affect your assessment? Explain.

Chapter 2

1. Compare the effects of achieving increases in productivity and profitability by the various methods discussed by Richard Douthwaite, Jonathan Greenberg, and John Miller. Considering their arguments, do you think efforts should be made to limit or regulate the free market? Why or why not?

2. Richard K. Vedder writes that government intervention disrupts the economy; Jonathan Greenberg says that government failures to intervene are disruptive. Compare their arguments, then formulate your own rules for the government's role in the marketplace. Explain your reasoning.

Chapter 3

1. Statistics show that married women and their children are less likely to live in poverty than are single women and their children. The Family Research Council draws very different conclusions from these data than Roberta Spalter-Roth and

Heidi Hartmann do. Which viewpoint makes a better case for its proposed solutions to the poverty of women and children? Explain.

2. Shelby Steele has said that "the very last message that poor blacks need to hear [is] that they should wait for the beneficence of society at large to reach down somehow and pull them up into the mainstream of American life." Roger Wilkins counters that "poor black people may be poor, but that does not mean that they are stupid. . . . They know that they have been slammed to the wall. And they know it because more of them . . . have tried like hell to climb out of the hole they're in, but there have been no jobs and few services to help them. I'm all for personal responsibility and empowerment, but people have to have something to stand on before they can begin to climb." What responses would John E. Jacob and Elizabeth Wright have to Steele and Wilkins? Use examples from the viewpoints to illustrate.

3. How are the situations of poor blacks and poor American Indians alike, according to the viewpoints in this chapter? How are they different?

Chapter 4

1. John Kenneth Galbraith argues that the comforts of capitalism rely on an underclass willing to supply them; Jack Kemp maintains that it is a failure of capitalism that has created an American underclass. On what points do Galbraith and Kemp agree?

2. James Q. Wilson, Myron Magnet, Murray Weidenbaum, and William Raspberry all feel that the American underclass has been created or perpetuated by skewed values. What values would help people escape the underclass, in your opinion? How would you suggest getting people to adopt these values?

Chapter 5

1. Do you think Robert L. Woodson would agree or disagree with Mickey Kaus's plans for reforming welfare? Explain your reasoning.

2. After reading the four viewpoints on the housing crisis, formulate a set of guidelines for making shelter or housing available for the homeless in your community. Address the fact that many people would prefer not to have housing for the poor in their communities.

Organizations to Contact

The editors have compiled the following list of organizations that are concerned with the issues debated in this book. All have publications or information available for interested readers. For best results, allow as much time as possible for the organizations to respond. The descriptions below are derived from materials provided by the organizations. This list was compiled at the date of publication. Names, addresses, and phone numbers of organizations are subject to change.

Americans for Indian Opportunity (AIO)
681 Juniper Hill Rd.
Bernalillo, NM 87004
(505) 867-0278

AIO promotes self-government and economic self-sufficiency for American Indian tribes and individuals. Its publications include *You Don't Have to Be Poor to Be Indian* and *The Family Systems Report*.

The Brookings Institution
1775 Massachusetts Ave. NW
Washington, DC 20036-2188
(202) 797-6195

The institution is devoted to nonpartisan research, education, and publication in economics, government, foreign policy, and the social sciences. Its principal purposes are to aid in the development of sound public policies and to promote public understanding of issues of national importance. It publishes the quarterly journal *The Brookings Review*, which periodically includes articles on poverty, and numerous books, including *The Urban Underclass*.

Center on Budget and Policy Priorities
777 N. Capitol St. NE, Ste. 705
Washington, DC 20002
(202) 408-1080

The center promotes better public understanding of the impact of federal and state governmental spending policies and programs primarily affecting low- and moderate-income Americans. It acts as a research center and information clearinghouse for the media, national and local organizations, and individuals. The center publishes numerous fact sheets, articles, and reports, including *The States and the Poor: How Budget Decisions Affected Low-Income People in 1992*.

Center of Concern
3700 13th St. NE
Washington, DC 20017
(202) 635-2757

Center of Concern engages in social analysis, theological reflection, policy advocacy, and public education on issues of justice and peace. Subjects of its programs and writings include international development, women's roles, economic alternatives, and a theology based on justice for all peoples. It publishes the bimonthly newsletter *Center Focus* as well as numerous papers and books, including *Opting for the Poor: A Challenge for North Americans.*

Children's Defense Fund (CDF)
25 E St. NW
Washington, DC 20001
(202) 662-3510

CDF provides a strong and effective voice for the children of America, who cannot vote, lobby, or speak for themselves. It pays particular attention to the needs of poor, minority, and disabled children. Its publications include *The State of America's Children 1992* and *Outside the Dream: Child Poverty in America.*

Coalition on Human Needs
1000 Wisconsin Ave. NW
Washington, DC 20007
(202) 342-0726

The coalition is a federal advocacy organization that works in such areas as federal budget and tax policy, housing, education, health care, and public assistance. It lobbies for adequate federal funding for welfare, Medicaid, and other social services. Its publications include *How the Poor Would Remedy Poverty* and the bimonthly newsletter *Insight/Action.*

Economic Policy Institute
1730 Rhode Island Ave. NW, Ste. 200
Washington, DC 20036
(202) 775-8810

The institute was established in 1986 to pursue research and public education to help define a new economic strategy for the United States. Its goal is to identify policies that can provide prosperous, fair, and balanced economic growth. It publishes numerous policy studies, briefing papers, and books, including *State of Working America* and *Declining American Incomes and Living Standards.*

Food Research and Action Center (FRAC)
1875 Connecticut Ave. NW, Ste. 540
Washington, DC 20009
(202) 986-2200

FRAC is a research, public policy, and legal center that works to eradicate hunger and undernutrition in the United States. Its publications include *Hunger and Poverty in the United States Information Packet* and the bimonthly *Foodlines: a Chronicle of Hunger and Poverty in America.*

Fourth World Movement
7600 Willow Hill Dr.
Landover, MD 20785-4658
(301) 336-9489

The movement defines the Fourth World as the poorest and most excluded families of society. Staffed by volunteers, the organization works to bridge the gap between the Fourth World and other sectors of society while emphasizing cooperation, peace, and growth. Its publications include *The Human Face of Poverty* and *The Fourth World Chronicle of Human Rights*.

Freedom from Hunger
1644 DaVinci Court
Davis, CA 95617
(916) 758-6200

Freedom from Hunger assists communities, organizations, and institutions in Africa, Asia, Central America, South America, and the United States to eliminate the causes of chronic hunger through leadership development and self-help projects. Its publications include the quarterly *Newsbriefs* and *A Geography of American Poverty*.

Institute for Food and Development Policy
145 Ninth St.
San Francisco, CA 94103
(415) 864-8555

The institute is a research, documentation, and public education center focusing on the social and economic causes of world hunger. It believes that there is enough food in the world to adequately feed everyone but that hunger results "when people lack control over the resources they need to produce food." It publishes the quarterly *Food First Action Alert* as well as numerous articles, pamphlets, and books, including *Food First: Beyond the Myth of Scarcity*.

The National Alliance to End Homelessness
1518 K St. NW, Ste. 206
Washington, DC 20005
(202) 638-1526

The alliance is a national organization committed to the ideal that no American should have to be homeless. It works to secure more effective national and local policies to aid the homeless. Its publications include *What You Can Do to Help the Homeless* and the monthly newsletter *Alliance*.

National Student Campaign Against Hunger and Homelessness (NSCAHH)
29 Temple Pl., Fifth Fl.
Boston, MA 02111
(617) 292-4823

NSCAHH is a network of college and high school students, educators, and other leaders who work to fight hunger and homelessness in the United States and around the world. Its mission is to create a generation of student/community activists who will explore and understand the root causes of poverty and who will initiate positive change through service and action. It publishes the quarterly newsletter *Students Making a Difference* as well as numerous manuals, fact sheets, and handbooks.

Population Reference Bureau, Inc. (PRB)
1875 Connecticut Ave. NW, Ste. 520
Washington, DC 20009-5728
(202) 483-1100

PRB gathers, interprets, and disseminates information on national and world population trends. Its publications include the quarterly *Population Bulletin* and the monthly *Population Today.*

Poverty and Race Research Action Council (PRRAC)
1711 Connecticut Ave. NW, Rm. 207
Washington, DC 20009
(202) 387-9887

PRRAC was established by civil rights, antipoverty, and legal services groups. It works to develop new antiracism and antipoverty strategies and provides funding for research projects that support advocacy work. It publishes the bimonthly newsletter *Poverty & Race.*

Progressive Policy Institute (PPI)
316 Pennsylvania Ave. SE, Ste. 555
Washington, DC 20003
(202) 547-0001

PPI develops policy alternatives to the conventional Left-Right political debate. It advocates social policies that move beyond merely maintaining the poor to liberating them from poverty and dependency. Its publications include *Microenterprise: Human Reconstruction in America's Inner Cities* and *Social Service Vouchers: Bringing Choice and Competition to Social Services.*

Bibliography of Books

Elijah Anderson — *Streetwise: Race, Class, and Change in an Urban Community.* Chicago: University of Chicago Press, 1990.

Lourdes Beneria and Shelley Feldman, eds. — *Unequal Burden: Economic Crises, Persistent Poverty, and Women's Work.* Boulder, CO: Westview Press, 1992.

Harry Browne and Beth Sims — *Runaway America: U.S. Jobs and Factories on the Move.* Albuquerque, NM: Inter-Hemispheric Education Resource Center, 1993.

Robert D. Bullard, ed. — *Confronting Environmental Racism: Voices from the Grassroots.* Boston: South End Press, 1993.

Gary Burtless, ed. — *A Future of Lousy Jobs? The Changing Structure of U.S. Wages.* Washington, DC: Brookings Institution, 1990.

Angela L. Carrasquillo — *Hispanic Children and Youth in the United States: A Resource Guide.* New York: Garland, 1991.

Linda Chavez — *Out of the Barrio: Toward a New Politics of Hispanic Assimilation.* New York: Basic Books, 1991.

Phoebe H. Cottingham and David T. Ellwood, eds. — *Welfare Policy for the 1990s.* Cambridge, MA: Harvard University Press, 1989.

Pamela D. Couture — *Blessed Are the Poor? Women's Poverty, Family Policy, and Practical Theology.* Nashville: Abingdon Press, 1991.

Osha Gray Davidson — *Broken Heartland: The Rise of America's Rural Ghetto.* New York: Free Press, 1990.

Theresa Funiciello — *Tyranny of Kindness.* New York: Atlantic Monthly Press, 1993.

Irene Glasser — *More Than Bread: Ethnography of a Soup Kitchen.* Tuscaloosa: University of Alabama Press, 1988.

William W. Goldsmith and Edward J. Blakely — *Separate Societies: Poverty and Inequality in U.S. Cities.* Philadelphia: Temple University Press, 1992.

Andrew Hacker — *Two Nations: Black and White, Separate, Hostile, Unequal.* New York: Scribner's, 1992.

Joel F. Handler and Yeheskel Hasenfield — *The Moral Construction of Poverty: Welfare Reform in America.* Newbury Park, CA: Sage, 1991.

Herbert Hill and James E. Jones Jr., eds.	*Race in America: The Struggle for Equality.* Madison: University of Wisconsin Press, 1993.
Christopher Jencks	*Rethinking Social Policy: Race, Poverty, and the Underclass.* Cambridge, MA: Harvard University Press, 1992.
Christopher Jencks and Paul E. Peterson	*The Urban Underclass.* Washington, DC: Brookings Institution, 1991.
James Jennings, ed.	*Race, Politics, and Economic Development: Community Perspectives.* New York: Verso, 1992.
Jacqueline Jones	*The Dispossessed: America's Underclasses from the Civil War to the Present.* New York: Basic Books, 1992.
Michael B. Katz, ed.	*The "Underclass" Debate.* Princeton, NJ: Princeton University Press, 1993.
Mickey Kaus	*The End of Equality.* New York: Basic Books, 1992.
Charles A. Kroloff	*Fifty-Four Ways You Can Help the Homeless.* Southport, CT: Hugh Lauter Levin Associates, 1993.
Dwight R. Lee and Richard B. McKenzie	*Failure and Progress: The Bright Side of the Dismal Science.* Washington, DC: Cato Institute, 1993.
Nicholas Lemann	*The Promised Land: The Great Black Migration and How It Changed America.* New York: Knopf, 1991.
Sar A. Levitan, Frank Gallo, and Isaac Shapiro	*Working but Poor: America's Contradiction.* rev. ed. Baltimore: Johns Hopkins University Press, 1993.
Elliot Liebow	*Tell Them Who I Am: The Lives of Homeless Women.* New York: Free Press, 1993.
Laurence E. Lynn Jr. and Michael G.H. McGeary, eds.	*Inner-City Poverty in the United States.* Washington, DC: National Academy Press, 1990.
George T. Martin Jr.	*Social Policy in the Welfare State.* Englewood Cliffs, NJ: Prentice Hall, 1990.
Douglas S. Massey and Nancy A. Denton	*American Apartheid: Segregation and the Making of the Underclass.* Cambridge, MA: Harvard University Press, 1993.
Philip Mattera	*Prosperity Lost.* Reading, MA: Addison-Wesley, 1991.
Lawrence M. Mead	*The New Politics of Poverty: The Nonworking Poor in America.* New York: Basic Books, 1992.

R. Shep Melnick   *Between the Lines: Interpreting Welfare Rights.* Washington, DC: Brookings Institution, 1994.

Rebecca Morales and Frank Bonilla, eds.   *Latinos in a Changing U.S. Economy: Comparative Perspectives on Growing Inequality.* Newbury Park, CA: Sage, 1993.

Robert M. Moroney   *Social Policy and Social Work: Critical Essays on the Welfare State.* New York: Aldine de Gruyter, 1991.

William P. O'Hare et al.   *Real Life Poverty in America: Where the American Public Would Set the Poverty Line.* Washington, DC: Center on Budget and Policy Priorities, 1990.

William P. O'Hare and Brenda Curry-White   *The Rural Underclass: Examination of Multiple Problem Populations in Urban and Rural Settings.* Washington, DC: Population Reference Bureau, 1992.

Marvin Olasky   *The Tragedy of American Compassion.* Washington, DC: Regnery Gateway, 1992.

Gary Orfield and Carol Ashkinaze   *The Closing Door: Conservative Policy and Black Opportunity.* Chicago: University of Chicago Press, 1991.

Valerie Polakow   *Lives on the Edge: Single Mothers and Their Children in the Other America.* Chicago: University of Chicago Press, 1993.

Harrell R. Rodgers Jr.   *Poor Women, Poor Families: The Economic Plight of America's Female-Headed Households.* rev. ed. Armonk, NY: M.E. Sharpe, 1990.

William E. Scheuerman and Sidney Plotkin   *Private Interests, Public Spending: Balanced-Budget Conservatism and the Fiscal Crisis.* Boston: South End Press, 1993.

William Tucker   *Zoning, Rent Control, and Affordable Housing.* Washington, DC: Cato Institute, 1991.

Richard K. Vedder and Lowell E. Gallaway   *Out of Work: Unemployment and Government in Twentieth-Century America.* Oakland, CA: Independent Institute, 1993.

William Julius Wilson   *The Truly Disadvantaged: The Inner City, the Underclass, and Public Policy.* Chicago: University of Chicago Press, 1987.

Paul E. Zopf Jr.   *American Women in Poverty.* Westport, CT: Greenwood Press, 1989.

Index